The Psychology of
Sexual
Victimization

A HANDBOOK

Edited by
Michele Antoinette Paludi

GREENWOOD PRESS
Westport, Connecticut • London

Library of Congress Cataloging-in-Publication Data

The psychology of sexual victimization : a handbook / edited by
  Michele Antoinette Paludi.
      p.   cm.
    Includes bibliographical references and index.
    ISBN 0–313–30248–0 (alk. paper)
    1. Sex crimes—Psychological aspects.   2. Sexual harassment—
Psychological aspects.   3. Dating violence—Psychological aspects.
4. Family violence—Psychological aspects.   5. Child abuse—
Psychological aspects.   6. Sexual abuse victims.   I. Paludi,
Michele Antoinette.
    HV6556.P78   1999
    364.15′3—dc21   98–14239

British Library Cataloguing in Publication Data is available.

Library of Congress Catalog Card Number: 98–14239
ISBN: 0–313–30248–0

First published in 1999

Greenwood Press, 88 Post Road West, Westport, CT 06881
An imprint of Greenwood Publishing Group, Inc.
www.greenwood.com

Printed in the United States of America

The paper used in this book complies with the
Permanent Paper Standard issued by the National
Information Standards Organization (Z39.48–1984).

10 9 8 7 6 5 4 3 2

For Carmen A. Paludi, Jr.
who gives me an understanding of our family's heritage
and who shares with me a vision of our family's future.

We carry on for Spike and Nino.

Contents

Acknowledgments

I thank the chapter contributors for their dedication to research, teaching, and advocacy in the area of sexual victimization. I especially thank Nita Romer at Greenwood Press for her encouragement and assistance.

I also acknowledge the following colleagues who worked with me on the United States Department of Education Subpanel on the Prevention of Sexual Harassment, Violence, and Alcohol and Other Drug Abuse in Higher Education: Leah Aldridge, Maggie Cretella, Lavonna Grow, Jackson Katz, Sue Klein, Mary Koss, Bernice Sandler, Oliver Williams, and Cheryl Vince-Whitman. I continue to learn so much from them.

I also thank Rosalie Paludi, and Lucille Paludi. My appreciation is extended to students working with me at Union College for their insightful comments.

Introduction

I began outlining the issues discussed in this book after some experiences I had as principal of my own firm that deals with education, training, and expert witness consulting in academic and workplace sexual harassment and as a member of several organizations dealing with educational and work equity. One of the first experiences was attending a conference on child abuse, with Matilda Cuomo (her husband, Mario, was a former New York State governor) presiding. I was attending this conference on behalf of the Schenectady, New York, and New York State Chapter of the Business and Professional Women's Organization, of which I was a member and officer. In a paper I presented, I indicated that each week in New York State, an average of four women are murdered as a result of domestic violence. The extremes of this violence are demonstrated by the fact that women in North America are more likely to be killed by their partners than by anyone else. More women are abused by their husbands or boyfriends than are injured in car accidents or muggings. Being battered has direct implications on a mother's effectiveness as a parent. Her role as a parent is demeaned through their victimization because the dysfunction and disorganization of the home offer little nurturance, support, structure, or supervision for children.

The Business and Professional Women's Organization pointed out to Mrs. Cuomo that battering is a workplace concern and that employers must respond to the needs of the mothers and children, in collaboration with community agencies. According to New York State's Office for the Prevention of Domestic Violence, approximately 25% of workplace problems, such as lower productivity, absenteeism, and excessive use of health benefits, are primarily due to domestic violence. Statistics from New York's Victim Service Agency report on the costs of domestic violence suggest that three-fourths of employed battered women are harassed at their workplaces by their abusive husbands or lovers, either in person or over the telephone. This harassment contributes to 56% of them being late for work at least five times a month, 28% of them leaving early at least five days a month, and 54% of them missing at least three full days of work per month. We recommended that New York State employee assistance programs provide therapeutic support for battered women—therapy that validates their perceptions and helps them regain belief in their own abilities, including their parenting skills.

As a result of this experience, I began lobbying New York State senators and assembly members, offering research findings and comments from women, men, and children themselves about battering. I lobbied on behalf of the Schenectady chapter of the Business and Professional Women's Organization and the Schenectady branch of the American Association of University Women. I helped form a coalition of women's organizations in Schenectady, New York, entitled WINS (Women's Issues Network of Schenectady) and lobbied with my colleagues on behalf of this coalition (which included women from the League of Women Voters, Republican Women, Democratic Women, American Association of University Women, Business and Professional Women, Soroptimists International, Zonta, Church Women United, Planned Parenthood, and the YWCA).

Part of my advocacy work involved volunteering as a legislative advisor on women's issues for James Tedisco, a member of the New York State Assembly. I co-authored a textbook, *Missing Children: A Psychological Approach to Understanding the Causes and Consequences of Stranger and Non-Stranger Abduction of Children* (SUNY Press, 1996) with Mr. Tedisco. This book discusses the fact that children suffer more victimizations than do adults, including more family violence, and forms of violence unique to children such as family abduction. Furthermore, most individuals believe that child abductions could never touch their lives—that they happen to other people. This "just-world hypothesis" is supported by the silence surrounding child abductions and sexual victimization in our culture. The silence contributes to our illusion of invulnerability for nonvictims.

Following the publication of our book, we were invited to do some book signings and give some presentations on the issue of missing children in general and our book specifically. I was always amazed at the number of parents who did not even want to look at our book display but rather walked quickly away from us (while their children were walking around the store and outside on the street unattended and in possible danger). I began offering advice for parents on how to teach their children about safety and strangers. I knew that most abductions occur by family members and began offering suggestions for parents on how not to use their children as pawns in their divorce proceedings and child custody battles. This led to my involvement with Child Find of America, offering research and legislative advice to them. I subsequently was elected to the board of directors of Child Find.

Tedisco and I offered the royalties from our book sales to various organizations that would work with us in educating and helping children and their parents about abductions and sexual victimization. We selected the following for the first year: Northeast Parent and Child Association in Schenectady, New York, the Schenectady and Saratoga Big Brothers/Big Sisters Program, Family and Child Guidance Center of Schenectady, the Schenectady Police Athletic League, and Union College.

At the time of the publication of our book, I was teaching part time at Union College, where I was primarily responsible for courses in the psychology of sex and gender, adolescent psychology, human resource management, and the psychology of race, gender, class, and ethnicity. It was in this last course, during a discussion of child abductions, that an undergraduate student offered her own account of being abducted by a parent and taken to Mexico to live, with no contact with other relatives. Her discussion in our class included her thanks for bringing up the issue; no other course had ever discussed the topic. I realized that students may want to learn about an issue with which they have dealt or are currently dealing from an academic perspective first—it's a little more removed for them—and then seek some referral for counseling to deal with the issue.

Subsequent to this student sharing her experiences in class, I developed a number of pedagogical techniques for dealing with sexual victimization in the courses I teach. I have also offered colleagues suggestions for incorporating this information in their own courses. I have talked directly with students about sexual victimization, through training programs I offer on sexual harassment awareness, and in my writing, including the chapter on sexual violence in my book, *The Psychology of Women* (Prentice Hall, 1998). The advice for students includes resources for therapeutic counseling; how to help a friend who is raped, a victim of incest, is sexually harassed, or is battered; and what to do to empower themselves if they are victims. I have also offered advice to men students about not using aggression and victimization as ways to resolve conflict with women (and with other men).

My work as a consultant with colleges about sexual harassment led to my appointment to the United States Department of Education's Subpanel on the Prevention of Violence, Sexual Harassment, Alcohol, and Other Drug

Abuse in Higher Education. I was subsequently elected chairperson of this subpanel. Through my involvement with colleagues on this panel as well as those working in the Department of Education and the Higher Education Center in Newton, Massachusetts, I learned more about the incidence of sexual victimization, especially of women, which leads to many women dropping out of college and never completing their degrees. My work for this subpanel has led me to describe college and university campuses as "violent institutions," as my colleague, Mary Koss, described the home for women as a violent institution. For example, research has suggested that approximately one-third of all American college students report using or being victims of courtship violence, with pushing, grabbing, shoving, slapping, and throwing of objects being the most common forms of violent behavior in dating relationships. In addition, current estimates of sexual harassment of college students by professors approximate 50%, ranging from sexual come-ons to sexual coercion (e.g., faculty threatening to lower students' grades for noncompliance with faculty's requests for sexual activity). For certain student groups, the incidence of sexual harassment by faculty appears to be higher than others:

Women of color, especially those with token status.

Graduate students, whose future careers are often determined by their association with a particular faculty member.

Female students in male-populated careers.

Lesbian women, who may be harassed as part of homophobia.

Physically or emotionally disabled students.

The incidence for student-to-student sexual harassment is higher than that reported for faculty-student sexual harassment.

As another example of sexual violence, between 8% and 15% of college women have disclosed they were raped, according to its legal definition, which includes acts involving nonconsensual sexual penetration obtained by physical force, by threat of bodily harm, or when the victim is incapable of giving consent by virtue of mental illness, mental retardation, or intoxication. The majority of women report knowing their attacker and having the rape occur while on a date.

Equally disturbing as these prevalence rates is that these acts of violence and sexual harassment are perpetrated on college campuses. Male violence against women on college campuses crosses lines of sexual orientation, age, ethnicity, and economic status. Many acts of sexual violence on college campuses involve the use of alcohol and other drugs.

Although the incidence of sexual violence among college women is high, with significant impact on several areas of their emotional and physical well-being, students are not likely to label their experiences as sexual violence, despite the fact that the behaviors they are experiencing fit the legal definitions of sexual victimization. Consequently, they may not label their stress-related responses as being caused or exacerbated by the sexual violence. Furthermore, students may not be aware that their experiences should be reported to campus authorities, since they do not know whether their experiences constitute sexual violence and do not know whether what they've experienced can be dealt with through organizational means.

For example, I recently reported that college students, when asked to identify the activities that would be summarized under the heading "campus violence," generated the following terms: *hazing, rape, assault, battering, emotional abuse*, and *date rape*. The term *sexual harassment* was not mentioned. This omission from a list of behaviors that constitute campus violence indicates how strong the messages they are socialized with that suggest that men should initiate sexual contact in any setting, including academic institutions, and that their campus could not help them deal with the issue. Furthermore, their responses reflect the silence that still surrounds sexual harassment on college campuses. Sexual harassment remains a hidden issue, as Bernice Sandler, a colleague on the subpanel, referred to it in 1978.

Sexual violence confronts victims with perceptions that are often invalidated by those around them. Victims' experiences get relabeled as anything *but* sexual violence. Most victims of sexual harassment doubt their experiences; they are encouraged to conform to their professors' and campus administrators' relabeling of the experiences.

In recent years I have been describing institutions' response to sexual violence, especially sexual harassment, against a backdrop of a classic experiment in social psychology that was conducted in the 1950s by Solomon Asch. The experiment was one concerning social influence—how people alter the thoughts, feelings, and behavior of others. In short, it is an experiment in conformity, of when we change our behavior in order to adhere to social norms.

In Asch's experiment, a participant would enter a laboratory room with six people and be told the experiment concerns visual discrimination. The task was simple: individuals were shown two cards. On the first card a single line was drawn. On the second, three lines were drawn and numbered 1, 2, 3. One of the three lines on this second card was the same length as the line on the first card. Participants were instructed to call out one a time which of the three lines was the same length as the line on the first card. Unbeknown to one of the seven individuals—the real participant in the study—the remaining six were confederates of the researcher and had pre-arranged a number of incorrect responses. For example, five of these confederates would say "1" when the correct answer was "3." When confronted with five people responding with the objectively incorrect answer, would the participant conform to erroneous group judgment or not conform? Asch reported that this experiment was an uncomforting experience. Individuals doubted their judgments; their discomfort was caused by the pressure to conform. Asch reported that 75% of participants went along with the crowd rather than assert what they knew to be the right answer.

I believe this experiment illustrates how sexual violence can confront individuals with perceptions that are often invalidated by those around them. Like the participants in the Asch study, victims of sexual violence come to doubt what they see with their own eyes; they are encouraged to conform to their mate's, professor's, parent's or campus's perspectives. This social conformity is even more pronounced for children, who are often not believed or are told to reinterpret their experiences by a stranger or parental abductor or abuser.

All of these experiences—as a researcher, advocate, lobbyist, professor, and author—led me to understand the importance of a textbook on sexual victimization that would be utilized by therapists, educators, attorneys, physicians, and students.

I have organized the chapters in this book according to themes. In Part I, we discuss sexual victimization of children by family members, including adult survivors of incest. In Part II, sexual victimization in dating and marital relationships is discussed, including courtship violence and battering. Part III deals with sexual victimization of women by strangers. In Part IV, sexual victimization in educational and workplace settings is discussed. Part V contains presentations of sexual victimization from legal and legislative perspectives. The final part is devoted to resources for teaching about sexual victimization and advocacy work, including the development of an organization to help survivors of educator abuse. The appendices identify resources—for example, organizations that deal with sexual victimization, audiovisual material, and popular books on sexual victimization.

The chapter contributors bring a vast array of experiences to the issue. Some are college or university faculty and researchers, others are trainers and directors of not-for-profit agencies, one is an attorney, some are students, one is a mother whose sons were sexually abused by their teacher. All of these voices are needed to understand and deal with sexual victimization of children, adolescents, and adults, especially understanding sexual victimization in the context of individuals' cultures.

I hope that a companion text will be published that includes issues not addressed in this book, including new research on campus and workplace hate crimes, including gender, sexual orientation, and disability in the categories that may motivate hate crimes.

I hope that you will find this book helpful in your efforts to deal with sexual victimization. I invite you to contact the contributors for additional information related to research, training, and lobbying. I will be pleased to share material related to my own work.

PART I

SEXUAL VICTIMIZATION BY FAMILY MEMBERS

1

The Resilience of the Human Psyche: Recognition and Treatment of the Adult Survivor of Incest

Paula K. Lundberg-Love

The past decade has witnessed the emergence of a burgeoning literature on the recognition and treatment of adult survivors of childhood incest and other types of sexual abuse. Indeed, women and men who had never told anyone began to tell, and clinicians who had never inquired about the possibility of sexual abuse during their clinical interviews began to do so. As a result, clinicians and clients alike learned that childhood incest is more prevalent than previously thought and that, without therapeutic intervention, childhood sexual abuse can result in the development of an array of long-term psychological and behavioral sequelae.

The research data and treatment interventions described in this chapter were collected and implemented over the past decade. The impetus for this research program lay in the observation that the successful treatment of depression, eating disorders, substance abuse and similar other problems in adult survivors of childhood sexual abuse often require some resolution of their unaddressed childhood trauma. Because there were no articles in 1985 that described specific, comprehensive approaches to the treatment of adult incest survivors, this program was conceived in response to the clinical challenges presented by clients, and it evolved as the knowledge base in the field of posttraumatic stress disorder and trauma recovery expanded.

This chapter describes research that sought to determine the personality and behavioral characteristics of adult incest survivors as compared to three other groups of women devoid of a history of childhood sexual abuse and to evaluate the impact of an abuse-focused treatment program. After a general description of the prevalence of childhood sexual abuse in general, and incest in particular, as well as the long-term consequences associated with such trauma, the design, methodology, and results of the research study will be discussed. Then the specific content of the treatment program will be delineated.

EPIDEMIOLOGY

The exact prevalence of child sexual abuse in the general population is not precisely known because most sexual abuse is not reported at the time of its occurrence (Finkelhor, Hotaling, Lewis, & Smith, 1990). Since there is no national reporting system for crimes against children, official crime and child abuse statistics typically underestimate the magnitude of the problem and therefore tend to be unreliable. Additionally, the definition of child sexual abuse varies across the states. As a result, the best mechanism for determining the prevalence of child sexual abuse is through retrospective surveys of adult nonclinical populations. But even then, the results of these surveys exhibit variability depending on the sample surveyed, the methodology of the survey (e.g., telephone versus face-to-face interviews), the definitions employed, and the type and numbers of screening questions used (Finkelhor, 1994). The gold standard studies of the prevalence of child sexual abuse are those of Russell (1984) and Wyatt (1985). The Wyatt study was conducted in Los Angeles, where subjects were contacted via random digit dialing, and 126 black women and 122 white women were interviewed extensively. The definition of sexual abuse used in this study was any form of contact of a sexual nature that occurred prior to age 18. Wyatt found that 45% of her sample reported contact sexual abuse. When noncontact offenses were included, a victimization rate of 62% was obtained. Incestuous abuse was reported by 21% of the participants of the study. The Russell (1986) survey, conducted in San Francisco, consisted of in-person interviews with 930 randomly selected adult female residents. The definition of incestuous abuse used in this survey was any kind of exploitative sexual contact or attempted contact that occurred between relatives, no matter how distant the relationship, before the victim turned 18 years old. Russell found that 38% of the women had experienced contact childhood sexual abuse. When noncontact abuse was included, the rate of victimization was 54%. Overall, 16% of the participants were survivors of incest; when Russell considered only the rate of incestuous victimization among women ages 18 to 36, it was 19%. Extrapolation of these data suggested that at least 160,000 per million children and adolescents are incest survivors.

Two more recent studies investigated the prevalence of child sexual abuse. A telephone survey of a national probability sample of adults revealed that 27% of women and 16% of men reported a contact sexual offense by age 18 (Finkelhor et al., 1990). Also, in a mailed questionnaire to a national, stratified random sample, 32% of females and 13% of males reported a history of contact sexual abuse (Elliott & Briere, 1995).

The Russell study provided a wealth of descriptive data regarding incestuous victimization. The identities of the perpetrators were as follow: 25% were uncles, 24% were fathers (including biological, foster, and step-), 16% were first cousins, 13% were brothers, 8% were other male relatives, 6% were grandfathers, 4% were brothers-in-law, 2% were female first cousins, 2% were other female relatives, and 1% were biological mothers. Father-daughter incest was found to be the most traumatic form of incest. Fathers were more likely to have imposed vaginal intercourse on their daughters. They also abused their daughters more frequently, were more likely to use force or violence, and were at least 20 years older than their daughters at the time of the abuse. The average age at which fathers committed incest was 39.6 years. With respect to demographics, middle-class women reported as much sexual abuse as lower-class women. Indeed, upper-middle-class women were overrepresented among incest victims. African-American women and Caucasian women had similar rates of victimization. The rates were lower for women of Asian descent, and those for Hispanic women were somewhat higher. Wyatt (1985) also reported similar results with respect to the prevalence of child sexual abuse in African-American and Caucasian women.

LONG-TERM SEQUELAE OF CHILD SEXUAL ABUSE

Childhood sexual abuse is a major risk factor for a myriad of psychological problems during adulthood. The number and nature of the effects are not uniform. Some survivors report few symptoms; others describe their childhood experience as permeating most aspects of their adult life. Regardless of the severity of their symptomatology, the effects they exhibit are extensions of those found in child victims. Like child victims, adult survivors tend to internalize their psychological pain, resulting in symptoms such as anxiety or depression; when they externalize it, interpersonal problems arise.

Results from research studies (Herman, 1981; Meiselman, 1978; Lundberg-Love, Marmion, Ford, Geffner, & Peacock, 1992; Briere & Runtz, 1988) have noted high frequencies of depressive symptoms in incest survivors they have studied. Depression is the most frequently reported symptom in a number of studies (Browne & Finkelhor, 1986). Stein, Golding, Siegel, Burnam and Sorensen (1988) suggested that adult sexual abuse survivors may have as much as a fourfold increase in the risk of developing major depression at some point in their lifetime. Additionally, Peters (1984) found that childhood sexual assault was associated with depression and alcohol abuse in a random sample of women living in Los Angeles. Bagley and Ramsey (1985) reported higher levels of depressive symptomatology in Canadian women who were survivors of childhood sexual abuse. Feelings of stigmatization, alienation, and isolation have been reported (Courtois, 1988; Finkelhor & Browne, 1985; Herman, 1981; Lundberg-Love et al., 1992). Couple those feelings with chronic betrayal, disempowerment, guilt, helplessness, and low self-esteem (Finkelhor & Browne, 1985; Peters, 1988), and it is not surprising that adult survivors frequently report suicidal ideation. In two samples of outpatient women, those with an abuse history were twice as likely to have attempted suicide as compared to their non-abused peers (Briere & Runtz, 1987; Briere & Zaidi, 1989). Similarly, in a community sample (Saunders, Villeponteaux, Lipovsky, & Kilpatrick, 1992), 16% of adult survivors had attempted suicide, whereas less than 6% of nonabused women reported such attempts.

Anxiety is another commonly reported symptom related to the internalization of traumatic experience. Adult survivors have a five times greater likelihood than their nonabused counterparts of being diagnosed with an anxiety-related problem, including panic disorder, phobias, obsessive-compulsive disorder, and generalized anxiety disorder (Saunders et al., 1992). Sedney and Brooks (1984) studied female college students and found that those with histories of sexual abuse experienced higher levels of anxiety, depression, and sleep disturbance. According to Briere and Elliott (1993) anxiety-related symptoms may manifest themselves cognitively (preoccupation with and hypervigilant responses to danger) (Jehu, 1988), as classically conditioned responses (sexual dysfunction, phobias), and somatically, most likely related to chronic sympathetic nervous system arousal or hyperreactivity (e.g., headaches, gastrointestinal problems, chronic pelvic pain, back pain, and muscle tension) (Springs & Friedrich, 1992; Walker, Katon, Alfrey, Bowers, & Stenchever, 1991; Walker, Katon, Roy-Byrne, & Jemelka, 1993). Posttraumatic stress disorder (PTSD) is one of the most common diagnoses received by adult survivors of childhood sexual abuse. PTSD manifests itself as a chronic reexperiencing of the traumatic events through nightmares, flashbacks, and intrusive thoughts. As many as 36% of adult survivors reported PTSD, and if the abuse involved penetration, the frequency for PTSD increased to 66% (Donaldson & Gardner, 1985; Saunders et al., 1992). Because the reliving of the childhood trauma through the intrusive symptoms of PTSD is experienced as not being under the control of the individual, feelings of powerlessness are enhanced, and symptoms of avoidance of the perceived triggering stimuli are avoided.

Dissociation is another common response to traumatic events that is often observed in clinical populations of adult survivors of sexual abuse (Kluft, 1985; Putnam, 1990; Ross, 1989), and has been reported in other research studies (Briere & Runtz, 1987; Chu & Dill, 1990). Dissociation involves the disruption of the integrated functions of consciousness, memory, identity, or perception of the environment. It is thought to be a mechanism wherein the psyche defends against the complete awareness of trauma-related thoughts, feelings, and behaviors (van der Kolk & Kadish, 1987). As a result, adult survivors of child sexual abuse may meet the diagnostic criteria for particular dissociative disorders, including dissociative amnesia, dissociative fugue, depersonalization disorder, and sometimes dissociative identity disorder. In particular, dissociative amnesia, a memory disturbance "characterized by an inability to recall important information usually of a traumatic or stressful nature that is too extensive to be explained by ordinary forgetfulness" (APA, 1994), has been documented to occur in adult survivors. In a follow-up study of girls whose sexual abuse was documented at a county hospital, 38% did not recollect that experience an average of 17 years later (Williams, 1994). Although the women were not informed of the purpose of the study at follow-up, they were asked questions regarding any history of sexual abuse. An analysis of the responses of the women who did not report the index case of sexual abuse strongly suggested that they did not recall the event. It did not appear that the participants were merely reluctant to disclose the abuse, because more than half of the subjects in question revealed other abusive experiences that had occurred in childhood (Williams, 1994). Additional research has suggested that a substantial proportion of sexual abuse survivors have reported a partial or complete loss of memory for their abusive experiences (Briere & Conte, 1993; Elliott & Briere, 1995). Dissociation of traumatic memories appears to be correlated with maltreatment that occurred at an early age, was long in duration, or was violent in nature (Briere & Conte, 1993: Herman & Schatzow, 1987; Putnam, 1990). Dissociation also has been associated with early abuse by a family member (Williams, 1994).

Childhood sexual abuse can compromise the development of coping mechanisms as a result of the chronic hyperarousal, memory restimulation, and emotional pain experienced by adult survivors. As a result, the survivors often exhibit seemingly disruptive behavioral responses that actually are methods for reducing internal tension—for example, self-harm activities such as trichotillomania (pulling out hair) or cutting, hitting, or burning oneself (van der Kolk, Perry, & Herman, 1991; Walsh & Rosen, 1988); engaging in sexual activities in response to painful affect (Briere, 1992); binging and purging to neutralize feelings of emptiness (Piran, Lerner, Garfinkel, Kennedy, & Brouillette, 1988; Steiger & Zanko, 1990); and the use of alcohol or drugs to obliterate psychic pain (Singer, Petchers, & Hussey, 1989). Briere (1992) conceptualizes these behaviors as the survivor's attempt to reduce overwhelming pain and reestablish a sense of internal equilibrium. The various behaviors can be activated by anger, anxiety, guilt, powerlessness, sadness, or a sense of isolation or alienation. Subsequent to the engagement in these behaviors, survivors often report a sense of relief, escape, or pleasure. However, at some point, a rebound experience of shame, guilt, or self-loathing again precipitates the tension-reduction behavior, and the cycle repeats itself.

As a result of the numerous psychological symptoms experienced by adult survivors, it is not surprising to find that their ability to form and sustain interpersonal relationships may be disrupted. Childhood sexual victimization impairs the ability to trust that others will act in the survivor's best interest, thus impeding the formation of stable relationships. Furthermore, the violation and the betrayal of boundaries that occurred within the context of intimate childhood relationships can create an interpersonal ambivalence that renders it difficult to sustain subsequent adult relationships. Hence, survivors report a greater fear of both men and women (Briere & Runtz, 1987; Lundberg-Love, 1990). They are more likely to remain single, and if they marry, they are more likely to divorce or separate from their partners as compared to women without a history of sexual abuse (Russell, 1986). They report having fewer friends (Gold, 1986), less satisfaction and greater discomfort in their relationships, and more maladaptive interpersonal patterns (Elliott, 1994; Lundberg-Love, 1990).

With respect to possible interpersonal sequelae, perhaps the most frequently reported problems are sexual ones. These can include a variety of sexual dysfunctions (Lundberg-Love, 1990; Maltz & Holman, 1987) and involvement in multiple, brief, superficial relationships (Courtois, 1988). Furthermore, sexual abuse survivors appear to have a greater propensity for becoming involved in abusive sexual or romantic relationships (Browne & Finkelhor, 1986) and are more likely to be sexually revictimized in their adult relationships (Russell, 1986; Sorenson, Siegel, Golding, & Stein, 1991).

THE EFFECTS OF CHILDHOOD INCESTUOUS VICTIMIZATION UPON ADULT SYMPTOMATOLOGY

The preceding discussion consists of a nonexhaustive review of the literature regarding the psychological sequelae reported to occur in adult survivors of sexual abuse. But when the research described in this chapter was initiated, the preponderance of the data just described was nonexistent. Then and, to the best of our knowledge, now, this is the only clinical study that has systematically assessed the long-term consequences of incestuous abuse, as well as the impact of treatment using standard psychological measures, and compared those results to those of female control groups devoid of any history of sexual abuse. Indeed, the inclusion of three control groups who lack a history of childhood sexual abuse is a particularly noteworthy feature of this study. These three control groups consisted of women participating in psychotherapy, women participating in a clinical exercise physiology program, and women who were part of the clinical exercise physiology program but were not engaging in any health-related intervention. The purpose of the study was to determine the impact of incestuous victimization on the scores obtained on the Minnesota Multiphasic Personality Inventory (MMPI) and the Millon Behavioral Health Inventory (MBHI) at the outset of treatment and after six months and one year of abuse-focused psychological treatment.

Prior clinical experience and pilot data had suggested that incest survivors would report greater numbers and higher levels of psychological symptoms, particularly those symptoms involving depression, anxiety, rumination, poor self-esteem, and social introversion. Additionally, the pilot data revealed that the most frequent two-point MMPI code obtained by incest survivors was 4–8. That is, the highest mean scores on the various MMPI clinical scales were those obtained for scale 4 (Psychopathic Deviate) and scale 8 (Schizophrenia). Other research articles had reported a 4–8 or 8–4 two-point code (Briere, 1989; Tsai, Feldman-Summers, & Edgar, 1979), and because the MMPI profiles for incest survivor pilot data were nearly identical to those of Scott and Stone, it was anticipated that the incest survivors might obtain a 4–8 or 8–4 two-point MMPI code more frequently than the other groups

The MHBI assesses four general behavioral health areas: (1) basic personality-related coping styles when interacting with health personnel, services, and medical regimens; (2) psychogenic attitudes that represent the personal feelings and perceptions of an individual regarding different aspects of psychological stress that can enhance somatic susceptibility or aggravate the course of an existing disease; (3) psychosomatic correlates as they relate to the exacerbation of allergic inclinations, gastrointestinal susceptibilities, or cardiovascular-related tendencies; and (4) prognostic indexes that seek to identify future treatment problems or difficulties that may arise during the course of an individual's chronic illness. Based on clinical experience, it was hypothesized that adult incest survivors, would score higher on coping styles and psychogenic attitudes that related to or were influenced by feelings of alienation, a sense of hopelessness or helplessness, lack of emotional support particularly by significant others, and the perception of overwhelming stressors in their lives. Furthermore, because it appeared that the survivors seemed to develop somatic symptoms in conjunction with the various stressors and recollections characteristic of their life histories, it was anticipated that they would report higher scores relative to the control groups on the gastrointestinal susceptibilities and cardiovascular tendencies scales due to the chronic feelings of anxiety and sustained vigilance characteristic of this population.

METHODOLOGY

Subjects

All women who participated in this study were volunteers from the East Texas area. The 103 women in this study were divided among four treatment and control conditions: incest victims entering treatment for a wide array of clinical conditions (INC-T), women entering psychological treatment without a history of sexual abuse (NoINC-T), women engaged in a clinical exercise physiology research study involving the impact of aerobic (walking/jogging) exercise on bone density as it relates to osteoporosis (EX-C), and women who were a no-treatment control group participating in the same exercise physiology study (NoEX-C). The exercise prescription and performance for the aerobic exercise group were conducted on an individualized basis. The last two groups were part of a concurrent research study and were included as comparisons in our study to eliminate such confounds as the Hawthorne effect (i.e., change in scores attributable to mere exposure or participation in a research study). They served the purpose of placebo and no-treatment control groups.

Recruitment of the incest treatment group (INC-T) and the therapy control group (NoINC-T) was achieved via referrals from three local crisis centers, local private therapists, and word of mouth. Participants were informed that the purpose of the study was to document the types of behavioral issues encountered by East Texas women in general and individuals participating in therapy in particular. Participants were also informed that the impact of a six-month experience of psychotherapy, aerobic exercise, or no treatment would be assessed. In order to be included in the target treatment group, a participant had to be female, at least 18 years of age, devoid of any participation in a specific treatment program for adult survivors of sexual abuse prior to entering the present study, not currently abusing any psychopharmacological agents, free of any chronic disease that would have on impact on MMPI or MBHI scores (e.g., multiple sclerosis), free of any psychotic disorders, and devoid of any organic brain disorder. Inclusion in the NoINC-T group required that a participant have no history of any type of sexual abuse and that all other subject inclusion criteria be fulfilled. Incestuous abuse was defined as unwanted sexual contact (fondling, oral, anal, or vaginal penetration) or noncontact sexual abuse perpetrated by a family member at least two years older than the victim prior to the victim's eighteenth birthday. All of the incest survivors in this study experienced some type of contact sexual abuse and all of the individuals actually experienced incestuous abuse before their sixteenth birthday.

Recruitment of the exercise (EX-C) and the no-treatment control (NoEX-C) groups occurred from referrals from local physicians and word-of-mouth publicity. All participants, regardless of experimental group, were volunteers. The women participating in each of the three no-incest groups were interviewed individually after their baseline testing and again after six months in order to eliminate from the study those women found to have experienced childhood sexual abuse. Approximately 8% of the EX-C and NoEX-C groups and 42% of the NoINC-T group had to be dropped from the study because at some point during the six-month period, they had recalled some incident of sexual abuse. In the NoEX-C group, all of the women initially indicated that they had not been sexually abused and subsequently recollected such experiences while they were in therapy for reasons other than treatment of sexual abuse and without any suggestions from the therapist. These instances appeared to be cases of traumatic amnesia. Hence the groups had the following characteristics: INC-T, $N = 29$, mean age = 35 years; NoINC-T, $N = 27$, mean age = 34 years; EX-C, $N = 2$, mean age = 50 years; and NoEX-C ($N = 15$ mean age = 49 years). Although attrition in the NoINC-T group was substantial, this group remained comparable to the INC-T group. An explanation of the possible risks and benefits associated with participation in the study was provided, and a signed consent form was obtained from each participant.

Only the INC-T and the NoINC-T were tested one year after entry into therapy because the focus of the study after the initial six months was the impact of psychological treatment. Hence, during the course of the study some individuals were lost to final MMPI and MHBI testing. Therefore, the sizes of the INC-T and NoINC-T samples for whom three data points (baseline, 6, and 12 months posttreatment) were available were $N = 22$ and $N = 11$, respectively. Although these numbers again represent substantial attrition from both groups, the analyses over three measurements are restricted to these remaining subjects only, and failure to replicate the results of the larger (two repeated measures) design will be noted.

Instrumentation

Data was obtained from a 14-page demographic questionnaire designed specifically for this study by Kevin Ford, the MMPI (MMPI-2 was not available at the outset of this study), and the MBHI.

Part One of the demographic questionnaire elicited the following information:

age

gender

ethnicity

religious preference

current religious status (practicing or not)

current relationship status

number of marriages

number of children

educational level

present occupational status of self and spouse

educational level of mother and father during individual's childhood

each parent's occupational level during individual's childhood

parents' relationship status during individual's childhood

number of times each parent was married

Part Two of the questionnaire, relevant only to the incest survivors, inquired about the characteristics of the molestation experience(s). Specifically, questions were asked regarding the number of perpetrators, the frequency of perpetration, whether disclosure occurred, and if it did, whether the individual was seeking help, was believed, and whether she received help. Additionally, if an individual did disclose her abuse, the possible results of such a disclosure were ascertained, including parental divorce, the victim's removal from the home, the perpetrator's removal from the home, the perpetrator's arrest, some other action, or no action. If the abuse ended without disclosure, it was determined whether the perpetrator simply stopped or began abusing someone else, whether the victim stopped the abuse or left the home, or whether someone else stopped the abuse. The final sections asked the respondents to rate 36 possible initial or long-term consequences of incestuous victimization on a scale of 0 ("I did not experience this problem") to 4 ("This was constantly a problem").

This chapter (1) describes the demographic characteristics of the INC-T group as compared to the other three groups, (2) describes the characteristics of the molestation experienced by the incest survivors, (3) describes the frequency of victim disclosure, the attendant results and the manner in which the molestation ceased, and (4) discusses the relationship between the socioeconomic status of the subject, as well as that of her family of origin and variables associated with the incestuous abuse, and describes the relationship between the INC-T scores on the MMPI scales and the duration of abuse.

The MMPI is a well-known 566 true-false item instrument designed to assess the major types of psychological symptomatology (Dahlstrom, Welsh, & Dahlstrom, 1972). It provides a score for 10 clinical scales, 4 supplemental scales, 3 validity scales, and a wide array of additional scales.

The MBHI is a 150 true-false item instrument designed to aid clinicians who deal with physically ill and behavioral medicine clients. Its purpose is to facilitate the psychological understanding of these individuals and the steps required to formulate a comprehensive treatment plan. The results provide information regarding a client's likely style of relating to health care personnel, problematic psychosocial attitudes and stressors, and similarity to persons with psychosomatic complications or poor responses to illness in general or treatment interventions.

Procedure

At the outset of the study, each participant completed a battery of tests to assess behavioral style, stress-related somatic symptoms, and psychopathology. This required 2.5 to 3.0 hours of testing time. A discussion of the results from the demographic questionnaire, the MMPI, and the MBHI will be the focus of this chapter.

After the completion of baseline testing, participants experienced six months of a treatment program designed to aid adults in the recovery from childhood incestuous abuse, six months of a program designed to help women recover from psychological problems unrelated to sexual abuse, six months of a thrice-weekly one-hour endurance exercise program consisting of brisk walking and jogging, or no treatment for the same time period. Then all tests were readministered. All members of the EX-C and NoEX-C groups were questioned in a structured manner regarding any history of sexual abuse. Only the INC-T group completed Part Two of the demographic questionnaire, which elicited an array of details associated with their sexual victimization. Following six more months of treatment, all tests were read-ministered to the incest survivors and the other women who had been or were still in treatment.

Discussion

The women who participated in this study tended to be Caucasian (93.3%), Protestant (75.8%), and married (52.0%). The average ages of the INC-T and NoINC-T groups were 36 and 35 years, respectively. Although the EX-C and NoEX-C groups appeared to be older—51 and 50 years, respectively—the age variability within the four groups ranged from 8 years (NoEX-C) to 15 years (EX-C). With respect to relationship status, 55% of the single women were incest survivors. These data are similar to those of Russell (1986), who found that incest survivors were less likely to be married. Although there were few women of color in the sample, 5% of them were Native American and 1.7% were African American and all except one of the Native American women were members of one of the therapy groups.

Of the women who were not Protestant, 7.5% were Catholic, 0.8% were Jewish, 8.5% considered themselves affiliated with some other religion, and 7.5% were religiously unaffiliated. Of the last group, 66.7% were incest survivors, 22.2% were in the NoINC-T group, and 11.1% were members of the EX-C group. All subjects were asked whether they were practicing their religions. Overall, 52.2% of the INC-T, 76.0% of the NoINC-T, 90.0% of the EX-C, and 93.3% of the NoEX-C groups were practicing their religions. Of those who were not practicing their religions, 68.8% were incest survivors. The data on religious affiliation and practice reflect reports in the literature suggesting that incestuous abuse is often associated with the victim's feeling of abandonment by God or attendant problems in the realm of spirituality (Briere, 1989; Courtois, 1988; Russell, 1986).

The majority of women in this study had some college work. Values ranged from a low of 80.1% (NoEX-C) to 96.2% (NoINC-T) with the INC-T group reporting 80.5%. However, 10.8% of the last group had not completed high school, while all of the women in the other groups had completed high school. Incest survivors reported the lowest levels of educational attainment for spouse, mother, and father (75.8%, 35%, and 38.1%, respectively, completed some college, while 65.6% of mothers and 30.9% of fathers did not complete high school). Thus, overall current family attainment levels and family of origin attainment levels of the incest survivors were consistently lower than all other groups, with the exception of the spouse educational level of the NoINC-T group. These values were nearly equal. Consistent with the family attainment indexs, the family of origin so-cioeconomic status (SES) levels, as determined by the Hollingshead Index, were the lowest for the incest survivors.

When the correlations among the SES occupational-educational attain-ment levels and the abuse variables were computed, only four significant re-lationships were obtained. The higher the father's SES, educational, or occupational level, the less likely the incest survivor was to seek help. Also, the higher the parents' combined SES, the older the survivor was before she perceived that the incestuous relationship was atypical. Considered to-gether, these data suggest that SES levels operate to enhance the perceived power of the perpetrator in the eyes of the victim. How many victims have told clinicians that they didn't seek help because they felt nothing would be done or they wouldn't be believed? Indeed, there were three correlational trends that supported this premise. The higher the combined SES of the par-ents, the less likely it was that the victim was believed when she did dis-close. Also, the higher the mother's occupational level and the higher her individual SES, the more likely it was that the victim was believed when she did disclose. Thus, although a higher maternal status suggested that a victim might be believed if she disclosed, a higher parental status did not. Given the relationship between patriarchal values and the prevalence of family violence in general, this finding makes intuitive sense.

With respect to the victim's age when the abuse first occurred, the data suggested that the higher the SES and occupational level of the subject, the older she was when the first sexually abusive event occurred. This finding is consistent with the belief that the older one is at the time of victimization, the more coping skills may be available, and perhaps the greater the devel-oped resilience of the victim (Briere, 1989; Finkelhor, 1986).

There also were trends in the data suggesting that the higher the SES of the mother, the greater the duration of the abuse, while the higher the SES of the father, the shorter the duration of abuse. The former finding could be re-lated to outside-the-home employment of the mother, thus rendering her less available to her daughter and perhaps necessitating child care. The pos-sible interpretation of the inverse relationship with paternal SES is not ap-parent.

Data regarding characteristics of the perpetrator and the incestuous abuse indicated that, as in the case of the Russell (1986) data, the family member most likely to abuse the victim was a father figure. Biological fa-thers (23%) outnumbered stepfathers (15%) and foster fathers (4%); grand-fathers (15%) and male siblings were the second most common classes of perpetrators. The ages of the perpetrators ranged from 8 to 60 years, with modal points at 22, 30, and 45 years. The duration, frequency, and severity of the abusive acts were considerable. The mean age at onset of abuse was 7.5 years, and the mean age at which the abuse ended was 14.5 years. When disclosure by the victim did occur—and it did in nearly half the cases—the mean age of the child was 11.5 years. These data are consistent with those in the literature suggesting that latency-age children are the group most frequently abused and that the abuse tends to end when the victim becomes an adolescent (Finkelhor, 1986), perhaps because the victim realizes that the abusive behavior is not mainstream family behavior.

Although 26% of the incest survivors were abused for a total of "a few months," 4.3% were abused "a few times" per year, 4.3% nearly "once per month," 30.4% "a few times" per month, and 13% responded "daily." Clearly the frequency of abuse for this sample was considerable, with 34.7% being abused at least more than once per week. Similarly, the invasive nature of the abusive acts was rather severe, with 53% experiencing intercourse, 18% fondling, 12% anal sex, 10% were prostituted, and 8% experienced oral sex.

Nearly half (48%) of the sample disclosed their abuse. The majority of them told their mothers or stepmothers. Other infrequent recipients of the disclosure were a grandmother, a friend, a social worker, or a counselor. Of the individuals who disclosed their abuse, only 50% of them were believed, and only one person received any help. Typically, the abuse ended because the victim stopped it herself or left the environment (44%). The perpetrator stopped of his own accord or switched to a new victim in 24% of the cases, and someone else stopped the abuse in 20% of the cases.

Regarding the psychological consequences of incestuous abuse as it related to demographic variables, the duration of the abuse correlated positively with the survivor's scores on the Psychopathic Deviate (Pd) and Mac-Andrews (MAC) scales of the MMPI. Significant positive correlations were obtained between the duration of the abuse and the survivor's scores on the Harris-Lingoe MMPI scales entitled Authority Problems (Pd2) and Amorality (Ma2). These data suggest that the longer the incestuous abuse occurs, the more likely it is to be related to behaviors associated with personality disorders, distrust of authority figures, impulsivity, and drug or alcohol abuse. The numbers of the symptoms experienced immediately that related to the trauma of incest were correlated significantly with the numbers of long-term psychological consequences also attributable to the incest. These data support the belief that when children do not receive therapeutic intervention at the time of abuse, the psychological trauma does not resolve spontaneously. Rather, individuals often require treatment as adults for sequelae related to their childhood victimization.

The results of this study also supported the hypothesis that incest survivors reported greater psychological distress and higher levels of symptomatology than women in treatment devoid of a history of sexual abuse and the EX-C and NoEX-C groups. The scores of the INC-T group were significantly higher than those of all the control groups on the Hypochondriasis (HS), Depression (D), Psychopathic Deviate (Pd), Psychasthenia (Pt), Schizophrenia (Sc), and Social Introversion (Si) clinical scales of the MMPI (Lundberg-Love et al., 1992). Also, as hypothesized, incest survivors scored higher on the Anxiety scale and lower on the Ego Strength scale than all other control groups. Consideration of the scores of the incest survivors on the Harris-Lingoe and Serkownik subscales suggested that they were the most depressed, alienated, and socially introverted group studied. Additionally, they reported higher levels of somatic symptoms than all control groups on two different scales (Physical Malfunctioning and Physical-Somatic Concerns). Furthermore, they had significantly higher levels of Familial Discord and Ego Mastery problems (cognitive, conative, and defective inhibition). It appears noteworthy that of 57 MMPI scales, the INC-T group scored higher than all other groups on 38 (66%) of them. Hence, the INC-T group did report greater numbers and higher levels of particular psychological symptoms than the NoINC-T group. These data are important because many incest survivors who seek treatment do so for a wide array of reasons. Based on clinical experience, from 20 to 40% of incest survivors may not recollect part or all of their victimization histories at the outset of treatment. Sometimes even women who do recall their childhood abuse may not understand its possible relationship to their presenting clinical issues. Therefore, the finding that MMPI results could suggest the possibility of a history of childhood incestuous victimization has implications for the identification and subsequent treatment of adult survivors. Also, these MMPI data may support the position that there is some connection between childhood experience and adulthood symptomatology. Indeed, the development of the Trauma Symptom Inventory by Briere (1995) has strongly supported this notion.

Additionally, comparisons of MMPI two-point profile frequencies for the INC-T group with those of the other control groups suggested that a particular type of MMPI two-point profile might be observed more frequently in the incest survivor group. The data suggested that often the two highest elevations of an incest survivor MMPI profile were on scales 8 (Sc) and 4 (Pd). This finding was consistent with our initial pilot data (Lundberg-Love, Crawford, & Geffner, 1987) as well as the work of others (Briere, 1989; Scott & Stone, 1986; Tsai et al.,1979). The data of Scott and Stone (1986) were particularly relevant to my results. Although their clinical adult incest survivor sample was more demographically heterogeneous than ours, their mean MMPI profile was nearly identical to that obtained in this study. Moreover, this finding suggested that the long-term psychological consequences associated with incestuous abuse, as measured by the MMPI, exhibited considerable consistency. Additionally, the data suggested that contrary to the belief of some investigators (e.g., Finkelhor, 1986), the MMPI has some potential to identify women who might be incest survivors. At the very least, when the two-point code for a woman entering therapy is 4–8 or 8–4, it might be advisable for the therapist during the course of treatment to raise the issue of a possible history of sexual or incestuous abuse.

Particularly noteworthy was the disparity between the interpretations of the MMPI profiles rendered by Scott and Stone and that suggested by further scrutinization of these data. Historically, clinically significant elevations on the Pd and Sc have been interpreted as possible evidence of sociopathy and schizophrenia, respectively. Indeed, Scott and Stone (1986) concluded that the results of their testing indicated that incest survivors possessed a generalized deviancy from societal standards and a tendency to act out in antisocial, immature, and egocentric ways. Although such an interpretation was consistent with standard textbook knowledge (Dahlstrom et al., 1972), it did not coincide with our experience in the treatment of our incest survivor clients. Fairly extensive clinical experience with this population suggested that they were neither sociopathic nor schizophrenic in the traditional sense of those terms. Indeed, the bulk of our sample was quite productive, with no history of legal problems, hospitalizations, or issues of social deviancy.

Hence, we examined differences among incest survivors and control groups on the Harris-Lingoe subscales of the MMPI Pd and Sc clinical scales. In the case of the Pd scale, the clinical significance was due primarily to elevation on the Familial Discord (Pd1) subscale and secondarily to elevations of the Social Alienation (Pd4A) and Self Alienation (Pd4B) scales (T-scores > 70). The scores on the Problems With Authority (Pd2) scale were not at a clinically significant level. Nor were there significant differences among the scores on the Social Imperturbability (Pd3) scale. In the case of the Sc scale, elevations appeared to be due primarily to clinically significant scores obtained on the Social Alienation (Sc1A) scale, and secondarily to elevations on the Lack of Ego Mastery-Cognitive (Sc2A) and Lack of Ego Mastery-Conative (Sc3A) scales. Although the scores of the incest survivors were higher than those of the control groups on the Emotional Alienation (Sc1B) and Bizarre Sensory Experiences (Sc3C) scales, the scores were not at clinically significant levels. Thus, the elevations that incest survivors exhibited on the Pd scale appeared, not surprisingly, to be related to long-term family problems and a pervasive sense of alienation that are the legacy of incest. Elevations on the Sc scale appeared to reflect the survivors' difficulty in establishing mastery over their cognitive and affective perceptions of powerlessness, as well as their sense of social alienation, relative to other members of society.

Of the 10 clinical MMPI scales that were analyzed, only 4 showed no significant differences between the scores of the INC-T and the NoINC-T groups: the Hysteria (Hy), Paranoia (Pa), Masculinity/Feminity (MF), and Mania (MA) scales. Nevertheless, when the score on the Harris-Lingoe and Serkownek scales were analyzed, some significant differences among the INC-T and the control groups emerged. Members of the INC-T group scored significantly higher than all other groups on the Need for Affection, Persecutory Ideas, and Narcissism-Hypersensitivity scales. They scored significantly lower than all groups on the Naiveté scale. These differences were noted because some of them might represent key clinical issues for incest survivors. Clearly, additional research is required to determine the replicability of these subscale differences.

Because differences in MMPI interpretations predicted different approaches to the treatment of as well as the prognosis for incest survivors, it was critical that the impact of treatment be evaluated. If the Scott and Stone (1986) interpretation of the data were correct, then psychological treatment would have had minimal impact on symptomatology in general and scores on the Pd and Sc scales in particular. However, if our interpretation possessed credence, then psychotherapy directed toward cognitive and behavioral problem solving, conflict resolution, assertiveness, and empowerment should have improved scores on the MMPI. Indeed, after six months of treatment, there were significant decreases in the scores of the INC-T group on the Hypochondriasis (Hs), Depression (D), Psycasthenia (Pt), and Social Introversion (SI) scales and the Anxiety (A) scales of the MMPI. Although the scores on the Familial Discord Harris-Lingoe subscale of the Pd scale did not exhibit a significant difference after six months of treatment, there was a trend for a scale reduction, which possibly provided some support for the hypothesis that childhood sexual victimization might be associated with elevated Pd scores without rendering an individual classically "sociopathic."

The results obtained on the MBHI also were rather interesting. Although the EX-C and NoEX-C groups did not score in the clinically significant range on any of the eight behavioral coping scales, the INC-T group scored at clinical levels and significantly higher than all other groups on two particular behavioral coping styles with respect to their interaction with health care providers: the Inhibited and Sensitive styles. Interpretation data indicated that individuals who score at clinical levels on the Inhibited scale tended to be hesitant and were often shy and ill at ease. Thus, health care personnel should be careful dealing with incest survivors, since they may be easily hurt and often concerned regarding what others might do to them. Hence, extra effort may be required in order to establish rapport. Because of the sexual trauma they experienced and the possible resultant traumagenic dynamics of betrayal, powerlessness, and stigmatization, it is not at all surprising that the incest survivor client may be easily hurt and often concerned about what others may do to her. Indeed, individuals who score high on this scale fear that others might take advantage of them and tend to keep their problems to themselves. Nevertheless, they do seek understanding and attention. With a sympathetic attitude, consistency, and positive reinforcement, the health care professional can empower the incest survivor to become involved in her health care, particularly as it relates to preventive procedures.

Individuals who scored in the clinical range on Sensitive behavioral coping style may tend to be moody and unpredictable, and the mood changes may seem to occur for no clear-cut reason. They may seem displeased by their physical and psychological state and may complain about their treatment. They may be erratic in following a treatment program, sometimes overmedicating or undermedicating themselves without consulting their physicians. Thus, clients may alternate between complaints about treatment and expressions of guilt regarding their complaints. Although there were solid trends toward score reduction over a 12-month treatment period, the change was not statistically significant overall.

The MBHI contains three scales that purport to assess one's inclination for gastrointestinal, allergic, and cardiovascular disorders. Both the INC-T and the NoINC-T groups scored higher than the other groups on the Gastrointestinal Susceptibility scale. The INC-T group scored significantly higher than all three groups on the Allergic Inclination and Cardiovascular Tendency scales.

The three clinically significant psychogenic attitudes or stressors that were most problematic for the incest survivors were Premorbid Pessimism, Future Despair, and Social Alienation. The INC-T group scored significantly higher than all other groups on these scales. Premorbid Pessimism assessed the level of an individual's sense of hopelessness and helplessness—in effect, the feeling of being powerless. Since powerlessness is one of the traumagenic dynamics that results from childhood sexual abuse (Browne & Finkelhor, 1986), it is not surprising that the INC-T group scored high on this dimension. Individuals who score high on this scale tend to view life as a series of troubles and misfortunes. As a consequence, the physical and psychological discomfort experienced by incest survivors may tend to be more intense than that experienced by others who do not score high on this scale. Thus health care providers should assess the complaints of incest survivors carefully and objectively. Consistent support and reassurance may be necessary in order not to aggravate their symptomatology.

The Future Despair scale assesses response to current difficulties and circumstances as opposed to a general or lifelong tendency to view things negatively. Individuals who score high on this scale do not look forward to a productive future and tend to view medical difficulties as seriously distressing and potentially life threatening. Given that the incest survivors scored high on this measure, it is not surprising that they tend not to engage in preventive health care practices. Again these results suggest that health care professionals can be more effective with survivors by providing strong patient education tempered with encouragement and support.

The results of our earlier research indicated that childhood sexual abuse results in profound feelings of social and emotional alienation (Lundberg-Love et al., 1992). Hence, it is not surprising that the incest survivors scored in the clinically significant range on this scale and higher than all other groups. Individuals who score high on this measure perceive low levels of family and social support and tend not to seek health care assistance until an illness is extremely discomforting. Hence, it is critical for health care practitioners to make every effort to provide the incest survivor client with opportunities to develop significant rapport with and confidence in them.

We believe that the results of this study have important implications for the provision of optimal health care. While practitioners have recognized that childhood sexual abuse can result in a wide array of psychological consequences many years after the molestation (Lundberg-Love et al., 1992), the results of this study (Lundberg-Love, Ford, Marmion, Rogers, & Geffner, in press) clearly indicated that the psychological sequelae of childhood sexual abuse also can mediate a wide array of medical and health-related consequences, some of which can be life threatening. Because approximately one-fifth of the women in this country may be incest survivors (Russell, 1986) and one-third to perhaps even one-half of the women may be survivors of some type of childhood sexual abuse (Russell, 1986; Wyatt, 1985), it is critical that health care practitioners learn to identify these women in their caseload and modify their treatment programs accordingly. Our research has suggested that the MBHI can greatly assist in the former task. However, it is up to each health care provider to accomplish the second task.

The Treatment Program

The research findings indicated that our approach to treatment resulted in significant reductions in the scores on the Depression, Hypochondriasis, Psychasthenia, and Social Introversion subscales of the MMPI after six months and significant reductions in the MMPI scores obtained on the Conscious Anxiety, Subjective Depression (D1), Denial of Social Anxiety, (Hy1), Familial Discord (Pd1), Persecutory Ideas (Pa1), Social Alienation (Sc1A), Emotional Alienation (Sc1B), Inferiority–Personal Discomfort (Si1), and the Narcissism-Hypersensitivity (Mf1) scales after one year of treatment. All of the scales listed, with the exception of the Conscious Anxiety scale, are specific Harris-Lingoe scales that were of therapeutic interest. It is important to recall that our program was initially formulated nearly a decade ago and was consistently fine-tuned as deemed appropriate (Lundberg-Love, 1988; 1989, 1990, 1991, 1992; (Lundberg-Love & Geffner, 1988). Essentially, trauma-focused treatment consisted of four general modalities: anxiety management training, the identification of feelings and salient therapeutic issues, ventilation and assimilation surrounding the array of affective issues, and the resolution of concurrent behavioral issues.

Anxiety management was a critical initial intervention for adult trauma survivors. During the course of the treatment process, survivors often experienced situations that required the ability to diminish problematic feelings and sensations. As a result, it was incumbent on the therapist to provide clients with a mechanism for affect regulation when they experienced strong or painful emotions. Teaching clients a variety of anxiety management strategies was one mechanism for doing this. Acquiring proficiency in such techniques was empowering and promoted affective and cognitive mastery with respect to problematic issues. It also provided a therapeutic intervention that could be used outside sessions. Also, because most adult survivors of abuse struggle with control issues, especially those surrounding control over their bodies, the ability to perform relaxation exercises successfully minimized a wide array of symptoms. Stress-reduction exercises were particularly useful when problematic recollections occurred and as a mechanism for the titration of flashback experiences. Additionally, they provided a means for controlling pain, both physical and emotional. Thus, anxiety management training enabled clients to regulate various aversive internal states.

Anxiety management techniques ranged from progressive muscle relaxation, autogenic techniques, metaphoric imagery, and meditative approaches, to deep breathing and verbal cueing. Typically, I provided an audiotape containing a wide array of relaxation exercises. It was the responsibility of the clients to practice with the tape and develop their own procedures for anxiety management. This approach promoted a spirit of teamwork between therapist and client and facilitated the development of rapport. Additionally, the client began to achieve a sense of affective and cognitive mastery.

The identification of feelings, salient therapeutic issues, and their attendant relationships were a critical cornerstone in an effective treatment process. It is not uncommon for adult survivors of sexual abuse to experience difficulty identifying the fact that a particular feeling even exists, much less articulating its accurate label. Often the range of descriptive adjectives enumerated by the survivor as she attempted to elaborate her affective state was quite restricted. Therefore, three different lists of verbal affective adjectives and two lists of pictorial representations of affective states were given to clients to help them in their identification process. These lists could be used inside and outside the therapy office to help clients begin to identify, characterize, resolve, and thereby master emotional difficulties. With practice, this method expanded clients' descriptive repertoires, which improved their abilities to label and process their experiences. Over time, as they were able to draw on their enhanced verbalization skills during the intermittent dissection and examination of their traumata, they experienced emotional empowerment. To be able to attach precise labels to one's past cognitive, affective, and behavioral experience was one of the core aspects of healing, and one that was consistently honed during the therapeutic process.

The identification of salient therapeutic issues for a client usually began with the review of the results obtained from the various testing instruments. The goal was for the client to link present problems with past experience where it was relevant, and to begin to identify and address the cognitive errors associated with each issue. Education regarding the nature of the various types of cognitive distortions people use was critical to the success of this ongoing therapeutic issue. Typically clients identified and wrestled with issues such as their long-standing feelings of isolation, alienation, depression, low self-esteem, guilt, and shame. Additionally, difficulty with social skills, problems trusting others, and sometimes developmental discontinuities with respect to sexual behavior tended to be revealed over time. Because survivors were often powerless to stop their victimization, it is not surprising to find that they struggled with strong feelings of powerlessness in their adult lives. As a result, feeling in control and the myriad attendant mechanisms executed to achieve that sensation were often a driving force in their behavioral repertoire. The centrality of the powerlessness-control theme in the lives of adult survivors is one of the most common salient treatment issues and one reason that the therapeutic process focused on client mastery and its resultant empowerment.

Once the client was able to identify her salient treatment issues, and the feelings and cognitive distortions with which they were associated, and to modulate her affective states, the processes of ventilation and assimilation ensued. During the ventilation process, a variety of symbolic and metaphoric techniques were used to enable the survivor to divest herself of the problematic emotions that constitute the legacy of sexual victimization. Although anger is a key issue, so are the feelings of guilt, shame, sadness, and grief. In effect, ventilation is a sort of catharsis. As such, this was a stage of treatment in which the collective creativity of both therapist and client was stimulated. Therapists should encourage clients to develop modalities through which feelings can be symbolically expressed. Often artistic, musical, poetic, and dramatic modalities were used.

As clients became ready to ventilate various emotions, they, in conjunction with the therapist, devised some type of symbolic activity that felt appropriate for them: drawing, painting, creating collages, sculpting, writing, and musical modalities, for example. Clients were instructed that ventilation was not an exercise in artistic expertise. Rather, it was a means for expression. Regarding the ventilation of anger, there were two specific rules: not to hurt any living entity and not to destroy any property not expressly secured for that purpose.

A valuable consequence of a client's ventilation activities often was the discovery of previously unrecognized talents. Concurrent client empowerment and enhancement of self-esteem also were common sequelae of ventilatory exercises. Typically these activities needed to be performed a number of times in order to attenuate and resolve problematic feelings.

Although the emphasis of the ventilation phase of treatment was unfettered expression of feelings, the emphasis of the assimilation of phase of treatment was the appropriate expression of emotions. During this phase of treatment, clients were taught techniques for effective communication, such as assertiveness and conflict resolution. Therapist-client role plays were extensively used, permitting the therapist to model empowerment for the client. In general, cognitive-behavioral restructuring techniques improved a wide array of emotional symptoms.

In the resolution phase of treatment, the therapist worked with the client to address remaining problematic issues. While issues such as substance abuse and eating disorders were typically addressed prior to initiating trauma-focused therapy, issues surrounding sexuality, relationships, appropriate health-related self-care, relapse prevention, and prevention of revictimization were now addressed. Once a survivor had successfully resolved her trauma-related symptoms, therapeutic resolution of additional problems was relatively straightforward and less complicated than trying to resolve, say, sexual dysfunction without having addressed trauma-related symptomatology. This is an important observation given the current philosophy of managed care.

Critically important in the treatment of adult survivors is an emphasis on improving the client's levels of functioning during the course of therapy. The key to such an approach is a careful pacing of the therapeutic process. When therapists try to move too rapidly, client decompensation often results. Successful trauma-focused therapy is not unlike an intricate dance between therapist and client wherein, at times, each partner leads and each partner follows until the final destination of the therapeutic journey is reached.

CONCLUSIONS

This chapter described and summarized research and treatment results I have obtained in my study of adult survivors of incestuous abuse during the past decade. By systematically comparing incest survivors with three other groups of similar women, who to the best of our knowledge were devoid of a history of any type of sexual abuse, it was possible to identify certain long-term sequelae associated with childhood incestuous victimization as measured by certain standardized psychological tests (MMPI, MBHI) and to determine the effects of six months and one year of a trauma-focused treatment program. The results indicated that incest survivors scored higher than all other groups and at clinically significant levels on a number of MMPI scales, including Hypochondriasis, Depression, Psychopathic Deviate, Psycasthenia, Schizophrenia, and Social Introversion, and a number of MBHI scales including the behavioral styles called Inhibited and Sensitive, the psychogenic attitudes defined as Recent Stress, Premorbid Pessimism, Future Despair, Social Alienation, and Somatic Anxiety, as well as the psychosomatic correlates entitled Allergic Inclination and Cardiovascular Tendency. Additional differences were found on a number of the Harris-Lingoe scales of the MMPI that have relevance to some of the core treatment issues that appear to be indigenous to survivors of sexual trauma. Moreover, after the survivors experienced one year of trauma-focused therapy, scores on certain clinical and/or Harris-Lingoe MMPI scales were found to decrease after six months (Depression, Hypochondriasis, Psycasthenia, Social Introversion) or one year of treatment (Conscious Anxiety, Subjective Depression, Denial of Social Anxiety, Familial Discord, Persecutory Ideas, Social Alienation, Emotional Alienation, Inferiority–Personal Discomfort,

Narcissism-Hypersensitivity), suggesting that the treatment program resulted in clinical improvement. Additionally, these data indicate that although recovery from some of the sequelae associated with childhood victimization requires more than 10 to 12 therapeutic sessions, trauma-focused treatment can be achieved successfully, and in the long run is cost-effective with respect to mental health and medical health issues.

REFERENCES

American Psychiatric Association. (1994). *Diagnostic and statistical manual IV.* Washington, DC: APA.

Bagley, C., & Ramsey, R. (1985). Sexual abuse in childhood: Psychosocial outcomes and implications for social work practice. *Social Work Practice in Sexual Problems, 4,* 33–47.

Briere, J. (1989). *Therapy for adults molested as children: Beyond survival.* New York: Springer.

Briere, J. (1992). *Child abuse trauma: Theory and treatment of the lasting effects.* Newbury Park, CA: Sage.

Briere, J. (1995). *Trauma symptom inventory.* Odessa, FL: Psychological Assessment Resources.

Briere, J., & Conte, J. R. (1993). Self-reported amnesia for abuse in adults molested as children. *Journal of Traumatic Stress, 6,* 21–32.

Briere, J., & Elliott, D. M. (1993). Sexual abuse, family environment, and psychological symptoms: On the validity of statistical control. *Journal of Consulting and Clinical Psychology, 61,* 284–288.

Briere, J., & Runtz, M. (1987). Post-sexual abuse trauma: Data and implications for practice. *Journal of Interpersonal Relations, 8,* 367–379.

Briere, J., & Runtz, M. (1988). Post-sexual abuse trauma. In G. E. Wyatt & G. Powell (Eds.), *The lasting effects of child sexual abuse.* Newbury Park, CA: Sage.

Briere, J., & Zaidi, L. Y. (1989). Sexual abuse histories and sequelae in female psychiatric emergency room patients. *American Journal of Psychiatry, 146,* 1602–1606.

Browne, A., & Finkelhor, D. (1986). Impact of child sexual abuse: A review of the research. *Psychological Bulletin, 99,* 66–77.

Chu, J. A., & Dill, D. L. (1990). Dissociative symptoms in relation to childhood physical and sexual abuse. *American Journal of Psychiatry, 147,* 887–892.

Courtois, C. (1988). *Healing the incest wound: Adults in therapy.* New York: Norton.

Dahlstrom, W. G., Welsh, G. S., & Dahlstrom, L. E. (1972). *An MMPI handbook, Volume I: Clinical interpretation.* Minneapolis, MN: University of Minnesota Press.

Donaldson, M. A., & Gardner, R., Jr. (1985). Diagnosis and treatment of traumatic stress among women after childhood incest. In C. R. Figley (Ed.), *Trauma and its wake: The study and treatment of post-traumatic stress disorder.* New York: Brunner/Mazel.

Elliott, D. M. (1994). Impaired object relations in professional women molested as children. *Psychotherapy, 31,* 79–86.

Elliott, D. M., & Briere, J. (1995). Posttraumatic stress associated with delayed recall of sexual abuse: A general population study. *Journal of Traumatic Stress Studies, 8,* 629–648.

Finkelhor, D. (1986). *Sourcebook on child sexual abuse.* Beverly Hills, CA: Sage.

Finkelhor, D. (1994). Current information on the scope and nature of child sexual abuse. *Future of Children, 4,* 31–53.

Finkelhor, D., & Browne, A. (1985). The traumatic impact of child sexual abuse: A conceptualization. *American Journal of Orthopsychiatry, 55,* 530–541.

Finkelhor, D., Hotaling, G., Lewis, I. A., & Smith, C. (1990). Sexual abuse in a national survey of adult men and women: Prevalence, characteristics, and risk factors. *Child Abuse and Neglect, 14,* 19–28.

Gold, E. R. (1986). Long-term effects of sexual victimization in childhood: An attributional approach. *Journal of Consulting and Clinical Psychology, 54,* 471– 475.

Herman, J. L. (1981). *Father-daughter incest.* Cambridge, MA: Harvard University Press.

Herman, J. L., & Schatzow, E. (1987). Recovery and verification of memories of childhood sexual trauma. *Psychoanalytic Psychology, 4,* 490–494.

Jehu, D. (1988). *Beyond sexual abuse: Therapy with women who were childhood victims.* Chichester, UK: Wiley.

Kluft, R. P. (Ed.). (1985). *Childhood antecedents of multiple personality.* Washington, DC: American Psychiatric Press.

Lundberg-Love, P. K. (1988, March). *Sexuality issues in the treatment of adult incest survivors.* In P. K. Lundberg-Love (Chair), The impact of incest upon the sexuality of adult women. Symposium conducted at the Society of the Scientific Study of Sex biennial meeting, Dallas, TX.

Lundberg-Love, P. K. (1989, August). *Treatment of adult incest survivors.* In R. A. Geffner (Chair), Treating incest victims and offenders: Applying recent research. Invited symposium presented at the American Psychological Association annual meeting, New Orleans, LA.

Lundberg-Love, P. K. (1990). Treatment of adult incest survivors. In R. T. Ammerman & M. Herson (Eds.), *Treatment of family violence: A sourcebook.* New York: Wiley.

Lundberg-Love, P. K. (1991, August). *Effectiveness of a treatment approach for adult incest survivors.* In R. Geffner (Chair), State-of-the-art research in family violence: Practical applications. Symposium presented at the American Psychological Association annual meeting, San Francisco.

Lundberg-Love, P. K. (1992, August). *Recent advances in determining who is a survivor.* In S. A. Kirschner (Chair), Recent advances in the treatment of incest survivors. Symposium presented at the American Psychological Association annual meeting, Washington, DC.

Lundberg-Love, P. K., Crawford, C. M., & Geffner, R. A. (1987, April). *Personality characteristics of adult incest survivors.* In R. Geffner (Chair), Characteristics and treatment of adult incest survivors. Symposium presented at the Southwestern Psychological Association annual meeting, New Orleans, LA.

Lundberg-Love, P. K., Ford, K., Marmion, S., Rogers, K., & Geffner, R. (in press). Identification of adult sexual abuse survivors: Implications for preventive medicine. *Journal of Child Sexual Abuse.*

Lundberg-Love, P. K., & Geffner, R. (1988, April). *Treatment of adult incest survivors: Recount, repair, resolve.* In R. Geffner (Chair), Identification, treatment, and prevention of sexual abuse in the family. Symposium presented at the Western Psychological Association annual meeting, San Francisco.

Lundberg-Love, P. K., Marmion, S., Ford, K., Geffner, R., & Peacock, L. (1992). The long term consequences of childhood incestuous victimization upon women's psychological symptomatology. *Journal of Child Sexual Abuse, 1*(1), 81–102.

Maltz, W., & Holman, B. (1987). *Incest and sexuality: A guide to understanding and healing.* Lexington, MA: Lexington Books.

Meiselman, K. (1978). *Incest: A psychological study of causes and effects with treatment recommendations.* San Francisco: Jossey-Bass.

Peters, S. D. (1984). *The relationship between childhood sexual victimization and adult depression among Afro-American and white women.* Unpublished doctoral dissertation, University of California at Los Angeles.

Peters, S. D. (1988). Child sexual abuse and later psychological problems. In G. E. Wyatt & G. J. Powell (Eds.), *The lasting effects of child sexual abuse* (pp. 101–117). Newbury Park, CA: Sage.

Piran, N., Lerner, P., Garfinkel, P. E., Kennedy, S. H., & Brouillette, C. (1988). Personality disorders in anorectic patients. *International Journal of Eating Disorders, 7,* 589–599.

Putnam, F. W. (1990). Disturbance of "self" in victims of childhood sexual abuse. In R. P. Kluft (Ed.), *Incest-related syndromes of adult psychopathology* (pp. 113–132). Washington, DC: American Psychiatric Press.

Ross, C. A. (1989). *Multiple personality disorder: Diagnosis, clinical features, and treatment.* New York: Wiley.

Russell, D.E.H. (1984). *Sexual exploitation: Rape, child sexual abuse, and workplace harassment.* Beverly Hills, CA: Sage.

Russell, D.E.H. (1986). *The secret trauma: Incest in the lives of girls and women*. New York: Basic Books.

Saunders, B. E., Villeponteaux, L. A., Lipovsky, J. A., & Kilpatrick, D. G. (1992). Child sexual assault as a risk factor for mental disorder for women: A community survey. *Journal of Interpersonal Violence, 7*, 189–204.

Sedney, M. A., & Brooks, B. (1984). Factors associated with a history of child-hood sexual experience in a nonclinical female population. *Journal of the American Academy of Child Psychiatry, 23*, 215–218.

Singer, M. I., Petchers, M. K., & Hussey, D. (1989). The relationship between sexual abuse and substance abuse among psychiatrically hospitalized adolescents. *Child Abuse and Neglect, 13*, 319–325.

Sorenson, S. B., Siegel, J. M., Golding, J. M., & Stein, J. A. (1991). Repeated sexual victimization. *Victims and Violence, 91*, 299–308.

Springs, F. E., & Friedrich, W. N. (1992). Health risk behaviors and medical sequelae of childhood sexual abuse. *Mayo Clinic Proceedings, 67*, 527–532.

Steiger, H., & Zanko, M. (1990). Sexual traumata among eating disordered, psychiatric, and normal female groups: Comparison of prevalences and defense styles. *Journal of Interpersonal Violence, 5*, 74–88.

Stein, J. A., Golding, J. M., Siegel, J. M., Burnam, M. A., & Sorensen, S. B. (1988). Long-term psychological sequelae of child sexual abuse: The Los Angeles Epidemiologic Catchment Area Study. In G. E. Wyatt & G. J. Powell (Eds.), *The lasting effects of child sexual abuse* (pp. 135–154). Newbury Park, CA: Sage.

Tsai, M., Feldman-Summers, S., & Edgar, M. (1979). Childhood molestation variables related to differential impact of psychosexual functioning in adult women. *Journal of Abnormal Psychology, 88*, 407–417.

van der Kolk, B. A., & Kadish, W. (1987). Amnesia, dissociation, and the return of the repressed. In B. A. van der Kolk (Ed.), *Psychological trauma*. Washington, DC: American Psychiatric Press.

van der Kolk, B. A., Perry, J. C., & Herman, J. L. (1991). Childhood origins of self-destructive behavior. *American Journal of Psychiatry, 148*, 1665–1671.

Walker, E. A., Katon, W. J., Alfrey, H., Bowers, M., & Stenchever, M. A. (1991). The prevalence of chronic pelvic pain and irritable bowel syndrome in two university clinics. *Journal of Psychosomatics, Obstetrics and Gynecology 12(Suppl)*, 65–75.

Walker, E. A., Katon, W. J., Roy-Byrne, P. P., & Jemelka, R. P. (1993). Histories of sexual victimization in patients with irritable bowel syndrome, or inflammatory bowel disease. *American Journal of Psychiatry, 150*, 1502–1506.

Walsh, B. W., & Rosen, P. (1988). *Self-mutilation: Theory, research, and treatment.* New York: Guilford.

Williams, L. (1994). Recall of childhood trauma: A prospective study of women's memories of childhood sexual abuse. *Journal of Consulting and Clinical Psychology, 62,* 1167–1176.

Wyatt, G. E. (1985). The sexual abuse of Afro-American and white-American women in childhood. *Child Abuse and Neglect, 9,* 507–519.

PART II

SEXUAL VICTIMIZATION IN DATING AND MARITAL RELATIONSHIPS

2

Physical Violence in Dating Relationships

Kathryn M. Ryan, Irene Hanson Frieze, and H. Colleen Sinclair

This chapter reviews research on physical violence in dating relationships, looking primarily at studies of teenagers and young adults. Due to limitations in existing research, we focus on white heterosexual relationships, although we do examine homosexual violence briefly. It is clear that more research needs to be done on homosexual courtship violence. We have also largely limited ourselves to a discussion of physical violence rather than sexual or psychological violence. We discuss the frequency of courtship violence and some of its characteristics, causes, and consequences. We also note the absence of research on stalking as a type of courtship violence and the need for more research on serious courtship violence. We suggest several characteristics that might predict serious courtship violence. We end the chapter with some suggestions for practitioners.

IS COURTSHIP VIOLENCE A PROBLEM?

Physical violence in dating relationships is clearly a problem in America. Approximately one-third of all American college students report using or being victims of courtship violence (Sugarman & Hotaling, 1989a; White & Koss, 1991). Some racially diverse studies show similar rates for physical violence, whereas others indicate there may be racial differences (Sugarman & Hotaling, 1989a). For example, Clark, Beckett, Wells, and Dungee-Anderson (1994) show that 41% of African-American men and 33% of African-American women report receiving some level of physical violence from their heterosexual partners. Prevalence figures for Asian Americans and Latinos prove more difficult to obtain, for various reasons. However, Yoshihama, Parekh, and Boyington (1991) assure us that despite the "model minority myth," dating violence among Asian Americans is a reality.

Sugarman and Hotaling (1989a) examined racial differences in courtship violence in their review of several published studies. They note that results sometimes show relatively higher levels in African Americans, relatively lower levels for Asian Americans, and slightly higher levels for Hispanic Americans as compared to white or Anglo groups. However, White and Koss (1991) showed no race effects in their national survey of college students. Thus, we cannot make definitive conclusions about race differences in courtship violence levels.

Sugarman and Hotaling (1989a) were unable to draw firm conclusions about age and rural-urban comparisons; however, they report higher incidence levels among individuals in lower-income groups. Regionally, Sugarman and Hotaling (1989a) noted that the South had the highest average rates for dating violence, where 44% of their survey's samples had experienced relationship violence. Following the South were the West (28%), the Midwest (26%), and then the eastern states (23%). However, these regional effects were not replicated in the national survey of college students by White and Koss (1991). Moreover, apparent regional differences may be related to race or socioeconomic status.

TYPES OF VIOLENCE

The most common form of reported aggression in dating relationships is pushing, grabbing, or shoving (Arias, Samios, & O'Leary, 1987; Deal & Wampler, 1986; Marshall & Rose, 1987; Worth, Matthews, & Coleman, 1990). Slapping and throwing objects are also relatively common. More severe forms of aggression are less common, but they do occur. For example, 12 studies of dating violence, up to 7% of respondents said that they had beaten up or were beaten by their partner (Arias et al., 1987; Bookwala, Frieze, Smith, & Ryan, 1992; Cate, Henton, Koval, Christopher, & Lloyd, 1982; Deal & Wampler, 1986; DeKeseredy & Kelly, 1993a, 1993b; Henton, Cate, Koval, Lloyd, & Christopher, 1983; Marshall & Rose, 1987, 1990; O'Keeffe, Brockopp, & Chew, 1986; Roscoe & Callahan, 1985; Sigelman, Berry, & Wiles, 1984; Thompson, 1990). Estimates for threatening with a weapon are in approximately the same range. Other serious forms of violence found in courtship include choking (Bogal-Allbritten & Allbritten, 1985; Laner & Thompson, 1982; Makepeace, 1981), striking their partner with an object (Bogal-Allbritten & Allbritten, 1985; O'Keeffe et al., 1986; Thompson, 1990), and using sexual force (Koss, 1993; Muehlenhard & Linton, 1987; Sigelman et al., 1984).

A key issue often raised in studies of relationship violence is how violence should best be measured. Courtship violence is usually assessed by the Conflict Tactics Scale (CTS) (Straus, 1979), which focuses on violent acts and asks how frequently any of a variety of acts have occurred during a conflict situation for the couple. These acts are grabbing, punching, kicking, throwing objects at, and threatening with or actually using a knife or a gun. Other common types of violent acts are often not included—for example, burning the partner, wrestling, restraining the partner, forcing sexual activity, locking the partner out of the home, or destroying belongings of the partner (Island & Letellier, 1991; Renzetti, 1992). However, several of these acts are included in the Revised Conflict Tactics Scale (Straus, Hamby, Boney-McCoy, & Sugarman, 1995).

Also missing from this list is stalking, an issue that is receiving increasing media attention but has been little studied by researchers. Mullen and Pathe (1994) note that "the largest group of stalkers are ex-husbands and ex-lovers who either refuse to accept the relationship is at an end, or who seek retribution for what they perceive as rejection or infidelity" (p. 469). In their 1994 study, Mullen and Pathe wrote that victims endured "stalking behaviors that included following, loitering in victim's vicinity, approaching, telephoning, and sending letters . . . threaten[ing] . . . , violently assault[ing]—one fatally—and sexually attack[ing]" (p. 469). These acts are both psychological and physical, and often included extensive material and property damage. Furthermore, they cause considerable psychological trauma (Kurt, 1995; Pathe & Mullen, 1997).

As Renzetti (1992) puts it, there is no "typical" violence, so it is difficult to make any list of violent acts (including the CTS) inclusive. Nor can one expect such a listing of actions to represent the different intents, frequency, motivation, or intensity of a given act. Moreover, what is felt by the victim may not tell us what is intended by the aggressor. For instance, a stalker who is damaging property or making obscene telephone calls may have very much the same intent as that of a batterer: to terrorize and control. Alternately, a person calling every day and hanging up may be someone who is trying to get up the nerve to speak with a possible love interest and does not intend any ill effects. The issue of intent is even more complex for psychological violence. Island and Letellier (1991), Walker (1979), and others have suggested that psychological violence and material or property destruction may be as devastating as, if not more so than, physical violence.

Women often report using relatively more courtship violence than men when they rate their actions on the CTS (Bookwala et al., 1992; Marshall & Rose, 1987); however, this higher rate of violence by women may not reflect the actual reality of courtship violence. The CTS may overestimate female aggression and underestimate male aggression because behaviors can be assessed on the CTS only if they are acknowledged and remembered. Because of a norm that men should not hit women, men may tend to deny or minimize their courtship violence. We know this is true of wife batterers (Bernard & Bernard, 1984; Ptacek, 1988) and rapists (Koss, Gidycz, & Wisniewski, 1987; Scully, 1990). Furthermore, men may lie about their behavior even if they recognize and remember it (Dutton & Hemphill, 1992), because male-on-female aggression is judged more harshly than female-on-male aggression (Arias & Johnson, 1989; Greenblat, 1983; Marshall, 1992a, 1992b). When asked if they would admit to engaging in courtship violence on an anonymous questionnaire, men were significantly less likely than women to admit they would use verbal aggression (male $M = 3.54$, female $M = 4.12$), and they were less likely than women to admit they would use physical aggression (male $M = 2.40$, female $M = 2.80$). This difference was nonsignificant (Riggs, Murphy, & O'Leary, 1989), so it is difficult to compare violence estimates for men and women.

CHARACTERISTICS OF COURTSHIP VIOLENCE

Most of the research on courtship violence explores the causes and consequences of relatively low-level physical violence among middle-class white heterosexuals. This research shows several clear patterns. First, violence is often mutual (Deal & Wampler, 1986; Gwartney-Gibbs, Stockard, & Bohmer, 1987; Sack, Keller, & Howard, 1982; Thompson, 1990). Second, women are as likely as, or even more likely than, men to report engaging in courtship aggression (Bookwala et al., 1992; Deal & Wampler, 1986; Lane & Gwartney-Gibbs, 1985; Plass & Gessner, 1983). Third, courtship violence is frequently viewed as acceptable by all parties. As noted by Henton and her colleagues (1983), dating "violence is viewed by participating individuals as relatively nondisruptive to the relationship and sometimes is even seen as a positive occurrence" (p. 467). Only about 40% of victims of courtship violence see their relationship as abusive (Stets & Pirog-Good, 1989). In addition, almost half of college women say that it is sometimes acceptable to slap one's partner (48%), whereas only 30% say it is never acceptable to use violence (Roscoe, 1985). And violence is somewhat acceptable to approximately one-third of individuals who do not engage in violence themselves (Matthews, 1984).

Fourth, men, especially abusive men (Henton et al., 1983), have a less negative attitude toward relationship violence than women (Greenblat, 1983). Men also generally see relationship violence as more justifiable (Tontodonato & Crew, 1992). Moreover, attitudes toward relationship violence are more predictive of male aggression than of female aggression (Bookwala et al., 1992; Tontodonato & Crew, 1992).

Fifth, people view relationship violence as less serious if it is done by a woman to a man than by a man to a woman (Arias & Johnson, 1989; Greenblat, 1983; Marshall, 1992a, 1992b). Sixth, the best predictor of future violence is past violence (Deal & Wampler, 1986; O'Leary et al., 1989). Threats and verbal abuse are also excellent predictors of courtship violence (Ryan, 1995). Finally, individuals do not typically report courtship violence to authorities (Makepeace, 1981). Although women are more likely than men to tell someone (Stets & Pirog-Good, 1989), if they do tell someone, it is usually a friend or parent (Henton et al., 1983; Roscoe & Callahan, 1985; Roscoe & Kelsey, 1986; Stets & Pirog-Good, 1989).

VIOLENCE IN HOMOSEXUAL RELATIONSHIPS

There is little research on homosexual relationship violence. In the eyes of the law, there are battering relationships within the family, involving heterosexual, legally married couples, and then there is the category of "other," which includes all other forms of acquaintance battering, from dating partners and co-habitants to relatives. As Hendricks (1992) noted, it was not until the late 1980s that 38 states recognized that parties do not have to be married, or formerly married, to be abused. Accordingly, dating and, in six states, same-sex couples are recognized and protected under the definition of abuse. In one of these states, California, San Francisco police report responding to no fewer than 100 calls a month for violence in lesbian and gay relationships, approximating 1,200 a year in San Francisco alone (Island & Letellier, 1991). San Francisco's Community United Against Violence estimates the actual rate of incidence to be much higher, placing the "best guess" that half the gay male population in San Francisco has been victimized, for a total of 20,000 annually (Island & Letellier, 1991). Island and Letellier further calculate 500,000 victims of gay male battering nationally every year. All of these figures are just best guesses; there has yet to be any definitive research on the extent to which the male homosexual community is affected by intimate violence.

There is slightly more information to be found regarding lesbian battering. A study conducted by Lie and Gentlewarrier (1991) surveyed a nonrandom sample of lesbians in Michigan. Of the 1,109 participants, 50%

reported experiencing at least one instance of abuse from a female partner. Type of abuse varied from verbal and psychological violence to combined sexual, physical, and psychological abuse. The most frequent pattern was a combination of physical and psychological abuse, reported by 20% of the respondents. A follow-up study by Lie and fellow authors Schilit, Bush, Montagne, and Reyes (1991) verified similar reports of levels of violence from 350 lesbians in the Phoenix metropolitan area. Over half (52%) of women classified at least one past relationship as abusive. In addition, over half of this group (57%) had been sexually victimized, 45% were physically assaulted, and 65% reported psychological abuse. Moreover, 10% of these women were in currently abusive relationships. Renzetti (1992) studied a nonrandom sample of lesbian victims of partner violence. The victims reported experiencing a wide variety of abuse, including many different types of physical and psychological aggression. Finally, looking at sexual abuse alone, a sample of gay and lesbian couples in New York (Waterman, Dawson, & Bologna, 1989) revealed that 12% of men and 31% of women reported being victims of sexual assault by their current or most recent companion.

The lack of research on homosexual couples makes generalizations difficult, although it is clear that cohabiting homosexual couples experience domestic violence (Island & Letellier, 1991; Renzetti, 1992). This finding suggests that dating homosexual couples also experience courtship violence. Future work may indicate how many of the generalizations made in the remainder of this chapter apply as well to homosexual violence.

CAUSES OF COURTSHIP VIOLENCE

We do know a bit about the perceived causes of courtship violence from the perspective of the individuals involved. For example, anger and confusion are commonly mentioned causes of courtship violence, and love is mentioned as a cause of violence more often than hate (Cate et al., 1982; Henton et al., 1983; Roscoe & Callahan, 1985). In addition, jealousy is one of the most commonly mentioned causes of courtship violence (Makepeace, 1981; Roscoe & Kelsey, 1986). Gagn and LaVoie (1993) found that among teenagers, jealousy was the most frequently cited cause of courtship violence. Similar results were established by Stets and Pirog-Good in 1987: jealousy was the most common situation in which violence was exhibited by women.

Other causes of violence, such as disagreements over sex or over alcohol and drug use, are less frequently mentioned (Makepeace, 1981; Roscoe & Kelsey, 1986). Frustration over communication difficulties and their partner's perceived involvement in another relationship are additional reasons for courtship violence (Matthews, 1984). Finally, women are more likely than men to see their own aggression as a product of self-defense (36% of women, 18% of men), and men are more likely than women to see their own aggression as intimidative (21% of men, 7% of women) (Makepeace, 1986). Men and women are equally likely to view their aggression as due to retaliation (16% of men, 19% of women) and uncontrolled anger (28% of men, 24% of women).

One major difference between men's and women's courtship violence may be its function. Male courtship violence may be more instrumental, whereas female courtship violence may be more expressive. Berkowitz (1993) suggests that a similar dynamic may operate for female and male murderers, and Campbell (1993) believes that this may explain several sex differences in aggression, including those found in domestic violence. Instrumental aggression is an "action carried out deliberately . . . to achieve a purpose other than injuring the victim" (Berkowitz, 1993, p. 25). Aggression may be used by men to dominate and control their partners. Power and dominance motives are highly predictive of male relationship violence (Follingstad, Rutledge, McNeill-Harkins, & Polek, 1992; Frieze & McHugh, 1992; Mason & Blankenship, 1987). In addition, men are more likely to suggest intimidation as a cause of their aggression (Makepeace, 1986). Finally, because men are less negative in their view of relationship violence, they may use it more consciously in order to control their partner.

In contrast, aggression may be more expressive in women. Expressive (or emotional) aggression is "impelled by intense physiological and motor reactions within the individual . . . and is motivated more by an urge to injure the target rather than by a wish to achieve some purpose" (Berkowitz, 1993, p. 26). This may explain why women engage in courtship violence even though they are negative in their attitudes toward relationship violence (Bookwala et al., 1992; Tontodonato & Crew, 1992). Women's use of courtship violence may be more spontaneous and impulsive than men's. In addition, women's relationship violence appears to be more of a product of generalized aggression than men's (Bookwala et al., 1992; Malone, Tyree, & O'Leary, 1989). Thus, women may aggress in a less conscious or controlled manner than men do. Relationship violence in women may be more of a product of emotions like fear (Mason & Blankenship, 1987; Matthews, 1984) and jealousy (Bookwala et al., 1992; Renzetti, 1992) or a desire for self-defense (Makepeace, 1986; Saunders, 1986). This also may be why we see more reciprocal aggression in women than in men (Marshall & Rose, 1987, 1990; Mason & Blankenship, 1987). For some women, aggression may be a reaction to actual, predicted, or perceived aggression in their partner. Thus, it appears that courtship aggression may serve different purposes in men and women.

OUTCOMES OF COURTSHIP VIOLENCE

Violence is sometimes associated with dissatisfaction with the relationship—but not always. Several studies have reported that most individuals were still involved in the relationship after physical aggression occurred (e.g., Brodbelt, 1983; Cate et al., 1982; Sigelman et al., 1984). Some respondents even reported increased involvement in the relationship (Gryl, Stith, & Bird, 1991; Makepeace, 1981). In one study, the average length of the relationship after aggression first occurred was 62 days (Flynn, 1990). Individuals may stay in an aggressive relationship for a variety of reasons. They may still love their partner, they may accept the violence as a normal part of relationships (Billingham, 1987), or they may think they have few dating alternatives (Cate et al., 1982; Henton et al., 1983). Flynn (1990) found that level of love, length of the relationship, and amount of aggression were all positively associated with staying.

Individuals sometimes see aggression as beneficial and interpret it as an act of love rather than an act of hate (Cate et al., 1982; Henton et al., 1983). There is other provocative research linking relationship violence and love. Researchers and theorists have noted the passionate beginning of many domestic violence relationships (Frieze & Browne, 1989; Kelly & Loesch, 1983; O'Leary et al., 1989; Pagelow, 1984; Walker, 1983). This may explain why jealousy, an emotion that may stem from possessive love, is a frequently cited explanation for courtship violence (Makepeace, 1981).

It has been suggested that "violence may serve as a catalyst which moves the relationship to greater levels of commitment" (Billingham, 1987, p. 283). Numerous studies have noted that violence tends to be experienced more frequently in relationships at more serious levels of commitment than those at a casual dating stage (Arias et al., 1987; Billingham, 1987; Gryl et al., 1991; Stets & Straus, 1989). However, this difference does not mean that violence at the casual dating level should be disregarded, since it may be a precursor to later, more severe violence. In fact, high rates in more serious relationships may result from the couple's having accepted the violence as a legitimate conflict tactic from exposure to abuse early in the relationship (Billingham, 1987). Billingham (1987) argues that physical and emotional violence is a victimizer's test of the safety of a relationship and the true commitment of a partner. If the partner endures the violence, then the aggressor feels secure in moving the relationship to a more committed level. Accordingly, it could be interpreted that following a violent dispute to which the victimized partner does not react adversely, the aggressor feels the relationship is safe. Consequently, there is an advance in dating status that could be perceived as an improvement in the relationship. This improvement then would be reported as a greater commitment between partners.

An outcome frequently found in courtship violence research is that the relationship purportedly improves after the aggression: 11% to 43% of respondents reported that their relationship improved after the aggression (Bogal-Allbritten & Allbritten, 1985; Cate et al., 1982; Henton et al., 1983; Matthews, 1984; Roscoe & Callahan, 1985; Worth et al., 1990). Between 12% and 44% reported the relationship worsened, and between 20% and 41% reported no change in the relationship. Sigelman and her colleagues (1984) noted that although individuals in abusive relationships viewed their relations less positively ($M = 3.67$) than those in nonabusive relationships ($M = 3.31$; 3 = very good, 4 = good), they were not negative in their relationship evaluation overall.

Minimization and denial of violence may also increase the likelihood of relationships' persevering in spite of the presence of violence. In one study, only 40% of abused individuals labeled their relationship as "abusive" (Stets & Pirog-Good, 1989). And in another study, about one-third of individuals saw no negative effects of the courtship violence (Worth et al., 1990). Men are especially likely to see their partner's aggression as inconsequential (O'Leary & Arias, 1988), and they may minimize and deny their own courtship aggression as well. Makepeace (1986) found that women reported sustaining more injury and emotional trauma than men; however, men did not share the perception of women being injured. Minimization and denial of violence have also been found in wife batterers (Bernard & Bernard, 1984; McHugh, Frieze, & Browne, 1993; Ptacek, 1988) and rapists (Koss et al., 1987; Scully, 1990). Finally, individuals who fight back are more likely to deny that relationship violence occurred than those who do not reciprocate the aggression (Renzetti, 1992).

Some individuals do choose to terminate their relationship after aggression. Sigelman and her colleagues (1984) found that 46% of their respondents had ended their relationship; however, only 14% of them said it was due to the abuse. Another 33% said the abuse was one of several factors that led to the relationship's termination. And over half of all respondents who terminated their relationship did not mention abuse at all as a factor. Since estimates of the number of people who terminate their relationship after violence vary widely (from 12% to 73%), it is difficult to know just how common this is as a reason for breaking up (Bogal-Allbritten & Allbritten,

1985; Makepeace, 1981; O'Keeffe et al., 1986; Roscoe & Callahan, 1985; Roscoe & Kelsey, 1986; Sigelman et al., 1984; Worth et al., 1990).

Some people may be more likely to terminate a violent relationship than others. For example, Flynn (1990) found that women with less traditional sex role attitudes were more likely than traditional women to terminate their relationship after the first episode of violence. Length of the relationship is also a factor since it is more difficult to terminate a serious relationship than a casual one because of the greater investments (Rusbult, 1983). This may help to explain why physical aggression usually enters a relationship only after it has become serious (Cate et al., 1982; Laner & Thompson, 1982; Thompson, 1990, 1991) or why greater levels of aggression are found in more serious relationships (e.g., Laner & Thompson, 1982; Plass & Gessner, 1983). People may be more willing to terminate a relationship if aggression occurs before they are committed to it.

Laner (1989) suggests that the victim's interpretation of the aggressor's motives is an important factor in her or his response to courtship violence. How the aggressor behaves (e.g., guilt and apologies versus smugness and self-approval) may be important in influencing the victim's willingness to stay and their evaluation of the quality of their relationship. Most respondents said their partner was responsible for the aggression, or they saw both persons as equally responsible (e.g., Henton et al., 1983; Makepeace, 1988; Matthews, 1984; Roscoe & Callahan, 1985; Roscoe & Kelsey, 1986). Individuals rarely assume sole responsibility for the violence they experience. They often see themselves as the victim.

When exploring individuals' immediate response to the situation, Henton et al. (1983) found that victims felt more angry and hurt, whereas aggressors felt more sorry and hurt. Aggressors often apologized (69%), tried to make up (54%), talked (42%), cried (25%), or left (19%). Victims talked (51%), cried (44%), left (39%), and moved out of reach (26%). Matthews (1984) asked men and women who experienced courtship violence to report their response. Men reported more talking (61% versus 39% female), while women reported more crying (84% versus 16% male), going out of reach (62% versus 38%), and leaving the scene (63% versus 37%). Men felt more sorry (56% versus 44%). Women were more scared (86% versus 14% male), surprised (60% versus 40%), angry (59% versus 41%), and hurt (59% versus 41%). Finally, female college students who experienced dating violence reported higher levels of psychological distress than those not having experienced courtship violence (Coffey, Leitenberg, Henning, Bennett, & Jankowski, 1996). However, this study of over 900 undergraduate women also found that the women in violent courting relationships more often had been victims of sexual aggression and other forms of violence in their homes, so causal relationships are not clear.

Another response to courtship aggression is to fight back. Almost half of the victims indentified by Henton et al. (1983) said they reciprocated the violence. Women are more likely than men to report fighting back (women, 61%; men, 39%) (Matthews, 1984). We also know reciprocation is a common response because of research that shows that most courtship violence is mutual (Cate et al., 1982; Deal & Wampler, 1986; Gwartney-Gibbs et al., 1987; Henton et al., 1983; Sigelman et al., 1984; Worth et al., 1990). Cate and his colleagues (1982) found a correlation of .64 between the number of abusive acts used and received. Bookwala and her colleagues (1992, p. 297) report that "receipt of physical violence from one's partner was the largest predictor of expressed violence for both men and women." O'Keeffe and her colleagues (1986) believe that reciprocity works to keep the level of violence down in relationships because it provides negative consequences for the aggressive act. However, Billingham (1987) found that individuals in a mutually violent relationship showed the highest violence scores. He suggests that violence-prone individuals seek other violence-prone individuals as partners (Billingham & Sack, 1987).

These findings lead to the important possibility of violence escalating in the relationship, yet little research has addressed this subject. Makepeace (1981) found that about half of his respondents engaged in aggression more than one time. Bogal-Allbritten and Allbritten (1985) found a similar estimate, with about half of the respondents using aggression more than once and 22% of the respondents using aggression five or more times. Lane and Gwartney-Gibbs (1985) reported that 80% of the males and 44% of the females said they were aggressive more than one time or with more than one partner. In addition, Billingham (1987) noted that the "higher violence scores [were] found for those respondents in mutual violence relationships" (p. 287). Finally, Flynn (1990) found that repeated victimization was associated with more serious forms of violence.

COURTSHIP VIOLENCE

Johnson (1995) introduced the possibility that there are two forms of violence found in current domestic violence research: patriarchal terrorism, the product of systematic emotional and physical violence used to control one's partner, and common couple violence, which refers to "occasional outbursts of violence from either husbands or wives" (p. 283). Johnson suggests that four features distinguish patriarchal terrorism from common couple violence: a greater level of aggression in patriarchal terrorism, greater escalation of aggression in patriarchal terrorism, more reciprocity and female-initiated aggression in common couple violence, and an interpersonal dynamic in patriarchal terrorism that is marked by the use of multiple control tactics. We believe there may be two types of courtship violence: low level, marked by the relatively rare occurrence of minor physical aggression, and high level which involves serious or repeated physical aggression and sexual aggression. In this section, we focus on predictors of more serious violent relationships.

Psychological Aggression

One possible predictor of high-level courtship violence may be the presence of psychological or emotional aggression, which may take many forms. It includes verbal abuse (e.g., name calling, obscenities), symbolic aggression (e.g., punching walls, throwing objects), and displaced aggression (e.g., punishing pets or children). It may also include "playful" aggression (e.g., playful force during sex, playful threats, playful wrestling). Research on college students shows higher levels of psychological aggression than physical aggression (DeKeseredy & Kelly, 1993a; White & Koss, 1991). In addition, psychological aggression appears to be reciprocated. Women are especially likely to report engaging in mutual psychological violence (Mason & Blankenship, 1987). Psychological aggression is so commonly associated with physical aggression that one form of the CTS includes threats and throwing objects as instances of physical aggression (Straus, 1979). Psychological aggression is an important correlate of domestic violence (Dutton, 1995; Evans, 1992; Pence & Paymar, 1993). Psychological aggression is also a distinguishing feature of patriarchal terrorism (Johnson, 1995). Research on college men shows that threats, verbal abuse, and playful force during sex predict courtship violence (Ryan, 1995). It is possible that psychological aggression may be an important predictor of serious courtship violence in men and women as well.

Male Initiation and Retaliation

Another predictor of serious aggression in dating relationships may be the man's use of physical aggression. Women are more likely than men to engage in low-level relationship violence (Deal & Wampler, 1986; Lane & Gwartney-Gibbs, 1985; Plass & Gessner, 1983). However, men are more likely than women to engage in serious relationship violence (e.g., Lane & Gwartney-Gibbs, 1985; Makepeace, 1986; Plass & Gessner, 1983; Thompson, 1990). Thus, women may be better able than men to moderate their use of aggression. This may be because women have more guilt, fear, and anxiety about engaging in aggression or that women are generally less physically aggressive than men (Eagly & Steffen, 1986). It may be a significant factor in a relationship if the man is willing to violate the norm that "men should not hit women." Because of their greater size and strength, men may be expected to censure their own aggressive impulses with women and to endure their partner's aggression. When they do not do this, it may indicate that the relationship has the potential for escalating levels of violence.

Early Violence

Another potential predictor of high-level courtship violence may be the timing of the first aggressive act. Individuals who use aggression early in a relationship, before it becomes serious, may be more likely to escalate their aggressive acts later in the relationship. This may be because they are generally more aggressive people, have a lower tolerance for frustration, or have a higher need to control their partner. It is also possible that the early acceptance of a partner's aggression might mean that the individual will be even less willing to end the relationship later, when both the relationship and the aggression have become more serious. Moreover, as Billingham (1987) suggests, some individuals may aggress early in a relationship to test their partner's response. If their partner "passes the test," he or she may be subject to greater levels of abuse in the future. Finally, Makepeace (1988) found the most serious injury rates early in the relationship (before three months) and later in the relationship (after one year). The early period produced the highest serious injury rates, supporting Billingham's contention that some individuals aggress early in the relationship. It is possible that these individuals would become even more aggressive later if the relationship was to continue.

Witnessing Parental Aggression

Research shows that witnessing parental aggression predicts both domestic violence (Fagan, Stewart, & Hansen, 1983; Rouse, 1984; Sugarman & Hotaling, 1989b) and courtship violence (e.g., Bernard & Bernard, 1983; Gwartney-Gibbs et al., 1987). It also predicts the severity of domestic violence (Fagan et al., 1983; Sugarman & Hotaling, 1989b). Nevertheless, DeMaris (1990) found that witnessing parental abuse was positively related to serious courtship violence only for women and black men. White men showed the reverse pattern: those who witnessed parental abuse showed lower levels of serious courtship violence. Social learning theory suggests

that children learn much of their behavior by modeling their parents. Witnessing aggression between one's parents may foster the belief that relationship aggression is acceptable behavior. In addition, the child may learn that violence is rewarded, and he or she may not learn alternative negotiation strategies.

Social Support for Relationship Violence

Another factor that may increase the use of serious aggression during courtship may be an association with family members, peers, a social group, or a culture that accepts violence in relationships. Several experts on domestic violence have noted the role of patriarchy in fostering wife abuse (Dobash & Dobash, 1988). Research on dating violence also supports this theory (Schwartz & DeKeseredy, 1997). For example, DeKeseredy and Kelly (1993b) found that men's patriarchal beliefs and attitudes, their peers' patriarchal attitudes, and their peers' abusiveness toward women predicted men's physical and sexual aggression. They also found that informational support and attachment to abusive peers predicted physical aggression in college men (DeKeseredy & Kelly, 1993b, 1995).

Sexual Aggression

Individuals who use both sexual aggression (as measured by the SES) and physical aggression (as measured by the CTS) during courtship may be more likely to engage in high-level physical violence than those who use only physical aggression. Research shows that the most violent batterers are those who also rape their wives (Finkelhor & Yllo, 1983; Frieze, 1983; Shields & Hanneke, 1983). Ryan (1997) found nonsignificantly higher levels of physical violence on the CTS in men who also sexually aggressed ($M = 12.00$) than in men who only physically aggressed ($M = 2.21$). A similar pattern was found for sexually aggressive women, and it was statistically significant. Women who sexually and physically aggressed (2% of all women) showed higher levels of physical violence on the CTS ($M = 10.38$) than women who just physically aggressed ($M = 5.07$). Sexual aggression in an ongoing relationship may be used to humiliate the partner. It may reveal excessive anger, the need to control, or a lack of empathy—features that may also cause increasing levels of physical aggression. Finally, we must recognize that sexual aggression is serious physical aggression. It can result in pain and injury to the victim (Koss, Heise, & Russo, 1994) and cause considerable emotional trauma.

ADVICE TO PRACTITIONERS

Counselors, teachers, and other professionals working with young men and women must recognize that violence during courtship exists. We do not know what distinguishes high-level violence from low-level violence, so any physical aggression should be viewed seriously. Professionals must be open to the possibility that aggression exists between dating partners, and they must listen to young people's stories. They should realize that this behavior is rarely reported and strive to make young people more comfortable with sharing information about courtship violence. Young people should be routinely asked about experiences with dating aggression, just as they should be routinely asked about experiences with sexual aggression when they visit doctors, counselors, and other health care agents.

We need to create a society in which there is Zero Tolerance of aggression in intimate relationships. That means that it is not acceptable for anyone, including young women, to hit, slap, shove, or restrain their partner. As long as young women and men believe it is acceptable to use physical aggression, they may place themselves in danger of being themselves abused. They also corrupt their relationship, lowering trust, intimacy, and satisfaction.

Professionals must take steps to decrease minimization and denial of courtship violence in themselves and in young people. This may especially be the case for young men in abusive relationships and for those who reciprocate aggression. We must do more to educate young people about intimate relationships and the possibility of courtship violence. We should teach young people how to deal with conflict, frustration, and fears in relationships. They need to know that verbal abuse, jealousy, and physical aggression are not positive aspects of a relationship. They need to see more alternatives outside of staying with an abusive partner, including the possibility of finding a new partner or being temporarily on their own. Young people also need to learn more about anger management. Anger need not inevitably lead to aggression (Tavris, 1989). It can be used in a positive manner to express one's needs and to improve one's relationships.

Finally, people who care about adolescents and young adults may consider providing a forum for both victims and perpetrators of courtship aggression that is similar to survivor groups for battered women and batterer intervention programs. If we are successful at decreasing courtship violence, we may also be successful at decreasing domestic violence. Many people believe that courtship is the time when people learn how to manage close intimate relationships. Destructive patterns learned during courtship may continue into marriage. When pressures grow, violence may grow in

48   The Psychology of Sexual Victimization

frequency and intensity, and people who love each other may find they cannot live together.

REFERENCES

Arias, I., & Johnson, P. (1989). Evaluations of physical aggression among intimate dyads. *Journal of Interpersonal Violence, 4,* 298–307.

Arias, I., Samios, M., & O'Leary, E. D. (1987). Prevalence and correlates of physical aggression during courtship. *Journal of Interpersonal Violence, 2,* 82–90.

Bergman, L. (1992). Dating violence among high school students. *Social Work, 37*(1), 21–27.

Berkowitz, L. (1993). *Aggression: Its causes, consequences, and control.* New York: McGraw-Hill.

Bernard, J. L., & Bernard, M. L. (1984). The abusive male seeking treatment: Jekyll and Hyde. *Family Relations, 33,* 543–547.

Bernard, J. L., Bernard, S. L., & Bernard, M. L. (1985). Courtship violence and sex-typing. *Family Relations, 34,* 573–576.

Bernard, M. L., & Bernard, J. L. (1983). Violent intimacy: The family as a model for love relationships. *Family Relations, 32,* 283–286.

Billingham, R. E. (1987). Courtship violence: The patterns of conflict resolution strategies across seven levels of emotional commitment. *Family Relations, 36,* 283–289.

Billingham, R. E., & Sack, A. R. (1987). Conflict tactics and the level of emotional commitment among unmarrieds. *Human Relations, 40,* 59–74.

Bogal-Allbritten, R. B., & Allbritten, W. L. (1985). The hidden victims: Courtship violence among college students. *Journal of College Student Personnel, 26,* 201–204.

Bookwala, J., Frieze, I. H., Smith, C., & Ryan, K. (1992). Predictors of dating violence: A multivariate analysis. *Violence and Victims, 7,* 297–311.

Brodbelt, S. (1983). College dating and aggression. *College Student Journal, 17,* 273–277.

Campbell, A. (1993). *Men, women, and aggression.* New York: Basic Books.

Cate, R. M., Henton, J. M., Koval, J., Christopher, F. S., & Lloyd, S. (1982). Premarital abuse: A social psychological perspective. *Journal of Family Issues, 3,* 79–90.

Clark, M. L., Beckett, J., Wells, M., & Dungee-Anderson, D. (1994). Courtship violence among African-American college students. *Journal of Black Psychology, 20*(3), 264–281.

Coffey, P., Leitenberg, H., Henning, K., Bennett, R. T., & Jankowski, M. K. (1996). Dating violence: The association between methods of coping and women's psychological adjustment. *Violence and Victims, 11,* 227–261.

Deal, J. E., & Wampler, K. S. (1986). Dating violence: The primacy of previous experience. *Journal of Social and Personal Relationships, 3*, 457–471.

DeKeseredy, W., & Kelly, K. (1993a). The incidence and prevalence of woman abuse in Canadian university and college dating relationships. *Canadian Journal of Sociology, 18*, 137–159.

DeKeseredy, W. S., & Kelly, K. (1993b). Woman abuse in university and college dating relationships: The contribution of the ideology of familial patriarchy. *Journal of Human Justice, 4*, 25–52.

DeKeseredy, W. S., & Kelly, K. (1995). Sexual abuse in Canadian university and college dating relationships: The contribution of male peer support. *Journal of Family Violence, 10*, 41–53.

DeMaris, A. (1990). The dynamics of generational transfer in courtship violence: A biracial exploration. *Journal of Marriage and the Family, 52*, 219–231.

Dobash, R. E., & Dobash, R. P. (1988). Research as social action: The struggle for battered women. In K. Yllo & M. Bograd (Eds.), *Feminist perspectives of wife abuse* (pp. 51–74). Newbury Park, CA: Sage.

Dutton, D. G., with Golant, S. K. (1995). *The batterer: A psychological profile.* New York: Basic Books.

Dutton, D. G., & Hemphill, K. J. (1992). Patterns of socially desirable responding among perpetrators and victims of wife assault. *Violence and Victims, 7*, 29–39.

Eagly, A. H., & Steffen, V. J. (1986). Gender and aggressive behavior: A meta-analytic view of the social psychological literature. *Psychological Bulletin, 100*, 309–330.

Evans, P. (1992). *The verbally abusive relationship: How to recognize it and how to respond.* Holbrook, MA: Bob Adams.

Fagan, J. A., Stewart, D. K., & Hansen, K. V. (1983). Violent men or violent husbands? Background factors and situational correlates. In D. Finkelhor, R. J. Gelles, G. T. Hotaling, & M. A. Straus (Eds.), *The dark side of families: Current family violence research* (pp. 49–67). Beverly Hills, CA: Sage.

Finkelhor, D., & Yllo, K. (1983). Rape in marriage: A sociological view. In D. Finkelhor, R. J. Gelles, G. T. Hotaling, & M. A. Straus (Eds.), *The dark side of families: Current family violence research* (pp. 119–130). Beverly Hills, CA: Sage.

Flynn, C. P. (1990). Sex roles and women's response to courtship violence. *Journal of Family Violence, 5*, 83–94.

Follingstad, D. R., Rutledge, L. L., McNeill-Harkins, K., & Polek, D. S. (1992). Factors related to physical violence in dating relationships. In E. C. Viano (Ed.), *Intimate violence: Interdisciplinary perspectives* (pp. 121–135).Washington, DC: Hemisphere.

Frieze, I. H. (1983). Investigating the causes and consequences of marital rape. *Signs: Journal of Women in Culture and Society, 8*, 532–553.

Frieze, I. H., & Browne, A. (1989). Violence in marriage. In L. Ohlin & M. Tonry (Eds.), *Family violence* (Vol. 11, pp. 163–218). Chicago: University of Chicago Press.

Frieze, I. H., & McHugh, M. C. (1992). Power and influence strategies in violent and nonviolent marriages. *Psychology of Women Quarterly, 16*, 449–466.

Gagn, M., & LaVoie, F. (1993, Fall). Young people's views on the causes of violence in adolescents' romantic relationships. *Canada's Mental Health*, 11–15.

Greenblat, C. S. (1983). A hit is a hit . . . or is it? Approval and tolerance of the use of physical force by spouses. In D. Finkelhor, R. J. Gelles, G. T. Hotaling, & M. A. Straus (Eds.), *The dark side of families: Current family violence research* (pp. 235–260). Beverly Hills, CA: Sage.

Gryl, F. E., Stith, S. M., & Bird, G. W. (1991). Close dating relationships among college students: Differences by use of violence and by gender. *Journal of Social and Personal Relationships, 8*, 243–264.

Gwartney-Gibbs, P. A., Stockard, J., & Bohmer, S. (1987). Learning courtship aggression: The influence of parents, peers, and personal experiences. *Family Relations, 36*, 276–282.

Hendricks, J. E. (1992). Domestic violence legislation in the United States: A survey of the states. In E. C. Viano (Ed.), *Intimate violence: Interdisciplinary perspectives* (pp. 213–226). Washington, DC: Hemisphere Publishing.

Henton, J., Cate, R., Koval, J., Lloyd, S., & Christopher, S. (1983). Romance and violence in dating relationships. *Journal of Family Issues, 3*, 467–482.

Island, D., & Letellier, P. (1991). *Men who beat the men who love them.* New York: Haworth Press.

Johnson, M. P. (1995). Patriarchal terrorism and common couple violence: Two forms of violence against women. *Journal of Marriage and the Family, 57*, 283–294.

Kelly, E. M., & Loesch, L. C. (1983). Abused wives: Perceptions during crisis counseling. *American Mental Health Counselors Association Journal*, 132–140.

Koss, M. P. (1993). Rape: Scope, impact, interventions, and public policy responses. *American Psychologist, 48*, 1062–1069.

Koss, M. P., Gidycz, C. A., & Wisniewski, N. (1987). The scope of rape: Incidence and prevalence of sexual aggression and victimization in a national sample of higher education students. *Journal of Consulting and Clinical Psychology, 55*, 162–170.

Koss, M. P., Heise, L., & Russo, N. F. (1994). The global health burden of rape. *Psychology of Women Quarterly, 18*, 509–537.

Kurt, J. L. (1995). Stalking as a variant of domestic violence. *Bulletin of the American Academy of Psychiatry and Law, 23*, 219–230.

Lane, K. E., & Gwartney-Gibbs, P. A. (1985). Violence in the context of dating and sex. *Journal of Family Issues, 6*, 45–59.

Laner, M. R. (1989). Competition and combativeness in courtship: Reports from women. *Journal of Family Violence, 4*, 181–195.

Laner, M. R., & Thompson, J. (1982). Abuse and aggression in courting couples. *Deviant Behavior: An Interdisciplinary Journal, 3*, 229–244.

Lie, G., & Gentlewarrier, S. (1991). Intimate violence in lesbian relationships: Discussion of survey findings and practice implications. *Journal of Social Service Research, 15*(1–2), 41–59.

Lie, G., Schilit, R., Bush, J., Montagne, M., & Reyes, L. (1991). Lesbians in currently aggressive relationships: How frequently do they report aggressive past relationships? *Violence and Victims, 6*(2), 121–135.

Makepeace, J. M. (1981). Courtship violence among college students. *Family Relations, 30*, 97–102.

Makepeace, J. M. (1986). Gender differences in courtship violence victimization. *Family Relations, 36*, 383–388.

Makepeace, J. M. (1988). The severity of courtship violence and the effectiveness of individual precautions. In G. T. Hotaling, D. Finkelhor, J. T. Kirkpatrick, and M. A. Straus (Eds.), *Family abuse and its consequences: New directions in research* (pp. 297–311). Newbury Park, CA: Sage.

Malone, J., Tyree, A., & O'Leary, K. D. (1989). Generalization and containment: Different effects of past aggression for wives and husbands. *Journal of Marriage and the Family, 51*, 687–697.

Marshall, L. L. (1992a). Development of the severity of violence against women scales. *Journal of Family Violence, 7*, 103–121.

Marshall, L. L. (1992b). The severity of violence against men scales. *Journal of Family Violence, 7*, 189–203.

Marshall, L. L., & Rose, P. (1987). Gender, stress and violence in the adult relationships of a sample of college students. *Journal of Social and Personal Relationships, 4*, 299–316.

Marshall, L. L., & Rose, P. (1990). Premarital violence: The impact of family of origin violence, stress, and reciprocity. *Violence and Victims, 5*, 51–64.

Mason, A., & Blankenship, V. (1987). Power and affiliation motivation, stress, and abuse in intimate relationships. *Journal of Personality and Social Psychology, 52*, 203–210.

Matthews, W. J. (1984). Violence in college couples. *College Student Journal, 18*, 150–158.

McHugh, M. C., Frieze, I. H., & Browne, A. (1993). Research on battered women and their assailants. In F. Denmark & M. A. Paludi (Eds.), *Psychology of women: A handbook of issues and theories* (pp. 513–553). Westport, CT: Greenwood.

Muehlenhard, C. L., & Linton, M. A. (1987). Date rape and sexual aggression in dating situations: Incidence and risk factors. *Journal of Consulting and Clinical Psychology, 34*, 186–196.

Mullen, P. E., & Pathe, M. (1994). Stalking and the pathologies of love. *Australian and New Zealand Journal of Psychiatry, 28*, 469–477.

O'Keeffe, N. K., Brockopp, K., & Chew, E. (1986). Teen dating violence. *Social Work, 31*, 465–468.

O'Leary, K. D., & Arias, I. (1988). Assessing agreement of reports of spouse abuse. In G. T. Hotaling, D. Finkelhor, J. T. Kirkpatrick, & M. A. Straus (Eds.), *Family abuse and its consequences: New directions in research* (pp. 218–227). Newbury Park, CA: Sage.

O'Leary, K. D., Barling, J., Arias, I., Rosenbaum, A., Malone, J., & Tyree, A. (1989). Prevalence and stability of physical aggression between spouses: A longitudinal analysis. *Journal of Consulting and Clinical Psychology, 57*, 263–268.

Pagelow, M. D. (1984). *Family violence.* New York: Praeger.

Pathe, M., & Mullen, P. E. (1997). The impact of stalkers on their victims. *British Journal of Psychiatry, 170*, 12–17.

Pence, E., & Paymar, M. (1993). *Education groups for men who batter: The Duluth model.* New York: Springer.

Petersilia, J. (1994). Violent crime and violent criminals: The response of the justice system. In M. Costanzo & S. Oskamp (Eds.), *Violence and the law* (pp. 226–245). Newbury Park, CA: Sage.

Plass, M. S., & Gessner, J. C. (1983). Violence in courtship relations: A southern sample. *Free Inquiry in Creative Sociology, 11*, 198–202.

Ptacek, J. (1988). Why do men batter their wives? In K. Yllo & M. Bograd (Eds.), *Feminist perspectives on wife abuse* (pp. 133–157). Newbury Park, CA: Sage.

Renzetti, C. M. (1992). *Violent betrayal: Partner abuse in lesbian relationships.* Newbury Park, CA: Sage.

Riggs, D. S., Murphy, C. M., & O'Leary, K. D. (1989). Intentional falsification in reports of interpartner aggression. *Journal of Interpersonal Violence, 4*, 220–232.

Roscoe, B. (1985). Courtship violence: Acceptable forms and situations. *College Student Journal, 19*, 389–393.

Roscoe, B., & Callahan, J. E. (1985). Adolescents' self-report of violence in families and dating relations. *Adolescence, 20*, 545–553.

Roscoe, B., & Kelsey, T. (1986). Dating violence among high school students. *Psychology: A Quarterly Journal of Human Behavior, 23*, 53–59.

Rouse, L. P. (1984). Models, self-esteem, and locus of control as factors contributing to spouse abuse. *Victimology: An International Journal, 9*, 130–141.

Rusbult, C. E. (1983). A longitudinal test of the investment model: The development (and deterioration) of satisfaction and commitment in heterosexual involvements. *Journal of Personality and Social Psychology, 45,* 101–117.

Ryan, K. M. (1995). Do courtship-violent men have characteristics associated with a "battering personality"? *Journal of Family Violence, 10,* 99–120.

Ryan, K. M. (1997). *The relationship between courtship violence and sexual aggression in college students.* Manuscript submitted for publication.

Sack, A. R., Keller, J. F., & Howard, R. D. (1982). Conflict tactics and violence in dating situations. *International Journal of Sociology of the Family, 12,* 89–100.

Saunders, D. G. (1986). When battered women use violence: Husband-abuse or self-defense? *Violence and Victims, 1,* 47–60.

Schwartz, M. D., & DeKeseredy, W. S. (1997). *Sexual assault on the college campus: The role of male peer support.* Newbury Park, CA: Sage.

Scully, D. (1990). *Understanding sexual violence: A study of convicted rapists.* Boston: Unwin Hyman.

Shields, N. M., & Hanneke, C. R. (1983). Battered wives' reactions to marital rape. In D. Finkelhor, R. J. Gelles, G. T. Hotaling, & M. A. Straus (Eds.), *The dark side of families: Current family violence research* (pp. 132–148). Beverly Hills, CA: Sage.

Sigelman, C. K., Berry, C. J., & Wiles, K. A. (1984). Violence in college students' dating relationships. *Journal of Applied Social Psychology, 5,* 530–548.

Stets, Jan E., & Pirog-Good, M. A. (1987). Violence in dating relationships. *Social Psychology Quarterly, 50*(3), 237–246.

Stets, J. E., & Pirog-Good, M. A. (1989). Patterns of physical and sexual abuse for men and women in dating relationships: A descriptive analysis. *Journal of Family Violence, 4,* 63–76.

Stets, J. E., & Straus, M. A. (1989). The marriage license as a hitting license: A comparison of assaults in dating, cohabiting and married couples. In J. E Stets & M. A. Pirog-Good (Eds.), *Violence in dating relationships* (pp. 33–52). New York: Praeger.

Straus, M. A. (1979). Measuring intrafamily conflict and violence: The conflict tactics (CT) scales. *Journal of Marriage and the Family, 41,* 75–88.

Straus, M. A., Hamby, S. L., Boney-McCoy, S., & Sugarman, D. B. (1995). *The Revised Conflict Tactics Scale (CTS2).* Durham, NH: Family Research Laboratory, University of New Hampshire.

Sugarman, D. B., & Hotaling, G. T. (1989a). Dating violence: Prevalence, context, and risk markers. In M. A. Pirog-Good & J. E. Stets (Eds.), *Violence in dating relationships: Emerging social issues* (pp. 3–32). New York: Praeger.

Sugarman, D. B., & Hotaling, G. T. (1989b). Violent men in intimate relation-
    ships: An analysis of risk markers. *Journal of Applied Social Psychol-
    ogy, 19*, 1034–1048.
Tavris, C. (1989). *Anger: The misunderstood emotion.* New York: Touch-
    stone/Simon & Schuster.
Thompson, E. H. (1990). Courtship violence and the male role. *Men's Studies Re-
    view, 7* (1), 4–13.
Thompson, E. H. (1991). The maleness of violence in dating relationships: An ap-
    praisal of stereotypes. *Sex Roles, 24*, 261–278.
Tontodonato, P., & Crew, B. K. (1992). Dating violence, social learning theory,
    and gender: A multivariate analysis. *Violence and Victims, 7*, 3–14.
Walker, L. E. (1979). *The battered woman.* New York: Harper & Row.
Walker, L. E. (1983). The battered woman syndrome study. In D. Finkelhor, R. J.
    Gelles, G. T. Hotaling, & M. A. Straus (Eds.), *The dark side of families:
    Current family violence research* (pp. 31–48). Beverly Hills, CA: Sage.
Waterman, C., Dawson, L. J., & Bologna, M. J. (1989). Sexual coercion in gay
    male and lesbian relationships: Predictors and implications for support
    services. *Journal of Sex Research, 26*(1), 118–124.
White, J. W., & Koss, M. P. (1991). Courtship violence: Incidence in a national
    sample of higher education students. *Violence and Victims, 6*, 247–256.
Worth, D. M., Matthews, P. A., & Coleman, W. R. (1990). Sex role, group affilia-
    tion, family background, and courtship violence in college students.
    Journal of College Student Development, 31, 250–254.
Yoshihama, M., Parekh, A. L., & Boyington, D. (1991). Dating violence in
    Asian-American communities. In B. Levy (Ed.), *Dating violence* (pp.
    184–195). Seattle, WA: Seal Press.

3

Observers' Blaming of Battered Wives: Who, What, When, and Why?

Dee L. R. Graham and Edna I. Rawlings

Battering is a situation of coercion, backed up by the threat of and actual display of violence. If there is any situation in which the power of external forces to influence behavior cannot be denied, it is that of domestic violence.

Each year, on average, women experience 572,000 violent victimizations at the hands of intimate partners, and 70% of victims murdered by an intimate are women (U.S. Department of Justice, 1994). A woman is more likely to be victimized and physically injured by an intimate than by a stranger. She is also more likely to receive medical care (27% versus 14%) and require hospitalization (15% versus 8%) if attacked by an intimate rather than by a stranger (U. S. Department of Justice, 1994). The percentage of women who feared they would die during an aggravated assault was 100% for those victimized by their husbands and 82% for those victimized by persons other than a husband (Riggs, Kilpatrick, & Resnick, 1992). Women assaulted by an intimate partner were almost twice as likely to suffer injuries if they used physical or verbal self-protective measures, compared to those assaulted by a stranger (Bachman & Carmody, 1994). Yet 80% of those victimized by an intimate took self-protective action (U.S. Department of Justice, 1994), approximately the same percentage as women victimized by strangers. Despite the greater seriousness of intimate than stranger violence, arrest is less likely when victim and offender are married (Berk, Berk, & Newton, 1984, cited by Pagelow, 1992), and sentences for convicted spouse assailants are lighter than those for convicted stranger assailants (Goolkasian, 1986).

Unlike most other victims of crime, battered wives are likely to live with their assaulters. And unlike victims of most other crimes, battered wives are subjected to repeated episodes of violence by the same assaulter. This keeps the victim under her abuser's control, desperately trying to prevent future violence. Thus, the impact of wife abuse is both direct, through physical and emotional injury, and indirect, through the added stress of constant vigilance as to the abuser's typically vague, changeable desires. Follingstad, Brennan, Hause, Polek, and Rutledge (1991) found that with more severe and frequent physical violence, women experienced more physical and psychological symptoms, such as depression, anxiety, persistent headaches, and back or stomach problems. Estimates of the incidence of posttraumatic stress disorder (PTSD) in battered women range from 31% (Gleason, 1993) to 81% (Kemp, Green, Hovanitz, & Rawlings, 1995). More severe violence and less perceived social support resulted in more intense PTSD symptoms (Astin, Lawrence, & Foy, 1993; Kemp, Green, Hovanitz, & Rawlings, 1995).

Bachman and Saltzman (1995) found that compared to married women, divorced women were almost 9 times more likely to be victimized, and separated women were about 25 times more likely to be victimized. These statistics suggest that the most frequently battered wives do in fact leave, and battered women are least in danger when in a relationship with the abuser and most in danger early in the separation process. Leaving is likely to encourage, rather than end, violence (Wilson & Daly, 1993).

To understand the difficulties inherent in separating from an abusive partner, one must first consider the complex forces giving rise to women's intense bonds with their abusers. Graham and Rawlings (1991) investigated the literature on hostage behavior and found parallels with battered women's behavior. The authors found four precursor conditions that, together, encourage the development of an intense bidirectional bond between hostages and their captors. Based on a bank holdup and hostage situation in Stockholm, Sweden, in 1973, this bond has become known as the Stockholm syndrome. Its four precursor conditions are that (1) victims perceive a threat—physical or psychological or both—to their survival; (2) victims do not perceive a way to escape this threat; (3) victims are ideologically or physically isolated from others with perspectives differing from those of their captors or abusers; and (4) victims perceive kindness by their captor or abusers (Graham & Rawlings, 1991). In our focus on victim blame, we shall see how this syndrome is promoted from outside the battered women's relationship by police, medical doctors, courts, and therapists, whose attitudes and actions thwart battered women's escape from abuse.

Women who attempt to escape their abusers permanently often face seemingly insurmountable obstacles, in addition to the violence and threat of violence often used by batterers to prevent them from leaving. Other obstacles are the need for employment, clothing, shelter, furniture, education, transportation, child care, legal assistance, health care, and social support (Bowker, 1983; Gondolf, 1988; Sullivan, 1991).

The separation process, thwarted by violence and its threat as well as economic and other obstacles, takes an average of four (Pagelow, 1981) to six years after violence begins (Walker, 1979). On average, battered women in shelters return to their abusers five times before eventually leaving for good (Okun, 1986). Allen (1991, 1996; Rawlings, Allen, Graham, & Peters, 1994) has identified the unbonding process through which battered women appear to progress, as well as some of the associated variables (e.g., being employed, being unmarried). Her 1996 findings reveal the confluence of a wide range of situational and psychological variables that have an impact on this process.

Bowker (1983) found that following early incidents of violence, women tended to use personal strategies, such as trying to talk their partner out of the abuse, hiding from him, and threatening nonviolent action such as contacting the police. As violence continued, the women sought help first from informal sources, such as family and friends, and then formal sources, such as police, attorneys, clergy, and women's groups. The more frequent the violence, the more the women engaged in personal strategies and help-seeking behaviors. Similarly, Dobash and Dobash (1984) observed that battered women's help-seeking behaviors increased over time, as the women sought help from an increasing number and wider variety of people.

Research by both Bowker (1983) and Gondolf (1988), but not Sullivan (1991), has revealed that the help provided to battered women is important to their ability to leave their abusers. Help can come in a variety of forms: direct physical intervention during an altercation; provision of shelter; direct emotional, financial, material, and child care support funds for shelters and victim advocacy; creation of safety provisions in places of employment; arrest of batterers; informed, unprejudicial decision making in court trials; and support for legislation aimed at preventing and punishing spouse abuse, to name a few.

Rarely do battered women find the help they need to end the violence (Gondolf, 1988), regardless of to whom they have turned for help (e.g., the police, the legal system, social service agencies). However, women who did manage to escape the violence viewed help received from friends and family as important to their having done so (Bowker, 1983).

Despite this considerable evidence, people appear eager to deny that battered women's behavior is strongly affected by powerful external forces—the batterer's control through the use of violence and its threat, and the lack of available resources. Uninformed parties argue that if a woman does not like being abused, she can simply leave her batterer (Ewing & Aubrey, 1987; Pagelow, 1992), although these same people are unlikely to assume that a victim of a bank holdup could safely "just leave" the situation. Why do outside observers deny that violence is used to control victims' behavior in one situation but not in another? Such an attitude belies the terror inherent in the separation process for many, if not most, female victims of spouse abuse.

The difficulty battered women experience in order to separate from their abusers and survive is intensified if the public blames them. For example, Dobash and Dobash (1984) found that third-party witnesses to wife abuse played key roles in either the continuation or cessation of violence, according to the battered women interviewed. If witnesses communicated unequivocally to the batterer that his violence was unjustifiable, this reduced the probability of future violence "by providing a challenge to the man's sense of justification and rightful use of violence and by providing the woman with a possible escape from attack" (Dobash & Dobash, 1984, p. 282). On the other hand, when witnesses scrutinized how the women's behavior and words may have "caused" the violence, the batterers felt justified, the women felt further isolated, and future violence was more likely. Public attitudes can thwart abuse (when the batterer is held responsible for his actions) or encourage it (when the wife is held responsible for the batterer's violence).

Publicly stated attitudes often portray battered women as not working in their own behalf to end violence. The first author has frequently heard this argument, as a reason that prosecutors do not abjudicate spouse abuse cases involving a reluctant victim or witness: "If a battered woman doesn't help herself, why should we help her?" Medical staff were heard by Kurz and Stark (1988) to make similar comments. Such attitudes are at odds with the resourcefulness, skill, and ingenuity shown by battered wives each day in their efforts to prevent further abuse. For example, Stacey and Shupe (1983) note:

Throughout our research we came to see that learned helplessness does not describe the courage and resourcefulness of the [battered] women we met. After all, these women did take the initiative and made the decision to leave their homes. This was never done without great sacrifice, and often risk, to each woman. Often their journey to the shelter was a calculated, narrowly timed escape that involved the nerve and planning of a prison break-out. (p. 54)

Bowker (1983) too observes that "the efforts [of battered women] to end the abuse . . . were extensive and intensive, and were completely at variance with the image of the battered woman as passively accepting her fate" (p. 104).

Victim blaming flourishes to the extent that public attitudes reflect an ignorance of the powerful forces (e.g., threat to survival) acting on battered women. Using voter registration lists, Ewing and Aubrey (1987) examined the beliefs about battering held by a primarily white, married, well-educated, and middle-class sample. Among other things, they found that 64% of the respondents agreed that the battered woman would "simply leave" her assailant if she was really afraid. Eighty-four percent agreed that the victim could stay with her abuser and probably prevent future abuse by seeking counseling, implying that they believed she was to blame. Dodge and Greene (1991) found that even among researchers in the field of spouse abuse, there existed a lack of consensus regarding the "fact" that battered women are helpless to stop the beatings. Only 64% agreed.

Battered women's cries for help from police have been largely ignored. Lavoie, Jacob, Hardy, and Martin (1989) found that police "always consider the wife somewhat responsible" (p. 369), particularly when the husband alleged she was "looking for a fight," despite no tangible evidence, and when the husband threatened violence rather than actually committing it. Belknap (1995) found that 45.4% of police officers agreed that victims do not mean it when they request officers to arrest, while only 27% disagreed with such a statement. Related perhaps, when an assailant was an intimate, as compared to a stranger, police were less likely to make a formal report of the abuse and were less likely to search the scene for evidence (U.S. Department of Justice, 1994).

Prior to the enactment of pro-arrest legislation, Okun (1986) found that fewer than 10% of police calls for domestic violence resulted in an arrest of the batterer for assault. Worden and Pollitz (1984) found an arrest rate of 9%. With the enactment of pro-arrest laws, attention has turned to the role of the judicial system in permitting wife abuse to continue unpunished. Quarm and Schwartz (1983) found that approximately 81% of 1,408 domestic violence cases in Hamilton County, Ohio, were dismissed by judges. Following the institution of pro-arrest laws, Martin (1994) found that "a decision to arrest was unlikely to result in either punishment or treatment. Only 14% of 4,138 defendants were prosecuted" (p. 219). For 79% of the defendants, the court took no action. *The more severely the victim was injured, the more likely it was that the case would be dismissed.*

Attitudes and beliefs such as those described above may affect the help that battered women receive from friends, neighbors, family, public jurors, and therapists. For example, many mental health professionals ascribe to theories that battered women are masochistic in the sense of seeking out abusive partners (object relations theory; e.g., Celini, 1994), or are equally culpable with the batterer for the abuse they suffer (family systems theory; e.g., Bagarozzi & Giddings, 1983; Bograd, 1984). Bowker (1983) describes numerous examples of victim-disparaging attitudes expressed by, and non-supportive actions taken by, clergy, police, district attorneys, and others in response to battered women who sought their help.

Kurz and Stark (1988) describe the response of medical staff to battered women presenting for treatment as both neglectful and victim blaming. In fact, battered women who had attempted suicide were significantly less likely to receive a referral for mental health services than were nonbattered women who had attempted suicide (22% versus 96%). Although the women were not labeled as battered in medical records, pejorative labeling (e.g., "hysteric," "neurotic female," "depressed, anxious lady") was used both to express victim-blaming attitudes and justify neglectful treatment. Eighty-six percent of the women receiving pejorative labels were battered. Two views of battered women predominated among medical staff: battered women were either "evasive" (reluctant to discuss their abuse) or "repeaters" (they could help themselves but, from the medical staff's perspective, did not). The authors note, "None of the staff mention the obvious social and economic factors that make it difficult for women to leave their families" (p. 257). Both views portray the women, *not* their assailant's abuse of them, as the problem.

It is commonplace for those responsible for helping battered women—police, prosecutors, doctors, therapists—to rationalize their negligible assistance. They claim that battered women are not helping themselves or portray battered women as co-dependents or as having a choice to be beaten. These attitudes are also held by the general public. Thus, both help sources, formal and informal, remain oblivious to the coercive nature of intimate violence and uninformed about the needs of battered women. Although studies are needed to establish a causal link between people's beliefs about abuse situations, their victim-blaming attitudes, and their helping behaviors, it is highly probable that, besides overtly encouraging wife abuse, victim-blaming attitudes reduce one's willingness to help battered women. When expressed, such attitudes are also likely to discourage others from helping. Some people may think nothing can help.

The effects of victim blaming may be cyclical and cumulative. Victim-blaming attitudes—by encouraging wife abuse, increasing battered women's isolation from others who might help, making escape from abuse more difficult, and making the battered woman more dependent on her abuser's kindness—are likely to encourage women to (terror-) bond with their abusers (Graham & Rawlings, 1991). Because outsiders then misperceive that love, not inability to escape, is the reason women stay with their abusers, the victim blaming that encouraged such bonding is likely to generate still more victim blaming.

Victim-blaming attitudes, publicly stated and privately held, have in all likelihood encouraged public and private neglect of women's right to live free from the threat of harm. Perhaps the most pernicious result of victim blaming is that it obscures the sociopolitical aspects of wife battering by individualizing and privatizing the problem. This directs attention to changing or "curing" the unfortunate victims rather than eradicating the underlying social roots of battering: sexism, androcentrism, and patriarchy, which are also the roots of victim-blame and derogation.

QUESTIONS WE ARE INTERESTED IN ANSWERING

In this chapter, research on beliefs and attitudes toward battered wives will be reviewed to answer the following questions: (1) Are female victims blamed by the general public? (2) What variables (victim characteristics, batterer characteristics, contextual characteristics, and subjects characteristics) encourage female victim blaming? (3) What are the characteristics of whose who blame battered women? (4) What theories best account for victim blaming of abused wives? And (5) what kinds of research are needed? After reviewing relevant research, we compare attribution theories and feminist theory with respect to their abilities to account for findings replicated in at least two studies and make recommendations for future studies.

Three primary measures we used, as do other investigators in the research literature (e.g., Shaver, 1970), to assess victim blame are the extent to which subjects "blame" the victim for the violent incident, the extent to which they hold her "responsible" for the incident, and the extent to which they derogate her, as revealed through liking and other evaluative measures. Although we view all three measures as assessing the global construct of victim blame, we examine separately those findings relating to each measure, thereby staying true to the language investigators use in their communications with subjects.

ARE VICTIMS BLAMED?

Stark and McEnvoy (1970) found that approximately 20% of American adults approve of slapping a spouse under certain circumstances. Similarly, Gentemann (1984) found that although North Carolina women did not feel it was okay if "once in a while" a man slapped, punched, or kicked his wife, 19% believed that a man had a right to beat his wife under certain conditions: if she is flirting with other men, if she is having an affair with another man, if she is drunk, or if she nags. Over 20% of the women affirmatively answered the question, "Do you think that a woman usually causes the beatings she receives?" Richardson and Campbell (1980) reported that college students attributed only 51% of the blame for a spouse abuse incident to the battering husband, while 21.92% of the blame was attributed to the battered wife and 19% to the situation. Kalmuss (1979) found that 23.7% of respondents held the battered wife and battering husband equally responsible for an incident of physical abuse, and 3.3% attributed more responsibility to the wife than to the husband for the incident. Thus, a sizable minority of the American population overtly justify men's right to beat their wives by holding the victims complicit in their own abuse.

These studies thus suggest that at least 20% of the public engages in victim blaming. Morever, a majority of people in our society may harbor more or less victim-blaming attitudes that typically are not expressed except in subtle ways, under conditions of ambiguity, or when circumstances demanding rapid decision making (Devine, 1989). Evidence supportive of this view is provided by Role (1987), who found that victim blame was more apparent in responses to open-ended questions than in responses to forced-choice ones. In response to open-ended questions, 61% of subjects, "chose, without prompting, to talk about how the victim contributed to his/her eventual assault" (p. 73–74). Many spontaneously wrote about "how the victim in some way provoked the assault" (p. 74). According to one or more subjects, the victim—male or female—did so in one or more of the following ways: by taunting, or egging on the perpetrator; by being too stubborn, opinionated, or strong or by being too passive, weak, and naive; by letting the argument go too far; by not being sufficiently considerate of the perpetrator's feelings; by not being adequately cautious or wary; by not having anticipated the perpetrator's behavior and altered his or her behavior accordingly; by having poor communication skills or showing off superior communication skills; by allegedly being mentally disturbed; by being "bitchy" (if female) or a "prick" (if male); and just by being there. Role notes that although subjects attributed more blame to the perpetrator than to the victim, they spontaneously wrote more about the victim than the perpetrator, suggesting that in some sense they found the victim more culpable.

These findings leave unclear whether victim-blaming attitudes are held by only a minority of the population or whether they reflect the sentiments and stereotypes of most people under certain circumstances. If the latter is the case, situational variables rather than personal variables should be better predictors of such attitudes.

Given the often-stated view that victims are to be pitied and shown compassion, not derogated and thus further abused, victim blaming of battered women, even among 20% of the population, is a curious phenomenon that deserves study, as many before us have noted (Coates, Wortman, & Abbey, 1979; Lerner & Simmons, 1966). What are the characteristics of those who are likely to express such attitudes? What victim, perpetrator, and situational circumstances are more likely to elicit them? The review that follows helps to answer these questions.

VARIABLES AFFECTING OBSERVERS' VICTIM-BLAMING

The findings that follow were obtained from studies in which subjects responded to scenarios depicting spouse violence wherein victim, perpetrator, and situational characteristics were experimentally varied. We will primarily focus on scenarios in which women are the victims of battering since the majority of victims of intimate violence are female (Bachman & Saltzman, 1995). Most findings were based on the responses of college students as subjects. Effects of race of subject and of victim were not examined in any of the studies. No authors reported qualitative findings of subjects' responses to open-ended questions about the victim's role. These study omissions may strongly limit the generalizability of the findings, as well as call into question their validity.

What Victim Behaviors and Characteristics Promote Observers' Wife Blaming?

Victim Provocation

A caveat regarding provocation "effects" is that investigators often mention that there is no provocation that they consider a legitimate reason to abuse another person. Bograd (1984) has expressed this eloquently: "There is little logical and empirical support for the prevalent assumption that women provoke men into abusing them. . . . Men are solely responsible for their actions" (p. 561). For this reason, the words "provocation" and "provoked" are often placed in parentheses by investigators. However, findings show that subjects have viewed this issue differently than have most investigators.

Nonviolent Provocation. In the studies whose findings we reviewed here, provocation of violence, usually by wife or other victims, involved acts such as yelling and shouting obscenities (Harris & Cook, 1994; Kristiansen & Giulietti, 1990; Pierce & Harris, 1993), threatening to leave (Harris & Cook, 1994), the house being a mess (low-provocation condition; Hillier & Foddy, 1993), and suspected infidelity (high-provocation condition; Hillier & Foddy, 1993). These "provocations" have ecological validity, for Dobash and Dobash (1984) found that "the men were most likely to become physically violent at the point when the woman could be perceived to be questioning his authority or challenging the legitimacy of his behavior . . . or at points when she asserted herself in some way" (p. 274). No systematic study of the effects of different provocations—used by different investigators—on subjects' attributions has been published; thus, it cannot be assumed that, or which, provocations used by different investigators elicit similar or different subject attributions. In fact, studies by Gentemann (1984), Greenblat (1985), and Briere (1987) suggest that different provocations do elicit greater or lesser blaming of the battered wife. In addition, because investigators generally have used provocations that involve gender role–atypical behaviors, the findings reported here should not be viewed as reflecting the effects of gender role–typical provocations (e.g., crying or acting in a dependent or fearful manner).

A fairly strong finding is that victims have been held more responsible for their own victimization when they have in some way "provoked" the batterer than when they have not. This finding was replicated among samples of college students ($w^2 = .52$, with both female and male victims, Harris & Cook, 1994; $w^2 = .59$, with a female victim, Pierce & Harris, 1993), police officers (Home, 1994; Lavoie et al., 1989), and social workers (Home, 1994). A weaker finding is that victim provocation lessened the extent to which subjects held the perpetrator responsible for the violence, regardless of the sex of the batterer ($w^2 = .17$, with both male and female batterers; Harris & Cook, 1994; $w^2 = .20$, with a male batterer, Pierce & Harris, 1993). It has also been found that a wife or other victim who "provokes" her abusive husband is blamed more than one who does not (Kristiansen & Giulietti, 1990).

College student subjects reported more strongly endorsing the view that a battering husband should be convicted if he was not provoked than if he was provoked. Male subjects reported being less likely to call the police if a wife victim had verbally provoked her abusive husband, whereas women were likely to call for help regardless of whether the wife had acted provocatively (Pierce & Harris, 1993). Thus, it appears that male students', but not females', beliefs regarding their willingness to help the victim by calling the police were affected by whether the victim had in some way provoked the violence.

This sex difference in willingness to call the police may be explained by the following interactions of provocation with both sex of subject and race of perpetrator. Female subjects viewed the incident as more violent, while male subjects viewed the incident as less violent, if the battering husband was verbally provoked (as compared to not provoked). White college students also viewed the abusive incident as less violent when a black, as compared to a white, man was provoked. If the victim had not "provoked" abuse, the violence level was not perceived to differ for a white versus a black perpetrator. However, these findings were primarily due to white men viewing the battering incident as less violent if the battering husband was black, was verbally provoked, and the injury was explicitly (not implicitly) described, as opposed to the batterer's being white, being provoked, and the injury explicitly described. In contrast, women viewed the same provoked incident as more violent regardless of the perpetrator's race. However, both male and female subjects viewed the wife victim as bleeding less severely when she had provoked her husband than when she had not provoked him (Pierce & Harris, 1993). It is unclear why women viewed an event (a "provocation") associated with greater perceived violence as producing less severe bleeding.

In general, subjects viewed the perpetrator's actions as unjustified. However, if a battering husband was "provoked," male subjects viewed his violent actions as more justified than if he was not provoked and as more justified than did female subjects. When he was not provoked, men's and women's attributions did not differ regarding justification. White men, as compared to white women, viewed the battering husband as having more right to use physical force, but only if the perpetrator was white *and* provoked *and* the injury was implicitly described (Pierce & Harris, 1993).

Kristiansen and Giulietti (1990) found that the wife or other victim was derogated less if she had not "provoked" her abusive husband. College student subjects liked a victim who did not provoke the batterer more than one who did provoke the batterer (Pierce & Harris, 1993), regardless of the sex of the victim and batterer (Harris & Cook, 1994). Female respondents liked the victim significantly more than did male respondents, but only if the victim had not "provoked" the batterer (Harris & Cook, 1994). Women subjects liked the wife victim less if she provoked the man *and* the injury was implicitly described than in any alternative conditions created by the inter-action of provocation (present versus absent) and injury description (im-plicitly versus explicitly described; Pierce & Harris, 1993). Pierce and Harris also found that subjects liked a battering husband more if he was pro-voked than if he was not provoked.

In conclusion, victim "provocation" had profound effects on victim blame and derogation. It increased victim blame, increased victim responsi-bility for the violent incident (especially among male subjects), increased male subjects' view that the perpetrator's actions were justified, increased victim derogation, increased female subjects' perceived level of violence, reduced male subjects' perceived level of violence, led subjects to perceive less severe bleeding by the victim, reduced liking for the victim, reduced endorsement of the view that the perpetrator should be convicted, and re-duced male subjects' likelihood of calling the police. Given the breadth of this effect and the violent and neglectful responses associated with provoca-tion by observers, it seems important to remind readers of the trivial nature of the provocations examined: the house being a mess, yelling, shouting ob-scenities. Even the more serious provocations—threatening to leave and suspected infidelity, even if true—are acts that every woman has a right to exercise without the threat of violence. To deny women the right to the en-gage in these activities—ones that reflect their perspectives and desires—is to deny them freedom of self determination and speech.

Violent Provocation. Cook and Harris (1995) found that husband initia-tors of violence were held more responsible for incidents than were wife initiators, and this effect was quite strong ($w^2 = .86$). However, wives were viewed as more responsible for the incident than were husbands when wives had initiated it ($w^2 = .38$). Subjects more strongly believed that hus-band rather than wife initiators of violence should be convicted ($w^2 = .82$).

The higher accountability standard to which the husband perpetrator was held may be accounted for by subjects' perceptions that incidents were more violent when the husband, as compared with the wife, initiated vio-lence ($w^2 = .54$). The party against whom violence had been initiated, whether husband or wife, was viewed as having more right to use physical force in response. However, this effect was substantially stronger for the husband than for the wife recipient of initial violence ($w^2 = .50$ versus. .32), suggesting that although husbands were held more responsible than were wives for starting violence, they were viewed as more justified than were wives in responding violently when "provoked" by a spouse's violence. The finding that men's violence was viewed as more dangerous than women's helps explain college students' holding men more responsible than women for initiating violence and their believing that men more than women should be convicted for initiating it. However, Cook and Harris's curious finding that men were perceived as having more right than women to respond in kind to violence initiated against them by a spouse suggests several possible interpretations: that it is more acceptable for a husband to discipline a wife than for a wife to discipline a husband (as earlier findings regarding nonviolent provocations revealed); that husbands are given greater latitude than are wives to use violence when disciplining a spouse for violently provocative behavior; and that violence initiated by a wife against a husband is viewed as a greater wrong than violence initiated by a husband against a wife.

Alcohol Use as Provocation. Richardson and Campbell (1980) found that when the battered wife was intoxicated during the abusive incident, respondents attributed more blame to her and less to her battering husband. Dent and Arias (1990) surmise that "alcohol consumption is perceived as a possible 'provocation' in and of itself or as a factor creating other possible provocative behavior" (p. 191). Perpetrator drinking by either husband or wife did not influence subjects' evaluative ratings, but victim drinking (either husband or wife) produced more negative evaluations (Dent & Arias, 1990). For the wife only, this effect was found to be stronger among male than female subjects. Thus, female victims who were drinking received more blame for a battering incident and were more derogated by male respondents.

Determination to End Abuse

Home (1994) investigated the effects on battered wife blame of a wife or other victim's ambivalence versus determination to end an abusive situation by having the wife either file a complaint (for police who were subjects) or leave her husband (for social workers who were subjects). She found that a wife's determination versus ambivalence did not affect the extent to which subjects—police or social workers—held the wife responsible for the abuse.

Love Versus Hate for the Abuser

Using an open-ended question, the first author asked students in a Psychology of Women class to identify stereotypes of battered women who love and of battered women who hate their abusers. Several students reported viewing wives who love versus hate their abusive husbands as similar because "both allowed themselves to be battered." Others stated they viewed the hating and loving women similarly *if* both stayed with their abusers. However, many viewed the "hating" woman as more likely to leave her abuser and as being at a "more advanced" stage than the "loving"

woman. The primary cultural stereotypes for the woman who loves her batterer were that she was "weak," in denial with both herself and possibly others, and not standing up for herself. The woman who hates her batterer was
viewed as "strong," not in denial, and as standing up for herself. The woman
who loves her abusive partner was also viewed as self-blaming, feeling that
she deserves abuse, thinking things will change, a loving partner, "submissive," "stupid," but also as "sick" and "pathetic." The woman who hates her
abusive partner was also seen as a bad partner, "independent," "stupid," and
as malevolent ("dangerous," "aggressive," "revengeful," "sick," "ungrate-
ful," "selfish," "hostile," "malicious," "grudge holding," "hateful," "cold,"
"bitchy," "out-of-line," "whiny," "demanding," "bitter," and a "trouble-
maker").

These findings suggest that cultural stereotypes derogate battered wives
regardless of their emotional reactions to their abusive partners, for it is difficult to imagine a response of indifference. Cultural stereotypes appear
more derogating of a wife who hates her abuser than of one who loves him.
Apparently a woman who hates her batterer is viewed—despite being a victim—as too powerful, presumably because she is personally clear that her
husband's abuse of her is wrong and thus stands up for her rights. Yet four
times as many students viewed it as safer for a battered woman to hate than
to love her abuser.

Demographic Characteristics

Relationship Status. Summers and Feldman (1984) varied the relationship status of victims with the batterer—married, living together unmarried, or acquainted—and found that as the intimacy of the relationship
increased, subjects attributed more responsibility for the abuse to the female victim. As the intimacy of the couple decreased, subjects attributed
more blame to the battering male. Home (1994) did not find that relationship status—married versus common law—affected responsibility ratings,
however, the relationships examined may have been viewed by subjects as
reflecting comparable levels of intimacy. Shotland and Straw's (1976) findings regarding assumptions made by observers about victims of stranger
versus intimate violence are suggestive of reasons that observers' attributions differ for the two groups.

Other Demographic Characteristics. Few studies have examined such
effects of demographic characteristics of battered wives as age, race, and
socioeconomic class on victim blaming of battered wives. Greene, Raitz,
and Lindblad (1989) reported that jurors were in significantly stronger
agreement that a younger, as compared to an older, spousal abuse victim
would be likely to blame herself. Subjects viewed a self-blaming (rape) vic-

tim as more emotionally disturbed than one who either blamed chance or one about whom no blame information was provided (Coates et al., 1979). Jurors also believed that a young woman of high socioeconomic status (SES), as compared to an older woman of high SES, was more likely to provoke violence (Greene et al., 1989). Together these findings raise the question of whether younger battered wives are derogated by observers more than are older ones.

Greene et al. (1989) also found that subjects were more aware of situational constraints affecting battered women of low SES than battered wives of higher status. However, the SES of the scenario couple did not affect social workers' (Home, 1994) or police officers' (Home, 1994; Lavoie et al., 1989) responsibility ratings for victim, perpetrator, or couple. Obviously studies are needed that examine the victim's age, race, and socioeconomic class, as well as the interactions of these variables, to elucidate the relationship between these variables and wife blame.

What Male Perpetrator Behaviors and Characteristics Promote Observers' Wife Blaming?

Few studies have examined perpetrator behavior and characteristics. Generally, men who initiated violence were held more responsible than were wives who initiated it, probably because subjects viewed incidents initiated by men as more violent than those initiated by women. On the other hand, men were viewed as more justified than women in responding to violence initiated against them by a spouse (Cook & Harris, 1995).

Having consumed alcohol did not affect the evaluative ratings of the husband (or wife) perpetrator (Dent & Arias, 1990). Home (1994) found that police officers agreed more, and social workers agreed less, that responsibility for a husband's abusiveness was shared by husband and wife when the husband had consumed alcohol versus when he had not. In contrast, Lavoie et al. (1989) found police attributions to be similar to those observed by Home for social workers: when the battering husband had consumed alcohol, police were likely to view the couple as sharing less responsibility for the situation, and individual spouses as being more responsible.

The lone study that examined race of perpetrator used only white participants (Pierce & Harris, 1993). This study revealed that white male participants viewed white male batterers, as compared to black male batterers, as having more right to use physical force but only when their violence was "provoked" and their victims' injuries were implicitly, rather than explicitly, described. Finally, physical attractiveness of perpetrators was not found related to respondents' attribution of the wife's responsibility (Burke, Ames, Etherington, & Pietsch, 1990).

The paucity of experimental studies on male perpetrator behaviors and characteristics, compared to the relatively larger number of studies on female victim behaviors and characteristics, reflects the greater scrutiny of battered wives than of perpetrators by society and by the mental health profession. This focus on the victims as opposed to the perpetrators may itself be an indirect measure of victim blaming.

What Contextual Variables Promote Victim Blame?

History of Abuse

Kalmuss (1979) found that a husband batterer's having beaten his wife several times in the past, versus his having never beaten her before, did not affect attributions of responsibility to the husband and wife for an abusive incident. In contrast, in Sugarman and Cohn's (1986) study, more overall responsibility was attributed to the husband if similar incidents of abuse had previously occurred than if there was no prior history of abuse. In support of Sugarman and Cohn's finding, Home (1994) found that front-line police and social workers blamed a male wife batterer more when he had previously abused a child than when there was no such history of child abuse. However, Lavoie et al. (1989) did not find subjects' responsibility ratings to vary as a function of whether the wife-battering husband had previously hit children but subjects may not have viewed hitting children as "abusive."

Sugarman and Cohn (1986) also found that male respondents attributed more origin responsibility (responsibility for causing the abusive situation) and less solution responsibility (responsibility for terminating the abusive situation) to the battered wife when the duration of the abuse was longer (three years as opposed to one year). Female respondents attributed less origin responsibility and more solution responsibility to the battered wife when the duration of the abuse was longer.

Psychological Versus Physical Violence

Lavoie et al. (1989) found that police officers attributed more responsibility to the wife, more to the couple, and less to the husbands' when an abusive situation involved the husband making threats rather than doing physical violence. Similarly, Home (1994) found that groups of both social workers and police officers blamed the woman more and agreed more that responsibility was shared when the battering husband made threats rather than physically abusing his wife. They blamed the husband batterer more when he had physically abused rather than threatened his wife.

Physical violence, as compared to threat, was viewed by social workers and police officers as more serious and as putting the woman in greater danger. Police, but not social workers, viewed physical violence as creating a greater risk of the situation's worsening or recurring than did threat alone (Home, 1994). In support of social workers' views, Follingstad, Rutledge, Berg, Hause, and Polek (1990) found that "threat of abuse was a very strong predictor that physical abuse would follow" (p. 115). Both types of workers predicted worse long-term consequences for the woman's and children's mental health if physical violence, rather than threat, was present (Home, 1994). These findings belie the finding by Follingstad et al. that 72% of battered women experience emotional abuse as having a more severe impact on them than physical violence.

Severity and Frequency of Injury

Kalmuss (1979) found that women, but not men, respondents held a battered wife more responsible, and thus a husband batterer less responsible, for a physical violence incident when the consequences of the abuse were low (black eye) rather than high (internal injuries). Although Kalmuss varied both severity of injury and sex of subject, no interactive effects of past pattern of abuse with either or both of these variables were reported.

As such, Kalmuss's (1979) findings contradict those of Sugarman and Cohn (1986), who found that when suffering mild, as compared to serious, injury, the battered wife was attributed more overall responsibility when incidents of abuse were frequent, as compared to infrequent. When suffering serious, as opposed to mild, injury, the battered wife was attributed more overall responsibility when the abuse was infrequent rather than frequent.

Pierce and Harris (1993) found that an explicitly, as compared to implicitly, described injury increased the seriousness with which the injury, as well as the violence, was viewed, suggesting that explicitly described injuries are viewed as more severe than implicitly described ones. Explicitly described injuries also produced lower perceived victim responsibility (when the batterer was of the same race as the subject), more liking for the victim, and, so long as the victim had not provoked her batterer, an increase in perceived likelihood of calling the police. Pierce and Harris did not examine the role of abuse frequency and thus, did not test for a frequency by severity of violence interaction.

Home (1994) found that a sample of police officers and social workers blamed the woman more and agreed more that responsibility was shared by the woman and man when the man had made threats rather than committed physical abuse. Because Home found that physical violence was viewed as creating a more dangerous situation for the woman than were threats, these findings also lend support to the notion that battered wives are blamed more when abuse is more mild. Although Home manipulated the variable of frequency of violence in her study, she did not test for a frequency by severity of violence interaction.

Examining police attitudes, Lavoie et al. (1989), like Sugarman and Cohn (1986), found what amounts to a frequency by severity of violence interaction, though the nature of their interaction differed from that of Sugarman and Cohn. When police viewed an incident as less serious (that is, as involving threat but not actual physical violence), they assumed a "more neutral attitude" (p. 381), blaming the wife more than when they viewed it as more serious (that is, as involving physical violence). When a husband battered his wife physically, police blame of the wife decreased as the frequency with which she was abused increased.

A variety of differences between Kalmuss's (1979), Sugarman and Cohn's, and Lavoie et al.'s studies confound interpretation of their discrepant findings. The three sets of investigators used different samples: Kalmass used Detroit citizens, Sugarman and Cohn used college students, and Lavoie et al. used municipal police officers from Quebec. Kalmuss' questionnaire return rate was 49% to 55%, comparable to that of Lavoie et al.; it is unclear what selection factors may have led Sugarman and Cohn's subjects to participate in their study, because the subjects were fulfilling a research requirement for their Introductory Psychology course. Kalmuss used a single item to measure both female victim and male batterer responsibility; Sugarman and Cohn and Lavoie et al. had separate measures for victim and batterer. Due to these numerous study differences, further research is needed to ascertain whether history of abuse interacts with severity of injury and frequency of violence to affect subjects' attributions of victim overall responsibility, and whether history of abuse interacts with sex of subject to affect subjects' attributions of origin and solution responsibility to victims. We recommend use of Sugarman and Cohn's (1986) measures of responsibility over those of Kalmuss.

In conclusion, it appears that a wife victim of spousal abuse is held more responsible for more mild than severe injuries, although this finding conflicts with that of Martin (1994), who found that in spouse abuse court trials, severity of injury was associated with case dismissal. It is likely that the frequency with which a woman is abused is likely to modify the effect of severity of violence. Future studies are needed to help elucidate the nature of severity of violence and frequency of violence interactions, when they are observed, and the conditions under which they are observed.

Other Contextual Variables

Summers and Feldman (1984) found that when it was mentioned that the battering husband had lost his job, subjects' attributions for violence focused on environmental causes ("The couple is under stress because of their financial situation") and on internal or unstable reasons that the male hit the female ("John is feeling particularly upset right now because of his job" and "John is in a bad mood"). Subjects did not assume the husband lost his job because he was a violent person, whether at work or at home. When his job loss was *not* mentioned in the scenario, subjects attributed more responsibility for a violent incident to the battered female ("Mary allows people to treat her like this" and "Mary had provoked John previously").

Kalmuss (1979) found that a battering husband's having had a hard day at work *and* having had a verbal argument with his wife (as opposed to a day at work and no verbal argument) led to the wife victim's being held significantly more, and, necessarily, the batterer's being held less, responsible for his physically abusing her. However, this situational variable affected only women's, not men's, attributions of responsibility. These two studies lead to somewhat contradictory conclusions although methodological differences could account for the discrepancy between the two studies. For example, Kalmuss did not include a measure of blame due to environmental causes. Clearly more research is needed with respect to extenuating circumstances and the interaction of these situations with other variables.

What Subject Characteristics Encourage Observers' Battered Wife Blaming?

Examining cross-sectional survey data of adult North Carolina women, Gentemann (1984) found that women who justified wife abuse under certain circumstances were more likely to be older, less educated, nonwhite, low-income, and blue-collar workers than those not justifying wife abuse. Lower education level was the strongest predictor of attitudes justifying wife abuse; however, race continued to predict such attitudes even when education was controlled. On the other hand, Stark and McEvoy (1970), analyzing Louis Harris and Associates poll data, found that approval for slapping one's spouse increased as respondent income and education increased. Approval was also higher among males than females, blacks than whites, and younger than older respondents.

Most investigators in this area have used college student samples, and thus have examined the attributions of those who tend to be younger, more educated, and white. This limitation, and the question of whether findings from college student samples generalize to the population at large, should be kept in mind in the review of findings.

Sex of Respondent

In this section, research findings bearing on three questions are described, and the state of knowledge in this area is assessed. Do men blame wife abuse victims more than do females when victim "provocation" is described? Do men hold victims more responsible for their own abuse than do women?

Perceptions of "Provocation" of Abuse. Do women and men differ in the blame they attribute to a spousal abuse victim when the victim is described as acting in a "provocative" manner? Even with the "effects" of gender role attitudes partialed out, Hillier and Foddy (1993) found that sex continued to have a significant effect on victim blame. This was true for victim blame for both the low-provocation (messy house) and high-provocation (suspected infidelity) conditions. Male respondents blamed the wife victim more than did female respondents, and women blamed the husband perpetrator more than did men, suggesting either identification with the same-sex scenario target or identification of men with the batterer and identification of women with the victim.

In contrast, some studies have found females to be more victim blaming than males when victim "provocation" is introduced. Kristiansen and Giulietti (1990) found that females blamed the wife victim more than did males when she was portrayed as yelling and shouting obscenities before violence commenced (the provocation condition). This sex difference was absent from their no provocation condition. Pierce and Harris (1993), using the same scenario and provocation, failed to find a sex difference. And Kalmuss (1979), who found females held a wife victim more responsible than did men, confounded provocation with the husband's having had a hard day at work. No sex of respondent difference in blame was found by Richardson and Campbell (1980) who used a scenario in which the wife was mildly "provocative" of abuse. In this case, the provocation was failing to prepare a proper dinner and accusing her husband of not making sufficient money to provide decent food.

In sum, findings are mixed as to whether men or women are more victim blaming when there is "provocation." The fact of mixed findings suggests that one or more other variables may be modifying the effects of provocation on females versus males. An unexplored confound in studies of the effects of provocation on victim blaming is that virtually all of the provocations examined to date represent gender role violations for women. To what extent are wife victims being blamed simply because they have acted out of gender role? Would "provocations" that are not sex role violations (e.g., crying) yield similar findings? Or might anything that a woman does to stand up for her rights be viewed as a gender role violation? To what extent does the wife's doing anything, so long as her behavior does not thwart the husband's imminent violence, increase the blame attributed to her? Regardless, males more than females perceived a female victim as provoking violence by a male perpetrator (Summers & Feldman, 1984).

Perceptions of Responsibility for Abuse. Do women and men differ in the extent to which they hold victims responsible for their own victimization? Ewing and Aubrey (1987) found that more men than women agreed that the female victim "bears at least some responsibility"; however, Kalmuss (1979) did not find a main effect for sex of respondent. Sample differences are unlikely to explain the discrepant findings, for both Kalmuss's and Ewing and Aubrey's samples were members of the general public—one in Detroit and the other in Buffalo. Differences are more likely due to either year of study—Kalmuss's study occurred earlier than Ewing and Aubrey's—or to measurement artifact, for Kalmuss used a single item to assess both victim and batterer responsibility, while Ewing and Aubrey used separate measures of victim and perpetrator responsibility. A more recent study by Pierce and Harris (1993) supports the findings of Ewing and Aubrey. Using a college student sample and providing separate measures of victim and perpetrator responsibility, these investigators found that women held the wife victim less responsible and the husband batterer more responsible for the battering incident, than did men. Similarly, Otchet (1993) found that male college students blamed a victim of dating violence more than did their female counterparts, and females blamed the perpetrator more than did males.

Home (1994) too obtained data supporting the notion that women hold victims less responsible than do men. Police officers (mostly men) attributed more responsibility to the woman than did social workers (mainly women), and social workers attributed more responsibility to the man than did police. Male social workers attributed more responsibility to the woman than did female social workers.

In sum, it appears that men attribute greater responsibility for spousal abuse to the wife victim than do women. In addition, findings presented in earlier sections reveal that sex of respondent frequently interacts with other variables (e.g., high versus low consequences of injury, Kalmuss, 1979; duration of abuse, Sugarman & Cohn, 1986).

Victim Derogation. Are women or men more victim derogating? Findings are mixed. On the one hand, Ewing and Aubrey (1987) found that more women than men agreed that the battered woman who stays is "somewhat masochistic" and "emotionally disturbed," suggesting that more women than men are victim derogating. This attitude is probably related to another of their findings: that more women than men agreed that a battered woman could simply leave her abuser (women, 71%, versus men, 57%; though this finding appears in conflict with those of Dodge and Greene, 1991).

On the other hand, female respondents reported liking the victim more than did male respondents (Harris & Cook, 1994; Pierce & Harris, 1993). However, they did so only if the victim had not "provoked" the batterer (Harris & Cook, 1994).

Identification with Victim and Batterer. Despite mixed findings regarding whether women or men are more blaming of battered wives who have "provoked" their husbands and despite mixed findings regarding which sex is more victim derogating, a sex difference has been found for a variety of other dependent variables relating to the spousal abuse situation. These findings suggest that women are more victim-identified and men are more batterer identified. Among college students, women as compared to men reported viewing the husband as having less of a right to use force, seeing the incident as more violent, being more likely to report the presence of bleeding, being more likely to report that the wife was yelling, being more likely to believe that the wife victim had suffered several internal injuries, and liking the abuser less (Pierce & Harris, 1993). In addition, women more than men felt that the husband should be convicted of assault (Cook & Harris, 1995; Pierce & Harris, 1993) and that if they had witnessed the incident from the window next door, they would have called the police (Cook & Harris, 1995; Harris & Cook, 1994; Pierce & Harris, 1993).

Other investigators have found that men more than women believed a husband has the right to hit his wife (Summers & Feldman, 1984), viewed the incident as less violent (Harris & Cook, 1994), saw the abusive incident as more humorous (Cook & Harris, 1995), and were more lenient in sentencing the husband (Burke et al., 1990). And males reported being less likely to call the police if a wife victim had verbally provoked her abusive husband, whereas women were likely to call for help regardless of whether the wife had acted provocatively (Pierce & Harris, 1993).

Similarly, Home (1994) found that (predominantly female) social workers, as compared to (predominantly male) police officers, viewed an overall abusive situation as more serious, considered the woman victim to be in greater danger, felt there was a greater risk of the abusive situation's recurring, were more concerned that the situation would worsen, and were more concerned about the consequences of the situation for the mental health of the woman and that of her children. Further, female social workers viewed the situation as more dangerous than did male social workers or police officers.

A preponderance of the findings suggests that women, as compared to men, are more victim identified (revealed by measures concerning right to use force, right to hit, and liking), are likely to view the incident as more dangerous to victims (revealed by measures concerning immediate danger, seriousness, risk of recurrence, risk of situation worsening, violence, bleeding, yelling, and internal injuries, mental health consequences, and humor), and are more likely to engage in victim-aiding behaviors (hinted at by measures concerning calling police, conviction, and sentencing). By the same token, men appear more batterer identified than do women.

Harris and Cook's (1994) study, wherein both males and females were portrayed as both victim and batterer, suggests that women's identification is with the victim rather than with the female target: "Women reacted more strongly to the battering incident, regardless of who the victim was [the husband, the wife, or a gay male lover]. . . . Thus this finding . . . is not attributable solely to the women subjects' gender identification with the battered wife victim" (pp. 560–561). Similarly, using scenarios involving dating violence with both female and male aggressors and victims, Otchet (1993) found that female, as compared to male, college student subjects reported being more likely to be in a situation like that of the victim. In short, it appears that women identify with the victim more than do men and consequently view spousal violence as more dangerous to victims than do men and are thus more likely to help victims than are men.

Support for this view was obtained by Schuller, Smith, and Olson (1994). Using a mock trial format, these investigators found that compared to female jurors, male jurors attributed greater responsibility to the female defendant accused of murdering her abusive husband, were less likely to believe the defendant's claim of self-defense, were more likely to recommend punishment for the defendant, and, if exposed to expert testimony, were less likely to believe that the battered woman's syndrome applied to the defendant. Compared to men, women jurors were not only more knowledgeable about abuse prior to the trial, but were more open to (expert) information about abuse that mitigated the responsibility attributed to a woman accused of killing her abusive spouse. This effect was particularly strong for women who believed that injustices exist. Information about abuse from an expert paradoxically exacerbated male jurors' victim blaming. In contrast to the supportive findings of Schuller et al., the findings of Burke et al. (1990) revealed that male college students were as likely as female college students to find a husband guilty of assault against his wife. However, as expected, males were more lenient than females in sentencing the husband.

In conclusion, a plethora of sex differences suggest greater female than male identification with the victim, greater perceived dangerousness by females than males, and greater reported likelihood to help the victim. Still, it remains unclear whether women or men generally attribute more blame to the victim when the victim is portrayed as having "provoked" violence. More women than men derogated a wife victim, in the sense of viewing her as masochistic and emotionally disturbed, and women liked the wife victim more than did men.

Gender Roles

Although the relationships are observed in often complex ways, subjects with more traditional gender role attitudes, typically measured using the Attitudes Toward Women Scale, have reported more wife abuse justification, more victim blaming, less blaming of the perpetrator, more responsibility being allotted to victims for their own victimization, and more victim derogation than have their more egalitarian counterparts. Specifically, Kristiansen and Giulietti (1990) found that more traditional attitudes toward women were associated with more derogating of victims and with blaming the abusive husband less. Gentemann (1984) found that women with traditional sex role attitudes were significantly more likely than those with egalitarian attitudes to justify wife abuse in certain contexts. And Finn (1986) has found that those with more traditional sex roles report attitudes more supportive of the use of force in marriage.

Others have found the relationship between gender role attitudes and victim blame and derogation to depend on the presence versus absence of victim provocation and on sex of subject. Sometimes the relationship also depends on the extent to which subjects believe the world is just.

Hillier and Foddy (1993) found that, in general, traditional subjects blamed the victim more and the perpetrator less than did egalitarian subjects. Both traditional and egalitarian subjects blamed victims in the high-provocation condition more than they did victims in the low-provocation condition. However, subjects with traditional sex role values, as compared to those with more egalitarian attitudes, were more influenced by victim provocation level in assigning blame to victim and perpetrator. Although egalitarian subjects tended to place more blame on the perpetrator, regardless of victims' level of provocation, traditional subjects blamed the high-provocation victims at least as much as, if not more than, the perpetrator. A three-way interaction of sex of subject, provocation level, and sex role attitudes was not found.

Kristiansen and Giulietti (1990) found that, in general, college students attributed more blame to the victim as their attitudes became more traditional. A higher-order interaction revealed, however, that this relationship was present only in the provocation condition, where victim blaming was highest; it was absent from the no provocation condition. And, the effect was modified by subjects' sex and just-world beliefs: females with more egalitarian attitudes toward women were more blaming of the victim who had provoked her abuser as their belief in a just world became stronger. There was no relationship between belief in a just world and victim blaming among females with more traditional attitudes toward women (even in the provocation condition). In contrast, males' blaming of a spousal abuse victim who had "provoked" her abuser increased as their attitudes toward women became more traditional.

Kristiansen and Giulietti (1990) found that, in general, victim derogation was higher among subjects with more traditional sex role attitudes than among those with more egalitarian ones. A sex of subject × sex role attitudes × belief in a just world interaction uncovered that only more traditional sex role attitudes predicted greater victim derogation among males. Among females, neither sex role attitudes, nor belief in a just world, nor the interaction of these two constructs predicted victim derogation.

In conclusion, among men, more traditional gender role attitudes have been associated with more blaming and derogating of battered wives when the wives have "provoked" their battering husbands' violence. Concerning "blame," findings regarding women are mixed (see Hillier & Foddy, 1993, versus Kristiansen & Giulietti, 1990). Since much of what is considered "provocation" is behavior that violates gender roles, this role violation may be perceived as justification for violence, particularly among men. Thus, one function of battering of wives by husbands may be to maintain gender roles. Further research is needed to clarify the possible role of belief in a just world attitudes in modifying the relationship between victim blaming and sex role attitudes among females. Further research also is needed to determine if gender role–typical provocations and gender role–atypical ones similarly affect the two sexes' blaming of battered wives. Traditional sex role attitudes appear to be associated with increased victim derogation, but only among men. This relationship is not surprising, for Briere (1987) found that 79% of the college men reported at least some likelihood to batter, and the more traditional a man's reported attitudes toward women, the greater his reported likelihood of battering.

Age

Ewing and Aubrey (1987) found that the percentage of persons agreeing with two statements—that the female victim "bears at least some responsibility" and is "somewhat masochistic"—increased with age. To the extent that victim derogation is associated with misinformation about the situation of battered women, these findings are consistent with Dodge and Greene's (1991) findings that younger subjects hold more accurate beliefs about battered women than do older subjects. Younger (18 to 31 year olds), as compared to older (over 44 years), jurors expressed more accurate beliefs regarding the following issues: (1) a battered woman might believe her husband could kill her; (2) she might be persuaded to stay if her partner promised never to hurt her again; (3) she might believe that the use of deadly force is the only way for her to stay alive; (4) most battered women show signs of anxiety and depression; and (5) most battered women are not masochistic. The youngest jurors also held significantly more accurate knowledge than did the middle-aged jurors (32 to 44 year olds) regarding these issues: a battered woman shows signs of anxiety and depression, and she believes that the use of deadly force is the only way for her to stay alive. Accuracy of information was assessed in terms of similarity of subjects' response to that of researchers with expertise in the area of spousal abuse.

Race

Sex of subject has been found to interact with race of perpetrator in complex ways (see Pierce & Harris, 1993). Unfortunately, the effects of race of subject have not been examined, thereby limiting the interpretation of these findings. It is also unclear whether race of *victim* affects subjects' attributions of victim blame and derogation, or whether it interacts with sex of subject because investigators have not systemically varied the race of the victim.

Alcohol Use

Subjects' own alcohol use did not relate to attributions of responsibility for (drinking and nondrinking) husband or wife (Dent & Arias, 1990).

Personal Experience with Abuse

Dent and Arias (1990) found that subjects' own history of relationship violence was related to subjects' evaluations of the wife, but not the husband. Those who had "been violent in their own relationships," as compared to those who had not, evaluated the wife less negatively, whether she was the victim or the perpetrator. Pierce and Harris (1993) found that although battering-experienced and battering-nonexperienced women did not view the battering incident as differing in severity of violence, battering-nonexperienced males viewed the incident as less violent than did battering-experienced males.

Professional Experience with Abuse

Home (1994) examined the attributions of front-line workers—police officers and social workers—who had contact with battered wives as part of their jobs during the previous year. Police officers attributed more responsibility to the wife victim, the couple, and the socioeconomic situation of the couple than did social workers. Social workers saw the woman in greater danger than did police. The author noted that sex of worker was confounded with occupation; however, male social workers attributed less responsibility to the woman and saw the woman in greater danger than did male police officers.

Prior Beliefs

Beliefs about Abuse. Schuller et al. (1994) found that jurors in a mock trial who had more prior knowledge of abuse dynamics, thus more accurate beliefs about battering, attributed less responsibility to the battered woman and more to the battering husband. These informed jurors also viewed expert testimony on the battered woman's syndrome as more applicable to the female defendant on trial for murdering her battering husband and were more supportive of the syndrome.

Belief in a Just World. In the mock trial study (Schuller et al., 1994), participants who were weak believers in a just world were more likely to view the battered women's syndrome as applying to the defendant than were strong believers, thus, mitigating the guilt of the defendant. Kristiansen and Giulietti (1980) found that the stronger one's belief in a just world, the greater was the victim blaming. However, this relationship was observed only when "provocation" had occurred (where victim blaming was higher).

Prejudiced Beliefs. In a study of the relationship of battered wife blame to other prejudices, Graham et al. (1996) found that among college students, as battered wife blame increased, sexism increased, heterosexism tended to increase, and authoritarianism decreased. Once the effects of sexism were controlled, the significant positive relationships of battered wife blame, with racism, vanished and, with heterosexism, became only a trend. Males reported greater prejudice on all measures—racism, sexism, heterosexism, and battered wife blame—than did females. These findings suggest that in blaming battered wives, individuals are using sexist and, to a lesser extent, heterosexist ideologies. Because battered wife blame is about justifying the use of violence against women who are wives, it seems that it reflects a willingness to use violence or force to keep women in subordinate positions to, and in intimate relations with, men.

To summarize, those holding the most victim-blaming attitudes tended to be male rather than female. Particularly if they were male, those expressing higher battered wife blame tended to possess more traditional attitudes toward women. If female, they tended to hold stronger beliefs in a just world. These findings were strongest when a victim had "provoked" violence, though males were more likely to perceive provocation than were females. Those expressing more battered wife blame also tended to hold less accurate beliefs about battering, though this finding was typically confounded with sex of subject. Those persons holding the most victim-derogating attitudes tended to be men with less favorable attitudes toward women and older rather than younger individuals. No simple relationship between personal experience with intimate violence and victim blaming and derogation has been found.

PSYCHOLOGICAL THEORIES ACCOUNTING FOR VICTIM-BLAME

There are six replicated findings from our review for which an adequate theory of battered wife blame must account:

1. Females seem to identify with the victim and males with the perpetrator, and men are more victim blaming than women (Ewing & Aubrey, 1987; Harris & Cook, 1994; Pierce & Harris, 1993; Schuller et al., 1994).
2. Compared to men, women were both more knowledgeable about the effects of abuse on victims (Greene et al., 1989; Schuller et al., 1994; but see Ewing & Aubrey, 1987) and more open to such information (Schuller et al., 1994).
3. Having more traditional gender role attitudes was associated with holding more battered-wife-blaming attitudes, particularly among male subjects (Kristiansen & Giulietti, 1990), when the woman "provoked" abuse (Hillier & Foddy, 1993).
4. "Provocation" was associated with increased blaming of battered wives (Dent & Arias, 1990; Harris & Cook, 1994; Kristiansen & Giulietti, 1990; Pierce & Harris, 1993) and with minimizing of the "provoked" incident's seriousness (Pierce & Harris, 1993).
5. Age was associated with increased blaming of battered wives (Ewing & Aubrey, 1987; Gentemann, 1984; but see Stark & McEvoy, 1970) and decreased knowledge of abuse dynamics (Dodge & Greene, 1991).
6. Subjects' blaming of battered wives increased as their belief in a just world increased (Kristiansen & Giulietti, 1980; Schuller et al., 1994).

Battered wife blame increased as abuse became more mild and decreased as abuse became more severe (among women only, Kalmuss, 1979; among both sexes, Pierce & Harris, 1993; but see Martin, 1994). Because threats are viewed as a less serious form of abuse than physical violence, another way in which this finding was expressed is that: battered wife blame was higher when a husband threatened his wife than when he used physical violence against her (Home, 1994; Lavoie et al., 1989). While evidence supports making this replicated finding, the finding is called into question by the interaction between seriousness and frequency of injury observed by both Sugarman and Cohn (1996) and Lavoie et al. (1989), an interaction whose nature differed for the two sets of investigators finding it. Until we have more studies varying severity and frequency, it may be best to reserve judgment on how these variables separately or together affect victim blaming.

A number of psychological theories have been posited to account for observers' victim blaming in a range of situations (e.g., rape, car accidents). These theories address both intrapersonal and social variables, and motivational and cognitive reasons, that observers might blame the victim. The motivational theories are that victim blaming occurs so that observers can maintain their beliefs in a just world (Lerner, 1980), maintain a sense of control and thereby defend against their own vulnerability (Walster, 1966), and avoid blame should they be victimized (Shaver, 1970). Cognitively based theories include Janoff-Bulman, Timko, and Carli's (1985) "hindsight effect" wherein outcome knowledge increases both the perceived likelihood of that outcome and the blame attributed to a victim, whom observers believe should have been able to foresee that her behavior would lead to victimization, and Howard's (1984a, 1984b) notion that people fall back on stereotypes in making (victim-blaming) attributions (e.g., the stereotype that women are weak causes people to view women as characterologically responsible for their own victimization).

Shaver's theory (1970)—that attributions serve the function of helping observers avoid blame should they be victimized in the future, assuming they view themselves as similar to the victim—received the most support of the traditional psychological theories. The theory was supported by four of the six replicated findings: (1) that men, who identified more with the perpetrator, were more victim blaming than women, who identified more with the victim; (2) that given these sex-linked identifications, women were both more knowledgeable about the effects of abuse and more open to new information about these effects than were men; (3) for male subjects only, that victim "provocation" elicited more victim blaming (the same finding for women subjects suggests that females did not identify with a "provocative" victim—for example, they reported less liking for her); and (4) that older subjects were more victim blaming than younger subjects, for older persons are less likely to be abused than are younger persons (U.S. Department of Justice, 1994).

Although Shaver's theory was superior to alternative psychological theories in explaining the attributional patterns uncovered by the current reviewers, it fails to account for why women would view themselves as more similar to, or identify with, victims and men would view themselves as similar to, or identify with, perpetrators—assumptions crucial to the theory's success in accounting for the findings. Given these shortcomings, we now examine the utility of radical feminist theory in accounting for the findings.

A Radical Feminist Analysis

A radical feminist analysis of wife battering examines this behavior in a socio-political context of male domination, wherein male violence against women is used to preserve male dominance and female subordination. Inequality between men and women is built into gender roles that prescribe rules for the interaction between men and women, particularly in intimate relationships (Graham, 1996). Dominants have certain rights—to name reality and to create and enforce rules of behavior that maintain their dominance. Subordinates have responsibilities to serve dominants and to follow the rules set forth by dominants (Miller, 1976). Male dominance is maintained through an intricate web of gender roles, values, and institutions (legal, economic, scientific, etc.) that ultimately rests on men's aggression and violence (Graham, 1996). Victim blaming is a way of viewing reality that preserves the status quo by locating problems (e.g., wife abuse) in subordinates and thus obscuring the underlying system of oppression (Miller, 1976).

Looking at the reviewed studies on victim blaming in wife abuse through the feminist lenses of power and gender helps us understand how people operationalize these rules in making sense of social behavior such as wife battering. Due to power differences in our culture being assigned on the basis of sex, with men possessing more power than women, men are likely to identify more with the aggressor (the batterer) and women more with the victim, as was observed. Similarly, since men and women are situated differently in the power structure of society, and men are more invested in maintaining these unequal relations than are women (Graham, 1996), it is not surprising that many investigators find sex differences in men's and women's attributions of blame and responsibility in wife battering, with men attributing more blame to victims than do women (Finding 1).

As subordinates, women are more likely to experience the costs of abuse than are men, as dominants. For example, during intimate violence, women are more likely than men to receive an injury (Cantos, Neidig, & O'Leary, 1994; Cascardi, Langhinrichsen, & Vivian, 1992; Langhinrichsen-Rohling, Neidig, & Thorn, 1995; Vivian & Langhinrichsen-Rohling, 1994), to sustain a serious injury (Cantos et al., 1994; Cascardi et al., 1992), to report negative psychological impact (Vivian & Langhinrichsen-Rohling, 1994), and to report depression (Cascardi et al., 1992), marital dissatisfaction (Cascardi et al., 1992), and being afraid (Langhinrichsen-Rohling et al., 1995). Given the effects of this sex difference in power, it is not surprising that women are both more informed about the realities of abuse and more open to such information (Finding 2).

Not unexpectedly, those men most strongly embracing their rights to dominate women (those with more traditional gender role attitudes) blame women for being victimized more than do men who hold more egalitarian attitudes (Finding 3). Women, who are supposed to act in *men's* best interest, are considered legitimate targets for male violence when they act in *their own* best interest (e.g., cursing men for men's ill treatment of them). To use male-identified language, these women "provoke" their own victimization (Finding 4).

It is possible that the finding that victim blaming increased with age is due to older individual' possessing more traditional sex role attitudes (Finding 5). Similarly, because belief in a just world is incompatible with the feminist belief in group oppression, the finding that battered wife blame increased as belief in a just world increased (Finding 6) may be due to an association between traditional sex role attitudes and belief in a just world. The speculation—that traditional sex role attitudes account for both of these spurious findings—awaits additional research for empirical confirmation.

Battered wife blame and derogation are forms of male or batterer identification, whether expressed by males or females, for battered wife blame is in abusers', not victims', interests. Graham's (1996) societal Stockholm Syndrome theory explains why women as well as men blame battered wives. While behavioral self-blame in victims is adaptive for survival (Janoff-Bulman, 1982), it does not lead to women's changing their dangerous situations (Andrews, 1992).

Both Shaver's defensive attribution theory and radical feminist theory contribute important and unique insights. Radical feminist theory brings in a power-oppression dimension—providing an explanation as to why women identify with victims and men with perpetrators—which is lacking in Shaver's theory. Defensive attribution theory specifies psychological mechanisms that translate beliefs and ideologies into behavior. Since our knowledge is quite limited we need to be open to various theoretical options and combinations of theories.

RECOMMENDATIONS FOR FUTURE RESEARCH

We have a number of recommendations for future research. Many findings reviewed here were contradicted by other findings. For example, under what circumstances are women likely to be more victim blaming than men, and why? In some cases, these contradictions could be explained by methodological differences among studies. In other cases, they may be due to as-yet-unidentified moderator variables. Further study of potentially confounding variables is needed, as suggested in our recommendations. The replicability of many other findings needs evaluation. For example, are husbands held more responsible than wives for initiating violence, but viewed as more justified than wives for responding violently to "provoked" violence," as Cook and Harris (1995) found?

Sex differences in observers' (or subjects') perceptions of provocation and in the effects of provocation on wife-blaming attributions are likely to contribute to variability in findings across studies. For this reason, it is recommended that the effects of different types of provocations, particularly of those commonly used by investigators, be systematically examined as a function of subject sex and gender role attitudes (traditional versus egalitarian).

Because interactions between gender role attitudes and presence versus absence of victim provocation have frequently been observed, we recommend that the effects on victim blame of gender role–typical versus–atypical provocations be examined. Does a battered wife who is acting out of sex role receive more blame and less help, and are observers more likely to minimize her victimization, than one acting in role? Or are battered wives alleged to provoke incidents, as compared to those not viewed as acting provocatively, blamed regardless of the gender role nature of their "provocations?"

Noncollege populations deserve much more study. Studies of the demographics of those most likely to victim-blame are needed, as are studies of the relation between college student samples and samples representative of the population at large. Attempts to generalize findings from studies using only college students may lead to misleading conclusions.

The role of race, especially race of victim and subject, has been ignored in past research. Inclusion of race as a variable for investigation will help unravel why black men are more frequently arrested for spousal abuse than are white men (Belknap, 1995; Buzawa & Austin, 1993).

Actual examples of battered wife blaming and derogating need to be studied, as well as their relationship to victim helping. For example, what are the effects of battered wife blaming on people's—the public's, neighbors, family members', judges,' prosecutors,' and police officers'—willingness to help (e.g., willingness to convict)? Does battered wife blame affect therapists' treatment plans and if so, how? Studies of therapists' knowledge, attitudes, and treatment plans, similar to those done by Dye and Roth (1990) around sexual assault client issues and by Graham, Rawlings, Halpern, and Hermes (1984) around lesbian and gay client issues, are needed regarding intimate violence. While a wife victim's efforts to file charges against her partner and to leave her partner were not found to affect the responsibility observers attributed to her (Home, 1994), do these efforts, or their lack, affect people's willingness to help that victim? Friends and family of battered women could be surveyed to determine if there is a relationship between attitudes about battered women (and beliefs about abuse situations) and helping behaviors. To what extent do scenario studies yield findings similar to those observed in real-life situations?

Battered women presumably are not immune from the effects of public attitudes surrounding spouse abuse victims. Research by Snyder and Swann (1978) on behavioral confirmation suggests that the public's victim blaming of battered women, and its viewing battered women as possessing dispositional traits (e.g., co-dependence, masochism) that cause them to seek abusive partners and to stay in abusive relationships, are likely to cause battered women to blame themselves and respond to abuse in ways consistent with such victim-blaming attributions. Such effects are indeed consistent with the findings of Andrews (1992), who determined that the type of blame in which women engaged was associated with the type of help sought (e.g., legal, caring profession) and with whether women sought help. Although not significant, only one-third of the women with characterological self-blame sought any type of formal help, compared to two-thirds of the other women.

Battered women would seem particularly likely to take on the attitudes of others if fear or shame precluded them from refuting victim-blaming attributions made by those others, including batterers, during social interactions (Swann & Hill, 1982). Consistent with this notion, Andrews (1992) found that battered women engaged in more self-blame while still involved with their abusive partners and more partner blame when the relationship with him was over. However, the research by Swann and his associates was not undertaken with a sample of battered women, and Andrews's study does not help unravel what is cause versus effect. Do batterers' and the public's wife-blaming attitudes affect battered women's attitudes about themselves, and, if so, once internalized by battered women, do they alter women's help-seeking behaviors, serve to keep them in abusive relationships, help erode their self-esteem, or further disempower them?

Feminist theory underscores the importance of social power in understanding attitudes such as victim blaming. While the theory would predict victim blaming would be greater toward groups lower in social power (women, blacks, and lower socioeconomic classes), such attitudes may be revealed only under certain conditions. For example, scenarios in which the victim is described as acting in ways that can be (mis)perceived as "provocative," or response options that permit opened-ended as opposed to, or in addition to, forced-choice responses, may be more effective in uncovering victim blaming attitudes. The interactions of gender, race, and class may be useful in elucidating power issues in victim-blaming. Adding a measure of feminist identity of subjects may produce outcomes that are not obtained by merely examining more traditional versus more egalitarian gender roles.

By better understanding the who, what, when, and how of battered wife blaming, we will be able to design more effective educational programs to reduce blaming and increase helping behaviors in the public at large as well as among professional service providers who have frequent contact with battered women. For example, the training needs of predominantly male police officers would most likely be different from those of predominantly female social workers (see Home, 1994), and the training needs of male jurors are likely to differ from those of female jurors (see Schuller et al., 1994). Are programs designed to denounce the patriarchal underpinnings of woman abuse and battered wife blame more or less effective than those designed to thwart the defensive attributions of male participants? Future research should go beyond the identification of variables associated with wife blaming and examine what strategies are useful in changing attitudes and increasing the helping behaviors of various target populations. The findings of Lerner and Simmons (1966) suggest that when people believe that they personally have done something that will prevent a victim from suffering in the future, victim blaming is reduced. If people were educated about the ways to help avert battered women's future suffering and about ways of discerning improvements, however small, in battered women's situations, perhaps they would provide battered women more help and less blame.

NOTE

This review was prompted by the victim-blaming questions asked and attitudes expressed by many mental health workers, members of the media, and court staff—people who are allegedly in the business of helping battered women—when we have spoken publicly about intimate violence. This experience led us to the realization that as important as research on batterers and intimate violence victims is, research on observers' victim-blaming attitudes, and on how to change those attitudes, is of almost equal importance.

We thank Alethea Bennett and Harold Fishbein, Ph.D., for their editing of a draft of this Chapter.

REFERENCES

Allen, P. G. (1991). *Separation issues of battered women.* Unpublished master's thesis, University of Cincinnati, Cincinnati, Ohio.

Allen, P. G. (1996). *A test of the concurrent validity of the stages of unbonding scale.* Unpublished doctoral dissertation, University of Cincinnati, Cincinnati, Ohio.

Andrews, B. (1992). Attribution processes in victims of marital violence: Who do women blame and why? In J. H. Harvey, T. L. Orbuch, & A. L. Weber (Eds.), *Attributions, accounts, and close relationships* (pp. 176–193). New York: Springer-Verlag.

Astin, M. C., Lawrence, K. J., & Foy, D. W. (1993). Posttraumatic stress disorder among battered women: Risk and resiliency factors. *Violence andVictims, 8*(1), 17–28.

Bachman, R., & Carmody, D. C. (1994). Fighting fire with fire: The effects of victim resistance in intimate versus stranger perpetrated assaults against females. *Journal of Family Violence, 9*(4), 317–331.

Bachman, R., & Saltzman, L. E. (1995). *Violence against women: Estimates from the redesigned survey* (U.S. Department of Justice Publication No. NCJ-154348). Washington, DC: U.S. Government Printing Office.

Bagarozzi, D. A., & Giddings, C. W. (1983). Conjugal violence: A critical review of current research and clinical practices. *American Journal of Family Therapy, 11,* 3–15.

Belknap, J. (1995). Law enforcement officers' attitudes about the appropriate responses to woman battering. *International Review of Victimology, 4,* 47–62.

Bograd, M. (1984). Family systems approaches to wife battering: A feminist critique. *American Journal of Orthopsychiatry, 54*(4), 558–568.

Bowker, L. H. (1983). *Beating wife-beating.* Lexington, MA: Lexington Books.

Briere, J. (1987). Predicting self-reported likelihood of battering: Attitudes and childhood experiences. *Journal of Research in Personality, 21,* 61–69.

Burke, D. M., Ames, M. A., Etherington, R., & Pietsch, J. (1990). Effects of victim's and defendant's physical attractiveness on the perception of responsibility in an ambiguous domestic violence case. *Journal of Family Violence, 5*(3), 199–207.

Buzawa, E. S., & Austin, T. (1993). Determining police response to domestic violence victims. *American Behavioral Scientist, 36*(5), 610–623.

Cantos, A. L., Neidig, P. H., & O'Leary, K. D. (1994). Injuries of women and men in a treatment program for domestic violence. *Journal of Family-Violence, 9*(2), 113–124.

Cascardi, M., Langhinrichsen, J., & Vivian, D. (1992). Marital aggression: Impact, injury, and health correlates for husbands and wives. *Archives of Internal Medicine, 152*(6), 1178–1184.

Celini, D. P. (1994). *The illusion of love: Why the battered woman returns to her abuser.* New York: Columbia University Press.

Coates, D., Wortman, C. B., & Abbey, A. (1979). Reactions to victims. In I. H. Frieze, D. Bar-Tal, & J. S. Carroll (Eds.), *New approaches to social-problems* (pp. 21–52). San Francisco: Jossey-Bass.

Cook, C. A., & Harris, R. J. (1995). Attributions about spouse abuse in cases of bidirectional battering. *Violence and Victims, 10*(2), 143–151.

Dent, D. Z., & Arias, I. (1990). Effects of alcohol, gender, and role of spouses on attributions and evaluations of marital violence scenarios. *Violence and Victims, 5*(3), 185–193.

Devine, P. G. (1989). Stereotypes and prejudice: Their automatic and controlled components. *Journal of Personality and Social Psychology, 56,* 5–18.

Dobash, R. E., & Dobash, R. P. (1984). The nature and antecedents of violent events. *British Journal of Criminology, 24,* 269–288.

Dodge, M., & Greene, E. (1991). Juror and expert conceptions of battered women. *Violence and Victims, 6*(4), 271–282.

Dye, E., & Roth, S. (1990). Psychotherapists' knowledge about and attitudes toward sexual assault victim clients. *Psychology of Women Quarterly, 14,*191–212.

Ewing, C. P., & Aubrey, M. (1987). Battered women and public opinion: Some realities about the myths. *Journal of Family Violence, 2,* 257–264.

Finn, J. (1986). The relationship between sex role attitudes and attitudes supporting marital violence. *Sex Roles, 14*(5/6), 235–244.

Follingstad, D. R., Brennan, A. F., Hause, E. S., Polek, D. S., & Rutledge, L. L. (1991). Factors moderating physical and psychological symptoms of battered women. *Journal of Family Violence, 6*(1), 81–94.

Follingstad, D. R., Rutledge, L., Berg, B., Hause, E., & Polek, D. (1990). The role of emotional abuse in physically abusive relationships. *Journal of Family Violence, 5*(2), 107–120.

Gentemann, K. M. (1984). Wife beating: Attitudes of non-clinical population. *Victimology: An International Journal, 9*(1), 109–119.

Gleason, W. J. (1993). Mental disorders in battered women: An empirical study. *Violence and Victims, 8*(1), 53–68.

Gondolf, E. W., with Fisher, E. R. (1988). *Battered women as survivors: An alternative to treating learned helplessness.* Lexington MA: Lexington Books.

Goolkasian, G. A. (1986, November). Confronting domestic violence: The role of criminal judges. In *National Institute of Justice, Research in brief.* Washington, DC: U.S. Department of Justice.

Graham, D.L.R. (1996). *Victim/witness reluctance in spouse abuse cases.* Manuscript in preparation, University of Cincinnati.

Graham, D.L.R., & Rawlings, E. I. (1991). Bonding with abusive dating partners: Dynamics of Stockholm Syndrome. In B. Levy (Ed.), *Dating violence: Young women in danger* (pp. 119–135). Seattle, WA: Seal Press.

Graham, D.L.R., Rawlings, E. I., Halpern, H. S., & Hermes, J. (1984). Therapists' needs in counseling lesbian and gay male clients. *Professional Psychology, 15*(4), 482–496.

Graham, D.L.R., with Rawlings, E. I., & Rigsby, R. K. (1994). *Loving to survive: Sexual terror, men's violence, and women's lives.* New York: New York University Press.

Graham, D.L.R., Wilson, C., Rawlings, E. I., Fishbein, H., Hoover, R., & Langmeyer, D.(1996). *Prejudice against battered wives.* Manuscript in preparation, University of Cincinnati.

Greenblat, C. S. (1985). "Don't hit your wife . . . unless . . . ": Preliminary findings on normative support for the use of physical force by husbands. *Victimology: An International Journal, 10*(1–4), 221–241.

Greene, E., Raitz, A., & Lindblad, H. (1989). Jurors' knowledge of battered women. *Journal of Family Violence, 4*(2), 105–125.

Harris, R. J., & Cook, C. A. (1994). Attributions about spouse abuse: It matters who the batterers and victims are. *Sex Roles, 30*(7/8), 553–565.

Hillier, L., & Foddy, M. (1993). The role of observer attitudes in judgments of blame in cases of wife assault. *Sex Roles, 29*(9/10), 629–544.

Home, A. M. (1994). Attributing responsibility and assessing gravity in wife abuse situations: A comparative study of police and social workers. *Journal of Social Service Research, 19*(1/2), 67–84.

Howard, J. A. (1984a). The "normal" victim: The effects of gender stereotypes on reactions to victims. *Social Psychology Quarterly, 47*(3), 270–281.

Howard, J. A. (1984b). Societal influences on attribution: Blaming some victims more than others. *Journal of Personality and Social Psychology, 47*(3), 494–505.

Janoff-Bulman, R. (1982). Esteem and control bases of blame: "Adaptive" strategies for victims versus observers. *Journal of Personality, 50*(2), 180–192.

Janoff-Bulman, R., Timko, C., & Carli, L. L. (1985). Cognitive biases in blaming the victim. *Journal of Experimental Social Psychology, 21*, 161–177.

Kalmuss, D. (1979). The attribution of responsibility in a wife-abuse context. *Victimology: An International Journal, 4*(2), 284–291.

Kemp, A., Green, B. L., Hovanitz, C., & Rawlings, E. I. (1995). Incidence and correlates of posttraumatic stress disorder in battered women. *Journal of Interpersonal Violence, 10*(1), 43–55.

Kristiansen, C. M., & Giulietti, R. (1990). Perceptions of wife abuse: Effects of gender, attitudes toward women, and just-world beliefs among college students. *Psychology of Women Quarterly, 14*,177–189.

Kurz, D., & Stark, E. (1988). Not-so-benign neglect: The medical response to battering. In K. Yllo & M. Bograd (Eds.), *Feminist perspectives on wife-abuse* (pp. 249–266). Newbury Park, CA: Sage.

Langhinrichsen-Rohling, J., Neidig, P., & Thorn, G. (1995). Violent marriages: Gender differences in levels of current violence and past abuse. *Journal of Family Violence, 10*(2), 159–176.

Lavoie, F., Jacob, M., Hardy, J., & Martin, G. (1989). Police attitudes in assigning responsibility for wife abuse. *Journal of Family Violence, 4*(4), 369–388.

Lerner, M. (1980). *The belief in a just world: A fundamental delusion.* New York: Plenum.

Lerner, M. J., & Simmons, C. H. (1966). Observer's reaction to the "innocent victim": Compassion or rejection? *Journal of Personality and Social Psychology, 4*(2), 203–210.

Martin, M. E. (1994). Mandatory arrest for domestic violence: The courts' response. *Criminal Justice Review, 19*(2), 212–227.

Miller, J. B. (1976). *Toward a new psychology of women.* Boston: Beacon Press.

Okun, L. (1986). *Woman abuse: Facts replacing myths.* Albany: State University of New York Press.

Otchet, F. B. (1993). *College students' perceptions of homosexual and heterosexual abusive dating relationships.* Unpublished master's thesis, University of Cincinnati, Cincinnati, Ohio.

Pagelow, M. D. (1981). *Woman-battering: Victims and their experiences.* Beverly Hills: Sage.

Pagelow, M. D. (1992). Adult victims of domestic violence: Battered women. *Journal of Interpersonal Violence, 7*(1), 87–120.

Pierce, M. D., & Harris, R. J. (1993). The effect of provocation, race, and injury description on men's and women's perception of a wife-battering incident. *Journal of Applied Social Psychology, 23*, 767–790.

Quarm, D., & Schwartz, M. D. (1983). Legal reform and the criminal court: The case of domestic violence. *Northern Kentucky Law Review, 10*(2), 199–225.

Rawlings, E. I., Allen, P. G., Graham, D. L. R., & Peters, J. (1994). Chinks in the prison wall: Applying Graham's Stockholm Syndrome theory to the treatment of battered women. In L. VandeCreek, S. Knapp, & T. L. Jackson (Eds.), *Innovations in clinical practice: A source book* (Vol. 13, pp. 401–417). Sarasota, FL: Professional Resource Exchange.

Richardson, D. C., & Campbell, J. L. (1980). Alcohol and wife abuse: The effect of alcohol on attributions of blame for wife abuse. *Personality and Social Psychology Bulletin, 6*(1), 51–56.

Riggs, D. S., Kilpatrick, D. G., & Resnick, H. S. (1992). Long-term psychological distress associated with marital rape and aggravated assault: A comparison to other crime victims. *Journal of Family Violence, 7*(4), 283–296.

Role, T. A. (1987). *Blaming the victims of wife battering: Gender, relationships, and attributions toward assault victims.* Unpublished master's thesis, University of Cincinnati, Cincinnati, Ohio.

Schuller, R. A., Smith, V. L., & Olson, J. M. (1994). Jurors' decisions in trials of battered women who kill: The role of prior beliefs and expert testimony. *Journal of Applied Social Psychology, 24*(4), 316–337.

Shaver, K. G. (1970). Defensive attribution: Effects of severity and relevance on the responsibility assigned for an accident. *Journal of Personality and Social Psychology, 14*(2), 101–113.

Shotland, R. L., & Straw, M. K. (1976). Bystander response to an assault: When a man attacks a woman. *Journal of Personality and Social Psychology, 34*(5), 990–999.

Snyder, M., & Swann, W. B., Jr. (1978). Behavioral confirmation in social interaction: From social perception to social reality. *Journal of Experimental Social Psychology, 14,* 148–162.

Stacey, W. A., & Shupe, A. (1983). *The family secret: Domestic violence in America.* Boston: Beacon Press.

Stark, E., & McEnvoy, J. (1970, November). Middle class violence. *Psychology Today,* 52–54, 110–111.

Sugarman, D. B., & Cohn, E. S. (1986). Origin and solution attributions of responsibility for wife abuse: Effects of outcome severity, prior history, and sex of subject. *Violence and Victims, 1*(4), 291–303.

Sullivan, C. M. (1991). The provision of advocacy services to women leaving abusive partners: An exploratory study. *Journal of Interpersonal Violence, 6*(1), 41–54.

Summers, G., & Feldman, N. S. (1984). Blaming the victim versus blaming the perpetrator: An attributional analysis of spouse abuse. *Journal of Social and Clinical Psychology, 2*(4), 339–347.

Swann, W. B., & Hill, C. A. (1982). When our identities are mistaken: Reaffirming self-conceptions through social interaction. *Journal of Personality and Social Psychology, 43*(1), 59–66.

U.S. Department of Justice (1994 November). Domestic violence: Violence between intimates. In *Bureau of Justice statistics: Selected findings, Office of Justice programs* (NCJ-149259). Washington, DC: U.S. Government Printing Office.

Vivian, D., & Langhinrichsen-Rohling, J. (1994). Are bi-directionally violent-couples mutually victimized? A gender-sensitive comparison. *Violence and Victims, 9*(2), 107–124.

Walker, L. E. (1979). *The battered woman.* New York: Harper & Row.

Walster, E. (1966). Assignment of responsibility for an accident. *Journal of Personality and Social Psychology, 3*(1), 73–79.

Wilson, M., & Daly, M. (1993). Spousal homicide risk and estrangement. *Violence and Victims, 8*(1), 3–16.

Worden, R. E., & Pollitz, A. A. (1984). Police arrests in domestic disturbances: A further look. *Law and Society Review, 18*(1), 105–119.

PART III

SEXUAL VICTIMIZATION BY STRANGERS

4

Stranger Rape

Patricia Rozee

COMPARISONS OF STRANGER VERSUS ACQUAINTANCE RAPE

There is agreement among professionals, researchers, and activists that the majority of rapes, especially those that are unreported, are committed by dates or acquaintances. However, an estimated 20% to 50% of rapes each year are committed by strangers to the victim (Madigan & Gamble, 1991). Stranger rapes and acquaintance rapes are equally devastating to the victims (Koss, Dinero, Seibel, & Cox, 1988). Stranger rape is generally thought to involve more force, display, and use of weapons, and physical harm but also more resistance by the victim than acquaintance rape (Ullman & Siegel, 1993; Koss, Dinero, Seibel, and Cox, 1988). There is a curvilinear relationship between the amount of violence used by the perpetrator and the degree of acquaintance between victim and perpetrator. Although there is a belief that the most violent rapes are stranger rapes, Koss, Dinero, Seibel & Cox, (1988) found that the most violent are marital or familial rapes, followed by stranger rapes and then acquaintance rape.

Ullman and Siegel (1993) found no difference between stranger and acquaintance rape survivors in terms of ethnicity, age, income, education, or psychological symptoms. However, stranger rape survivors are more likely than acquaintance rape survivors to reach out to a friend, relative, or professional helper and are more likely to report the attack to the police (Siegel, Sorenson, Golding, Burnam, & Stein, 1989; Koss, Dinero, Seibel, & Cox, 1988).

Stranger rape differs in another way. It is stranger rape that women picture when they hear the word "rape." Stranger rapes are what Estrich (1987) refers to as "real rapes," meaning they are given more credibility and are more likely to receive legal remedies than are date or acquaintance rapes. Most people regard stranger rape as the more serious assault (Tetreault & Barnett, 1987), including victims themselves, as evidenced by their greater reporting of stranger rape. Stranger rape victims are also more likely to label their experience as rape (53%) than are acquaintance rape victims (23%) or date rape victims (Muehlenhard, Powch, Phelps, & Giusti, 1992; Koss, Dinero, Seibel, & Cox, 1988). Women attribute more responsibility to victims of acquaintance rape than stranger rape (Tetreault & Barnett, 1987; Bell, Kuriloff, & Lottes, 1994), even when they are the victim. However, in virtually every study, men blame the victim more and identify with her less than do women, regardless of the type of rape.

NORMATIVE RAPE

Rape is a socially constructed and socially legitimized phenomenon (Becker & Kaplan, 1991). Thus, even stranger rapes are often socially condoned or "normative" (Rozee, 1993). Rozee (1993) defines normative rape as genital contact that the female does not choose but is supported by social norms. In her random sample study of world societies, Rozee (1993) gives many examples of normative rape. Such socially approved rapes can be presumed when there is no punishment of the male; only the female is punished—for example, as "used goods"; rape is used as a punishment for errant females; rape is embedded in a cultural ritual such as an initiation ceremony or when the women's refusal would be punished by the community. Rozee concluded that rape is regulated, not prohibited, based on the finding that in most societies, there are examples of both normative and nonnormative (uncondoned) rapes operating concurrently. In nearly every society there are certain women whose rapes are not considered rape (e.g., wives, slaves, enemy women, prostitutes). As Muehlenhard et al. (1992) have pointed out, "As long as a society approves of or is silent about a form of sexual coercion, it is not considered rape" (p. 36).

Stranger rapes may be considered normative when jurors give undue weight to such extralegal factors as the victim's marital status, living arrangements, drinking patterns, and conformity to conservative gender role behaviors (Goldberg-Ambrose, 1992). In order to have suffered "real rape," a woman must be chaste, since prostitutes are considered unrapeable; have proof of penile penetration, since objects, fingers, and so on fall outside the legal definition of rape in most states; must show evidence of resisting, such as cuts and bruises, because without them, consent is implied; and should not have been involved in "provocative behavior," such as walking alone at night, wearing certain types of clothing, or consuming alcohol. Often the first question asked of a rape survivor is, "What were you doing out there by yourself?" or "What were you wearing?" or "Why did you let him in?" Each of these questions assumes that it was the victim's behavior that in some way caused or contributed to the assault. Rape law in the United States today, even when it involves rape by a stranger, is governed by the "law of exceptions." That is, rape is illegal, *except* when the victim dresses, looks, acts, or reacts in unacceptable ways.

THE CULTURAL CONTEXT OF STRANGER RAPE

Goodman, Koss, Fitzgerald, Russo, and Keita (1993) note the underrepresentation of women of color in prevalence studies of violence against women and suggest that street crimes such as rape by strangers are more prevalent among ethnic and poor women. According to Wyatt (1992) black women are more likely than white women to be raped by strangers. The former were significantly more likely to give explanations about their victimization that involved the riskiness of their living situation, such as use of public transportation, walking in unlit neighborhoods, and living in high-crime areas. Yet Koss and Dinero (1989) found lower victimization rates for black than white women when all types of rape were assessed. This may be explained by the finding that black women were less accepting of interpersonal violence, rape myths, adversarial sexual beliefs, and gender role stereotypes than white women (Kalof & Wade, 1995). Black women are significantly less traditional than white women. Holland and Eisenhart (1990) found that black women were more likely to profess principles of self-reliance, self-protection, and avoidance of interpersonal exploitation. They possessed a strong sense of self.

It is important to note that black women experience rape in the context of the historical sexual abuse of females during slavery. This heritage, coupled with the lingering societal belief that black women cannot be raped (Fonow, Richardsen, & Wemmerus, 1992), may result in a level of caution among black women about accepting that now things have changed and society wants to protect them from rape (Wyatt, 1992). According to Wyatt (1992), "If African American women perceive that society does not consider that they can be raped, and that they would not be believed if they disclosed their assault, the chances are minimal that they will disclose or seek help from authorities that represent societal views regarding 'real rape' " (p. 78). African-American women's beliefs about rape are couched in their own cultural experience of being black and female; rape may be seen as something that happens to them because they are black and female (Wyatt, 1992). Thus, there may be a heightened sense of vulnerability due to the historically accurate belief that society's institutions will not protect or defend them. In addition, black women may not find support in their own community, especially if their rape did not meet the perceptions of "real rape." If they did not fight back, there may be an assumption that they have become someone's "sexual property," and the consequent perception of being "ruined" may be part of the victim's belief system (Wyatt, 1992).

Sorenson and Siegel (1992) found that the lifetime prevalence of rape for white women was two and a half times higher than that for Latinas (20% versus 8%). Latina rape victims had more traditional attitudes and were more likely to subscribe to rape myths than either blacks or whites (Lefley, Scott, Llabre, & Hicks, 1993). They were also most likely to attribute victim-blaming views to most women and men in their own ethnic community. Lefley et al. (1993) note that there was remarkable correspondence between the perception that the community was victim blaming and the prevalence of psychological symptomology among victims. They also note that such assessment of community attitudes will also negatively affect help seeking by victims. Possibly because of this, Latinas are less likely to use health services than are white victims (Sorenson & Siegel, 1992).

In a sample consisting mainly of Asian-American students, Mills and Granoff (1992) found that while 28% of the women were rape or attempted rape victims by legal definition, only one-third of these so labeled themselves. Mori, Bernat, Glenn, Selle, and Zarate (1995) suggest that Asian women will thus be less likely to report the rape due to failure to recognize it, fear of negative repercussions, and self-blame. Some women resist the label of rape because the cultural meaning attached to it is intolerable (Holzman, 1994). Mori et al. (1995) report that Asians are more likely to endorse negative attitudes toward rape victims and greater belief in rape myths than whites. More acculturated Asians were more positive toward victims and less likely to believe rape myths (Mori et al., 1995).

As these studies illustrate, the impact of rape must be understood in the context of the survivor's own culture, religious beliefs, and experience as an immigrant or refugee (Holzman, 1994). Race, class, culture, age, and sexual orientation affect every aspect of recovery from the rape experience. According to Holzman (1994), "The dynamics of rape involve the ways in which power and violence are structured by a particular culture, not just the psychodynamics of the individual perpetrators or victims. Rape is both a tool and a consequence of an interlocking system of oppressions based on these factors. Those who have the least power in a society are the most vulnerable to rape" (p. 83).

Among the most vulnerable are immigrant women, especially the undocumented, and refugee women. Both are at risk for rape due to their general unfamiliarity with local customs and resources and language differences. Many of these women dare not risk turning to the usual institutions due to fear of deportation or fear of authority figures in general. In their work with Cambodian refugees, Rozee and Van Boemel (1989) report the absolute fear of authorities and institutions caused by the very real experience of being tormented, tortured, or seeing people killed by those in positions of authority among the Khmer Rouge communist guerrillas. Rape was something one did not speak of, even though most had come through the Thai refugee camps, where rape was "as common as the night." The refugee experience for women coming from war-torn countries is one of forced labor, torture, starvation, beatings, and rape (Van Boemel & Rozee, 1992). One of the so-called spoils of war is the raping of enemy women. Mollica (1986) reports that 95% of his Cambodian clients had experienced some form of sexual assault, yet it took three years of group therapy and trust building before the women would speak of it. In traditional cultures, a woman who loses her virginity, even by rape, is considered soiled; thus, the assault is always a matter of shame (Van Boemel & Rozee, 1992). Holtzman (1994) points out that Southeast Asian women are often sexually exploited and victimized by sexual tourism and by so-called R&R for U.S. military personnel. The female sex slave trade is also flourishing in Southeast Asia (Fund, 1993). Often immigrant and refugee women have not had access to protection and to legal recourse, and the consequent perception of being "ruined" may be part of their belief system (Wyatt, 1992).

There are several groups of women who are often left out of consideration in discussions of rape vulnerability: disabled women, older women, and lesbians. Disabled women are three times more likely to be raped than able-bodied women, and often the perpetrator is their caregiver on whom they are physically dependent (Holzman, 1994). There is very little published information on sexual assaults against disabled women.

Information about the rape of older women is more likely to appear in the public literature than the professional literature (Tyra, 1993). Older women are especially vulnerable to rape, and the outcomes can be profound and debilitating physical and psychological effects that can be permanent (Tyra, 1993). Older women are more likely to be raped by strangers and to experience robbery and physical injury in addition to the rape. The psychological effects stemming from loss of power and control may exacerbate existing issues in this area. Self-defense classes are in high demand among older and disabled women who recognize their special vulnerability and wish to empower themselves for self-protection.

Lesbians may be subjected to "punitive rape," defined as any rape that is used as a discipline or punishment (Rozee, 1993). People who challenge the system of power are often targeted by rapists as a form of punishment for presumed transgressions (Holzman, 1994). Thus, the rape of lesbians (and gay men) is often part of the enactment of a hate crime (Garnets, Herek, & Levy, 1993). Lesbians in particular are vulnerable to rapists, who describe them as "open targets" deserving of punishment because they are not under the protection of a man (Garnets et al., 1993). Lesbians have been sexually harassed and raped for being "out" as a lesbian (Funk, 1993). Lesbians must also confront the impact of victimization on their identity as lesbians. Rape may cause the lesbian victim considerable confusion, especially if there is any involuntary physiological response on her part during the rape. In addition, relationship problems may develop because significant others may be uncomfortable with the fact that she has been with a man, however involuntarily. (This is a common reaction among the male partners of heterosexual women victims as well.) Lesbian victims may also experience the rape as an attempt to undermine the worth of lesbian sexuality, thus contributing to fear or anxiety related to their normal sexual activities.

The psychological outcomes for lesbians are exacerbated by the undermining of their feelings of independence from the actions of men. As Garnets et al. (1993) describe it, "Because many lesbians are not accustomed to feeling dependent on or vulnerable around men, a sexual attack motivated by male rage at their life-style constitutes a major assault on their general sense of safety, independence, and well-being" (p. 584).

RAPE AND POWER

According to Madigan and Gamble (1991), rape is a reenactment of social dominance, no matter who the victim or the perpetrator is. Its motive is the subjugation of another person and demonstrates contempt and objectification of another. It is the acting out of power roles. Feminist theories that incorporate power analyses into explanations of rape can effectively explain both male-on-female rape and same-sex sexual assaults. Male power, domination, and physical force are part of the structure of U.S. society (Liddle, 1989), but male-dominance theories are not sufficient to explain why most men do *not* rape or why there are in female-perpetrated sexual assaults, as rare as these may be. That is because gender is but one of many power and status categories. Power roles can also be defined by economic status, physical size and strength, rank, or social status and be reinforced by personal traits such as aggressiveness, hostility, lack of empathy, and emotional unavailability.

WOMEN'S FEAR OF RAPE

Women fear rape by male strangers, not by females or even by male dates. As Funk (1993) points out, "Even though many men do not rape . . . and many are probably opposed to rape, all men benefit from rape and the constant threat of rape. If we benefit in no other way, we at least don't live with the constant threat of rape. . . . But all women are threatened, controlled, and victimized by the reality of rape and the constant threat that exists—represented by every man" (p. 32). Thus, in the context of this chapter, women's fear of rape takes on special meaning because it is at its root a fear of stranger rape and has as a major consequence the social control of women.

Women's fear of rape results in their use of many self-imposed restrictive behaviors intended primarily to avoid rape (Warr, 1985). Women use more precautionary behaviors than men (Riger & Gordon, 1981), and fear of rape is the best predictor of the use of isolation behaviors, such as not leaving the house (Riger, Gordon, & LeBailly, 1982). Women's fears are most likely to result in avoiding those activities they enjoy most, like visiting friends or going out for evening entertainment, because such behaviors are not "necessary." However, women also avoid night classes and night jobs if possible (Rozee, Wynne, Foster-Ogle, Compuesto, & Hsaio, 1996).

Women fear rape more than any other offense (including murder, assault, and robbery), and they report levels of fear three times higher than men's (Stanko, 1993). Rozee (1995) reports a high fear of rape among both community and college women. On the single item, "I am scared of rape," 46 percent of women marked the highest possible agreement: 6 or 7 on a 7-point scale. On the item, "Rape would be devastating to my life," nearly half of the women marked the highest possible agreement levels (Rozee-Koker, Wynne, & Mizrahi, 1989).

Rozee et al. (1996) proposed a three-factor model to explain women's fear of rape. Their study demonstrates that the fear of the consequences of rape may be the essence of women's fear. Some of the most serious and immediate consequences that women fear are AIDS, injury, death, and mutilation. As well, they fear the psychological and emotional consequences: the fear of seeing the rapist again, nightmares, flashbacks and intrusive thoughts, feelings of powerlessness, negative effects on their sex life, hate and mistrust of men, and permanent life changes, including pregnancy.

The second most powerful predictor of women's fear of rape is the perception of exposure to risk. Higher fear was related to more exposure to sexual intrusions, such as sexual comments, obscene phone calls, being leered or whistled at, being followed or hassled on the street, being grabbed or fondled or rubbed up against, being exposed to flashers or masturbators, sexual harassment, rape situations, attempted and completed rapes, incest, and molestation. Higher fear was also related to receiving more warnings from parents, friends, and intimates about sexual danger. Although actual experience with fearful events is important, it seems that much of the perception about danger is related to respected other people's worries and communications about them.

The third predictor of women's fear of rape delineated by Rozee et al. (1996) was lack of perceived control. Women who lacked a strong internal locus of control over future events were more fearful of rape. There were no differences based on the ethnicity of the women on any of the major variables.

If the communication of danger by others is a major contributor to women's fear of rape, then it can be presumed that the way in which the media portray rape will have an effect on women's assessment of rape exposure. Brinson (1992) found 132 suggestions of rape myths in 26 rape episodes in a survey of prime-time dramas (five per episode). Most of the myths were of the type that reduces or denies the injury in rape and implies that the woman asked for it, wanted it, or lied about it. The news media are not much better, according to Riger and Gordon (1989). A random sample survey of households conducted for the Census Bureau found that there are four attempted rapes for every one completed rape and that the press covers one attempted rape for every thirteen completed rapes that it covers. The press reports give the false impression that there are far more completed than attempted rapes, whereas the reverse is actually true. This is an important distinction because an attempted rape is a situation where a woman fought back and was not raped. If the Census Bureau figures are correct, then women are four times more likely to escape their would-be rapists than they are to be raped. The media reporting gives women the impression that they are 13 times more likely to be raped than to escape a would-be rapist. An attempted rape is not "news." Such sensationalist reporting does a disservice to women by exaggerating women's helplessness, instilling a lack of self-confidence in their ability to defend themselves, and thus increasing fear of rape.

The finding that other people's warnings exacerbate fear of rape coupled with the impression of the pervasiveness of rape given by the media demonstrate that firsthand experience with rape is not needed to instill a fear of

impact of rape (Koss, 1993). Some studies have found that stranger rape seems to be related to greater depression and fear (Ellis, Atkeson, & Calhoun, 1981), while others have found no difference in mental health outcomes among date, stranger, and marital rape survivors (Resick, 1993).

It is important to remember that not all victims are equally traumatized by a rape. There is considerable variability in response, and a number of factors (e.g. social support, community resources) may mediate the impact of rape. Many rape survivors can be expected to suffer problems in sexual function, intimate relationships, fear, and depression for sometimes years later (Koss & Burkhart, 1989). There may also be problems in self-esteem and self-efficacy and lowered affect.

Some women resist the label of rape because the personal or cultural meaning they attach to it is intolerable (Holzman, 1994). These researchers also point out that it is not necessary for a survivor to acknowledge rape to begin the process of recovery.

INTERVENTIONS WITH RAPE SURVIVORS

According to Koss and Burkhart (1989), few victims are willing to accept immediate postrape therapeutic intervention, preferring to put it out of mind and go on. They found that 31% to 48% of victims eventually sought professional psychotherapy, often years after the assault. Wyatt (1992) reports that of those incidents of sexual assault that were not disclosed to anyone until years later, 64% involved African-American women as compared to 36% for white women. Such delays can have negative effects on recovery and result in elevated levels of use of mental health services later on (Koss, 1993). Failure to disclose reduces access to resources and results in a lack of social support for the victim. Koss and Burkhart (1989) suggest that the primary role of clinicians may be in the identification and handling of chronic, posttraumatic responses to an event that is long past. However, they also point out that most of the literature addresses immediate postrape symptoms. (Specific treatment issues have been addressed extensively elsewhere. For an excellent in-depth discussion of clinical and community interventions, see Koss & Harvey, 1991.)

Some of the general goals that therapists and others can work toward with survivors of sexual assault have been outlined by Schwartz (1991):

1. Provide accurate information regarding sexual assault, focusing on societal blame rather than self-blame.
2. Promote healthy relationships and support systems.
3. Encourage positive actions she can take on her own behalf.

4. Help her set goals for herself and follow through on them.
5. Emphasize that you understand the challenges posed by rape and that recovery means increased strength, personal growth, and self-reliance for the majority of women.

Madigan and Gamble (1991) remind us that therapists can revictimize rape victims if they are ignorant and unwilling to accept the woman's reality once she tells it. It is difficult to hear a woman's rape story. Helpers must fight the tendency to distance themselves from victims by using feelings of personal invulnerability ("it can never happen to me because . . ."), searching for psychosexual motives, or viewing the rape as an individual problem, to the exclusion of viewing it as primarily a societal problem. Therapists must address their own feelings of disbelief. The attitudes of rape crisis counselors, emergency room workers, police officers, and other helpers will often influence a victim's opinions about whether it was "real rape" (Estrich, 1987). They must avoid trying to make the rape rational, to explain the unexplainable. One of the main components in most stranger rapes is sheer chance—being in the wrong place at the wrong time (Groth, 1990). It is important for those working with rape survivors to examine their own belief systems about rape, especially victim-blaming rape myths. Many men and some women believe rape myths to some degree. Maintaining a supportive nonstigma view of rape as a crime helps avoid victim blaming.

It is noteworthy that often those values that helpers hold most dear, such as autonomy, individual control, and open and direct communication, can be less than useful when dealing with clients from cultures where such values may be seen as intrusive or insensitive or simply impossible (Holzman, 1994). Holzman points out that the Euro-American values of self-determination, inner directedness, and individual autonomy are quite rate among other world cultures and may, in fact, clash with the values of cultures where deference to authority, especially male authority over women and the authority of elders, is considered most important. Sometimes the ability to make a successful intervention depends on the knowledge of and adherence to cultural values other than one's own. Rozee and Van Boemel (1989) describe the difficulty of two feminists having to come to terms with the values of deference to males in traditional Cambodian culture. They needed to ask the permission of the oldest male family member in order for a female family member to participate in a therapy group for Cambodian refugee women. Without his permission, the intervention would have been impossible. (For an excellent review of cultural considerations and values in therapeutic interventions see Holzman, 1994.)

Since rape survivors are reluctant to contact mental health professionals immediately after rape, it is important to provide information for lay helpers, who may be the persons of first resort. Tyra (1993) suggests the following guidelines for nontherapist helpers of rape survivors:

1. Be concerned and available.
2. Give the woman time to ventilate about the experience.
3. Help put the rape into perspective. She is not to blame.
4. Give information about resources and referrals.
5. Help identify emotionally supportive people in her life.
6. Offer to telephone the next day to see how she is feeling.

Sometimes there is no better help than simply a good listener with a calm and caring manner.

HEALTH EFFECTS OF SEXUAL ASSAULT

It is especially important for health workers to screen for victimization and identify victims during routine examinations. Sexual assault can affect health status by lowering normal resistance, exacerbating preexisting conditions and lowering tolerance (Koss & Harvey, 1991). In a random sample of 2,291 women primary care patients, Koss, Woodruff, and Koss (1991) found that 57% were victims of a crime. Rape victims report more negative health behaviors and more symptoms across body systems, perceive their health less favorably, and utilize physician services at twice the rate of nonvictimized women (Koss et al., 1991). Physician visits by victimized women increased 15% to 24% during the first year after the crime compared to only 2% among nonvictims. In fact Koss et al. (1991) reported that criminal victimization was a better predictor of physician visits than age or severity of health factors. Victims also disproportionately report certain physical symptoms, such as headaches, pelvic pain, and premenstrual symptoms (Koss & Heslet, 1992). Drug problems and high-risk sexual behaviors may also be seen.

FACTORS AFFECTING RECOVERY

Koss and Mukai (1993) point to a number of factors that have not been adequately studied for their effects on the recovery process, including the effect of participating in the criminal justice system, the effectiveness of the type of counseling provided, social support, coping methods by the victim, and victim attributions.

One area that has received considerable study is the effect of active resistance by the intended victim on her physical and psychological outcomes. Bart and O'Brien (1985) published the first large-scale study on successful survival strategies for women facing rape. Their work was significant in that it challenged, with data, the common notion that a woman should not fight a rapist because she would be hurt worse. Many police officers also share the common assumption that those who fight back get hurt more, but recent studies dispute this view (Brown, 1995; Bart & O'Brien, 1985; Ullman & Knight, 1991, 1993, 1995; Ullman & Siegel, 1993, 1991; Koss & Mukai, 1993; Zoucha-Jensen & Coyne, 1993; Kleck & Sayles, 1990).

Current research on self-defense concludes *unequivocally* that:

1. Women who fight back and fight back immediately are less likely to be raped than women who do not.
2. Women who fight back are no more likely to be injured than women who do not fight back. In fact, it has been shown that victim resistance often occurred *in response to* physical attack.
3. Pleading, begging, and reasoning are ineffective in preventing rape or physical injury.
4. Women who fight back experience less postassault symptomology due to avoidance of being raped.
5. Women who fought back had faster psychological recoveries whether or not they were raped.
6. Fighting back strengthens the physical evidence should the survivor decide to prosecute for rape or attempted rape.

Ullman and Knight (1995) also dispute the idea that physical resistance provokes increased violence in particular types of rapists, such as sadists (see Groth, 1990). Based on a sample of incarcerated stranger rapists, their study showed that overall, the efficacy of women's resistance strategies for avoiding sexual abuse and physical injury did not vary by rapist type. Women who fought in response to sadistic rapists were no more likely to experience physical injury than women who did not. Ullman and Knight (1995) admonish people from issuing warnings against the supposed dangers of physical resistance to sadistic rapists in the absence of any empirical data to support such claims. They also point out the futility of advising women to assess the "type" of rapist before determining whether to resist.

Victim resistance raises the cost of rape for the perpetrator (Kleck & Sayles, 1990). It makes rape completion more difficult, increases the effort required by the rapist, and prolongs the attack, thereby increasing the risk of discovery and capture. It also increases the probability of injury to the rapist, possibly leaving marks that will contribute to late discovery.

Given the prevalence of rape, it would seem that warning women not to fight back because they might get hurt is based in myth, not empirical evidence. Cooperation with the assailant does not guarantee safety and resistance does not increase risk (Koss & Mukai, 1993). Such myths serve only to ensure more victims for would-be rapists, and they do an immense disservice to women by absurdly encouraging them to "bargain" with criminals. Only 3% of rapes involve some additional injury that is serious; usually the rape itself is the most serious injury suffered (Kleck & Sayles, 1990). Thus, the myth that fighting back will get you hurt mistakes from where the real hurt comes: trying to recover from rape.

REFERENCES

Alexander, B. H., Franklin, G. G., & Wolf, M. E. (1994). The sexual assault of women at work in Washington State, 1980 to 1989. *American Journal of Public Health, 84*(4), 640–642.

Bart, P. B., & O'Brien, P. (1985). *Stopping rape: Successful survival strategies.* New York: Pergamon Press.

Becker, J. V., & Kaplan, M. S. (1991). Rape victims: Issues, theories, and treatment. *Annual Review of Sex Research, 2,* 267–292.

Bell, S. T., Kuriloff, P. J., & Lottes, I. (1994). Understanding attributions of blame in stranger rape and date rape situations: An examination of gender, race, identification, and students' social perceptions of rape victims. *Journal of Applied Social Psychology, 24,* 1719–1734.

Biden, J. R. (1993). Violence against women: The congressional response. *American Psychologist, 48*(10), 1059–1061.

Brickman, P., Rabinowitz, V. C., Karuza, J., Coates, D., Cohn, E., & Kidder, L. (1982). Models of helping and coping. *American Psychologist, 37,* 368–374.

Brinson, S. L. (1992). The use and opposition of rape myths in prime-time television dramas. *Sex Roles, 27*(7/8), 359–375.

Brown, M. (1995, July 23). Should you fight? No easy answers. *Sacramento Bee,* p. A10.

Bureau of Justice Statistics. (1992). *Criminal victimization in the United States: 1991.* Washington, DC: U.S. Department of Justice.

Burgess, A., & Holmstrom, L. (1974). Rape trauma syndrome. *American Journal of Psychiatry, 131,* 981–986.

Burgess, A., & Holmstrom, L. (1979). *Rape crisis and recovery.* Bowie, MD: R. J. Brady Co.

The Psychology of Sexual Victimization

Donat, P.L.N., & D'Emilio, J. D. (1992). A feminist redefinition of rape and sexual assault: Historical foundations and change. *Journal of Social Issues*, *48*(1), 9–22.

Ellis, E. M., Atkeson, B. M., & Calhoun, K. S. (1981). An assessment of long-term reactions. *Journal of Abnormal Psychology*, *90*, 263–266.

Estrich, S. (1987). *Real rape: How the legal system victimizes women who say no.* Cambridge, MA: Harvard University Press.

Fonow, M. M., Richardson, L., & Wemmerus, V. A. (1992). Feminist rape education: Does it work? *Gender and Society*, *6*(1), 108–121.

Funk, R. E. (1993). *Stopping rape: A challenge for men.* Philadelphia: New Society Publishers.

Garnets, L., Herek, G. M., & Levy, B. (1993). Violence and victimization of lesbians and gay men: Mental health consequences. In L. Garnets & D. Kimmel (Eds.), *Psychological perspectives on lesbian and gay male experiences.* New York: Columbia University Press.

Gidycz, C. A., & Koss, M. P. (1990). A comparison of group and individual sexual assault victims. *Psychology of Women Quarterly*, *14*, 325–342.

Goldberg-Ambrose, C. (1992). Unfinished business in rape law reform. *Journal of Social Issues*, *48*, 173–186.

Golding, J. M. (1996). Sexual assault history and women's reproductive and sexual health. *Psychology of Women Quarterly*, *20*(1), 101–121.

Goodman, L. A., Koss, M. P., Fitzgerald, L. F., Russo, N. F., & Keita, G. P. (1993). Male violence against women: Current research and future directions. *American Psychologist*, *48*(10), 1054–1058.

Groth, A. N. (1990). *Men who rape: The psychology of the offender.* New York: Plenum Press.

Gurin, P., Gurin, G., Lao, R. C., & Beattie, M. (1966). Internal, external control in the motivational dynamics of Negro youth. *Journal of Social Issues*, *25*(3), 29–51.

Holland, D. C., & Eisenhart, M. A. (1990). *Educated in romance: Women, achievement, and college culture.* Chicago: University of Chicago Press.

Holzman, C. G. (1994). Multicultural perspectives on counseling survivors of rape. *Journal of Social Distress and the Homeless*, *3*(1), 81–97.

Horney, J., & Spohn, C. (1991). Rape law reform and instrumental change in six urban jurisdictions. *Law and Society Review*, *25*(1), 117–153.

Kalof, L., & Wade, B. H. (1995). Secual attitudes and experiences with sexual coercion: Exploring the influence of race and gender. *Journal of Black Psychology*, *21*(3), 224–238.

Kleck, G., & Sayles, S. (1990). Rape and resistance. *Social Problems*, *37*(2), 149–162.

Koss, M. P. (1992). The underdetection of rape: Methodological choices influence incidence estimates. *Journal of Social Issues*, *48*(1), 61–75.

Koss, M. P. (1993). Scope, impact, interventions, and public policy responses. *American Psychologist, 48*(10), 1062–1069.

Koss, M., & Burkhart, B. (1989). A conceptual analysis of rape victimization. *Psychology of Women Quarterly, 13,* 27–40.

Koss, M. P., & Dinero, T. E. (1989). Discriminant analysis of risk factors for sexual victimization among a national sample of college women. *Journal of Consulting and Clinical Psychology, 57,* 242–250.

Koss, M. P., Dinero, T. E., Seibel, C. A., & Cox, S. L. (1988). Stranger and acquaintance rape: Are there differences in the victim's experience? *Psychology of Women Quarterly, 12,* 1–24.

Koss, M. P., & Harvey, M. R. (1991). *The rape victim: Clinical and community interventions.* Newbury Park, CA: Sage.

Koss, M. P., & Heslet, L. (1992). Somatic consequences of violence against women. *Archives of Family Medicine, 1,* 53–59.

Koss, M. P., Koss, P., & Woodruff, W. J. (1991). Deleterious effects of criminal victimization on women's health and medical utilization. *Archives of Internal Medicine, 151,* 342–357.

Koss, M. P., & Mukai, T. (1993). Recovering ourselves: Frequency, effects, and resolution of rape. In F. L. Denmark & M. A. Paludi (Eds.), *Psychology of women: A handbook of issues and theories.* Westport, CT: Greenwood Press.

Koss, M. P., Woodruff, W. J., & Koss, P. (1991). Criminal victimization among primary care medical patients: Prevalence, incidence, and physician usage. *Behavioral Sciences and the Law, 9,* 85–96.

Lebowitz, L., & Roth, S. (1994). "I felt like a slut": The cultural context and women's response to being raped. *Journal of Traumatic Stress, 7*(3), 363–390.

Lefley, H. P., Scott, C. S., Llabre, M., & Hicks, D. (1993). Cultural beliefs about rape and victims' response in three ethnic groups. *American Journal of Orthopsychiatry, 63*(4), 623–632.

Liddle, A. M. (1989). Feminist contributions to an understanding of violence against women—three steps forward, two steps back. *Canadian Review of Society and Anthropology, 26*(5), 759–775.

Madigan, L., & Gamble, N. C. (1991). *The second rape.* New York: Lexington Books.

Mantese, G., Mantese, V., Mantese, T., Mantese, J., Mantese, M., & Essique, C. (1991). Medical and legal aspects of rape and resistance. *Journal of Legal Medicine, 12,* 59–84.

Martin, B. A. (1989). Gender differences in salary expectations when current salary information is provided. *Psychology of Women Quarterly, 13*(1), 87–96.

Meyer, C. B., & Taylor, S. E. (1986). Adjustment to rape. *Journal of Personality and Social Psychology, 50,* 1226–1234.

Miller, D. T., & Porter, C. A. (1983). Self-blame in victims of violence. *Journal of Social Issues, 39*(2), 139–152.

Mills, C. S., & Granoff, B. J. (1992). Date and acquaintance rape among a sample of college students. *Social Work, 37*, 504–509.

Mollica, R. (1986, August). *Cambodian refugee women at risk.* Paper presented at the American Psychological Association Annual Meeting, Washington, DC.

Mori, L., Bernat, J. A., Glenn, P. A., Selle, L. L., & Zarate, M. G. (1995). Attitudes towards rape: Gender and ethnic differences across Asian and Caucasian college students. *Sex Roles, 32*(7/8), 457–467.

Muehlenhard, C. L., Powch, I. G., Phelps, J. L., & Giusti, L. M. (1992). Definitions of rape: Scientific and political implications. *Journal of Social Issues, 48*(1), 23–44.

Resick, P. A. (1993). The psychological impact of rape. *Journal of Interpersonal Violence, 8*(2), 223–255.

Riger, S., & Gordon, M. (1981). The fear of rape: A study in social control. *Journal of Social Issues, 37*(4), 71–94.

Riger, S., & Gordon, M. (1989). *The female fear.* New York: Free Press.

Riger, S., Gordon, M., & LeBailly, R. (1982). Coping with urban crime: Women's use of precautionary behaviors. *American Journal of Community Psychology, 10*, 369–386.

Rotter, J. B. (1966). Internal-external control of reinforcement. *Psychological Monograph, 80* (1, Whole No. 609).

Rozee, P. (1993). Forbidden or forgiven: Rape in cross-cultural perspective. *Psychology of Women Quarterly, 17*, 499–514.

Rozee, P. D., & Van Boemel, G. (1989). The psychological effects of war trauma on older Cambodian refugee women. *Women and Therapy, 8*(4), 23–50.

Rozee, P. D., & Wynne, C. (1994, August). *The importance of external locus of control among rape survivors.* Paper presented at the annual meeting of the American Psychological Association, Kona, HI.

Rozee, P. D., Wynne, C., Foster-Ogle, D., Compuesto, M., & Hsiao, M. (1996, March). *Fear of rape among campus women.* Paper presented at the annual meeting of the Association of Women in Psychology, Portland, OR.

Rozee-Koker, P., & Polk, G. A. (1986). The social psychology of group rape. *Sexual Coercion and Assault: Issues and Perspectives, 1*(2), 57–65.

Rozee-Koker, P., Wynne, C., & Mizrahi, K. (1989). *Workplace safety and fear of rape among professional women.* Paper presented at the annual meeting of the Western Psychological Association, Reno, NV.

Schwartz, I. L. (1991). Sexual violence against women: Prevalence, consequences, societal factors, and prevention. *American Journal of Preventative Medicine, 7*(6), 363–373.

Siegel, J. M., Sorenson, S. B., Golding, J. M., Burnam, M. A., & Stein, J. A. (1989). Resistance to sexual assault: Who resists and what happens? *American Journal of Public Health, 79*, 27–31.

Sorenson, S. B., & Siegel, J. M. (1992). Gender, ethnicity, and sexual assault: Findings from the Los Angeles epidemiological catchment area study. *Journal of Social Issues*, *48*(1), 93–104.

Stanko, E. (1993). Ordinary fear: Women, violence, and personal safety. In P. Bart & E. Moran (Eds.), *Violence against women: The bloody footprints* (pp. 155–165). Newbury Park, CA: Sage.

Tetreault, P. A., & Barnett, M. A. (1987). Reactions to stranger and acquaintance rape. *Psychology of Women Quarterly*, *11*, 353–358.

Tyra, P. A. (1993, May). Older women: Victims of rape. *Journal of Gerontological Nursing*, 7–12.

Ullman, S. E., & Knight, R. A. (1991). A multivariate model for predicting rape and physical injury outcomes during sexual assaults. *Journal of Consulting and Clinical Psychology*, *59*(5), 724–731.

Ullman, S. E., & Knight, R. A. (1993). The efficacy of women's resistance strategies in rape situations. *Psychology of Women Quarterly*, *17*, 23–38.

Ullman, S. E., & Knight, R. A. (1995). Women's resistance strategies to different rapist types. *Criminal Justice and Behavior*, *22*(3), 263–283.

Ullman, S. E., & Siegel, J. M. (1993). Victim-offender relationship and sexual assault. *Violence and Victims*, *8*(2), 121–134.

U.S. Senate Committee on the Judiciary. (1991). Violence against women: The increase of rape in America in 1990. *Response*, *14*(2), 20–23.

Van Boemel, G., & Rozee, P. D. (1992). Treatment efficacy for psychosomatic blindness among Cambodian refugee women. *Women and Therapy: A Feminist Quarterly*, *13*, 239–266.

Warr, M. (1985). Fear of rape among urban women. *Social Problems*, *32*(3), 238–250.

Wortman, C. B. (1976). Causal attributions and personal control. In J. H. Harvey et al. (Eds.), *New directions in attributing research*. Hillsdale, NJ: Erlbaum.

Wortman, C. B., Abbey, A., Holland, A. E., Silver, R. L., & Janoff-Bulman. (1980). Transitions from the laboratory to the field: Problems and progress. *Applied Social Psychology Annual*, *1*, 197–233.

Wyatt, G. E. (1992). The sociocultural context of African American and white American women's rape. *Journal of Social Issues*, *48*(1), 77–91.

Wyatt, G. E., Notgrass, C. M., & Newcomb, M. (1990). Internal and external mediators of women's rape experiences. *Psychology of Women Quarterly*, *14*(2), 153–176.

Zoucha-Jensen, J. M., & Coyne, A. (1993). The effects of resistance strategies on rape. *American Journal of Public Health*, *83*(11), 1633–1634.

SEXUAL VICTIMIZATION IN EDUCATIONAL AND WORK SETTINGS

PART IV

SEXUAL VICTIMIZATION IN
EDUCATIONAL AND WORK
SETTINGS

5

Sexual Harassment in Education and the Workplace: A View from the Field of Psychology

Michele A. Paludi, Darlene C. DeFour, Kojo Attah, and Jennifer Batts

In Chapter 6, Levy discusses issues in understanding sexual harassment from the legal perspective, including the legal definitions of quid pro quo and hostile environment sexual harassment and the way complaints are handled through the courts. Certainly it is important and necessary to know what the law says about sexual harassment, but it is equally necessary to have an understanding of the psychology of sexual harassment: what it is, why and how it affects students and employees, and how to handle situations at the school or workplace long before they reach the courts (Levy & Paludi, 1997; Petrocelli & Repa, 1995).

In this chapter we provide an overview of the psychology of sexual harassment, including empirical definitions, prevalence rates, attitudes about and attributions of sexual harassment, and explanatory models of why this form of victimization occurs in educational institutions as well as in workplaces. We also offer a critique of the psychological research published thus far and make suggestions for dealing with sexual harassment in the educational and workplace settings.

LEGAL AND EMPIRICAL DEFINITIONS OF SEXUAL HARASSMENT

Legal Definition

Sexual harassment is clearly prohibited within the school and college and university system as a form of sexual discrimination, under Title IX of the 1972 Education Amendments and within the workplace under Title VII of the 1964 Civil Rights Act. The Equal Employment Opportunity Commission states in its guidelines on sex discrimination:

Unwelcome sexual advances, requests for sexual favors, and other verbal or physical conduct of a sexual nature constitute sexual harassment when (1) submission to such conduct is made either explictly or implicitly a term or condition of an individual's employment, (2) submission to or rejection of such conduct by an individual is used as the basis for employment decisions affecting such individual, or (3) such conduct has the purpose or effect of substantially interfering with an individual's work performance or creating an intimidating, hostile, or offensive working environment.

This definition has been extended to academic environments as well.

Courts have called the first two conditions *quid pro quo* sexual harassment and the third condition *hostile environment* sexual harassment. Quid pro quo sexual harassment is a demand or request for sexual activity in exchange for a job-related or academic-related benefit (e.g., raises, grades, promotions, remaining in school, keeping one's job). The major elements of it for workplaces and school systems are as follows:

- The sexual advances are unwanted.
- The harassment is sexual.
- The submission is explicitly or implicitly a term or condition of employment or school status or is used as a basis for making decisions about the individual's school status or employee's work status.

Hostile environment sexual harassment refers to behaviors in the classroom or in the workplace that reasonably interfere with an individual's ability to learn or work.

Title IX of the Education Amendments prohibits discrimination on the basis of sex and covers all educational institutions that receive federal financial assistance and all federally funded educational programs in noneducational institutions. It also covers institutions whose students receive federal financial aid. Virtually all public and private institutions of higher education are covered, as well as all public elementary and secondary schools. Private elementary and secondary schools are covered ony if they receive federal funds. This federal statute is enforced by the Office of Civil Rights (OCR) at the U.S. Department of Education. According to OCR, sexual harassment is defined as "verbal or physical conduct of a sexual nature, imposed on the basis of sex, by an employee or an agent of [an institution] that denies, limits, provides different, or conditions the provision of aid, benefits, services, or treatment protected under Title IX."

This definition clearly covers sexual harassment or harassment of students by faculty and staff. OCR also interprets Title IX to cover peer sexual harassment of students (i.e., student-to-student sexual harassment).

Behavioral Definition

Sexual harassment takes many forms, from sexist remarks and covert physical contact (patting, brushing against another's body) to blatant propositions and sexual assaults. Researchers have developed five categories that correlate with legal definitions of sexual harassment and encompass the range of sexual harassment (Fitzgerald, 1996):

1. *Gender harassment*—generalized sexist remarks and behavior not designed to elicit sexual cooperation but rather to convey insulting, degrading, or sexist attitudes.
2. *Seductive behavior*—inappropriate and offensive sexual advances.
3. *Sexual bribery*—the solicitation of sexual activity or other sex-linked behavior by promise of reward (e.g., high grade, letter of recommendation, salary increase).
4. *Sexual coercion*—the coercion of sexual activity by threat of punishment (e.g., failure to give the grade earned, failure to grant a promotion, low performance appraisal).
5. *Sexual imposition*—including gross sexual imposition, assault, and rape.

Thus, behavioral examples of verbal sexual harassment include sexual innuendos, comments, and remarks; implied or overt threats related to students' grades; and sexual propositions or other pressures for sex. Behavioral examples of nonverbal sexual harassment include patting, pinching, brushing up against another's body, leering, ogling, obscene gestures, and the use of pornographic teaching materials in class discussions.

The most useful behavioral definition of sexual harassment has been offered by Fitzgerald and Omerod (1993): "Sexual harassment consists of the sexualization of an instrumental relationship through the introduction or imposition of sexist or sexual remarks, requests, or requirements, in the context of a formal power differential. Harassment can also occur where no such formal differential exists, if the behavior is unwanted by or offensive to the [individual]" (p. 556).

There are four main elements in this definition:

1. The behavior is unwanted and unwelcome.
2. The behavior is sexual or related to the sex of the individual.
3. The behavior typically occurs in the context of a relationship where one person has more formal power than the other.
4. The impact of the behavior, not the intent, is the most crucial to understanding whether sexual harassment has occurred.

These elements have been addressed specifically for students by Zalk, Paludi, and Dederich (1991):

The bottom line in the relationship is POWER. The faculty member has it and the student does not. As intertwined as the faculty-student roles may be, and as much as one must exist for the other to exist, they are not equal collaborators. The student does not negotiate indeed, has nothing to negotiate with. . . .

All the power lies with the faculty member—some of it real, concrete, and some of it is imagined or elusive. The bases of the faculty member's almost absolute power are varied and range from the entirely rational into broad areas of fantasy. Professors give grades, write recommendations for graduate schools, awards and the like, and can predispose colleagues' attitudes towards students. (pp. 101–102)

Definitional Problems

Many individuals are confused over the definition of sexual harassment, especially hostile environment sexual harassment. One major source for this confusion is that girls and women typically have different experiences within society than do boys and men (Doyle & Paludi, 1995). For example, Fitzgerald, Weitzman, Gold, and Ormerod (1988) found that male faculty members typically do not label their behavior as sexual harassment despite the fact that they report they frequently engage in behaviors that meet the legal definition of sexual harassment. Male faculty members denied the inherent power differential between faculty and students, as well as the psychological power conferred by this differential. Kenig and Ryan (1986) reported that faculty men were less likely than faculty women to define sexual harassment as including jokes, teasing remarks of a sexual nature, and unwanted suggestive looks or gestures. In addition, women faculty were more likely than men to disapprove of romantic relationships between faculty and students.

Furthermore, students and teachers have substantially different definitions of sexual harassment. Fitzgerald et al. (1988) reported that male faculty members who participated in their study typically denied that there is an inherent power differential between students and faculty. Students, however, recognize this power differential. Truax (cited by Fitzgerald, 1990) claimed, "There is often little disagreement with what has happened between student and professor, but rather, with what the conduct means. Professors will try to justify their behavior on the grounds that they are just friendly and trying to make a student feel welcome, or they thought that the student would be flattered by the attention." However, the interpretation given to the professor's behavior by women students is not flattery or friendliness. As high school students in Minnesota outlined, there is a distinction between flattery or flirtation and sexual harassment (Minnesota Department of Education):

Flirting	**Sexual Harassment**
Feels good	Feels bad
Makes me feel attractive	Is degrading
Is a compliment	Makes me feel cheap
Is two-way	Is one-way
Is positive	Makes me feel helpless
I liked it	I felt out of control

Some courts have determined that the standard for hostile environment sexual harassment claims should be whether a "reasonable woman" would be offended by the conduct, not a "reasonable man" or "reasonable person." Adopting this perspective requires an analysis of the differing perspectives females and males often have and a recognition that behavior that many boys and men find unobjectionable may offend girls and women. It is the power differential or the individual's reaction to the behavior or both, that are the critical variables.

Consensual Relationships

Margaret Mead (1978) once argued that a new taboo is needed that demands that teachers and faculty make new norms, not rely on masculine-biased definitions of success, career development, and sexuality. One important change needs to be in the mentor-protégé relationship, where women are protégés and men are mentors (Haring-Hidore & Paludi, 1991). This common arrangement by which men are in positions of power within mentoring relationships (as mentors) and women are in more vulnerable positions (as protégés) suggests the possibility of sexuality and sex as significant and complex factors within such relationships. Mentors are seen as essential because they generate power. The introduction of sexuality and sex into mentoring relationships can have negative implications for achievement for women protégés. Women who are suspected of having "slept their way to the top" are castigated by others, sometimes unfairly when the accusation is false. Women who have sex with their mentors may be unjustly deprived of their achievements if the achievements did not depend on an unfair advantage gained by a sexual mentoring relationship. Whether it is fair or not, achievements made in sexual mentoring relationships may never boost protégés' careers—and may in fact detract from their careers because of the stigma attached by others (Haring-Hidore & Paludi, 1991).

Neither Title IX nor Title VII prohibits consensual sexual relationships; however, a number of institutions are developing policies on this matter. While consensual relationships may not always be unethical, they always cause problems. This happens, according to Sandler and Paludi (1993), for the following reasons:

The situation involves one person exerting power over another.

The seduction of a much younger individual is involved.

Conflict of interest issues arise, e.g., How can a teacher fairly grade a student with whom they are having a sexual relationship?

The potential for exploitation and abuse is high.

The potential for retaliatory harassment is high when the sexual relationship ceases.

Other individuals may be affected and claim favoritism.

Stites (1996) noted how including consensual relationships as part of the definition of academic sexual harassment has been met with considerable resistance. There are a few campuses (e.g., University of Iowa, Harvard University, Yale University, Temple University) that prohibit sexual relationships between faculty and students over whom the professor has some authority (i.e., advising, supervising, grading, teaching). A few other campuses have "discouragement policies," in which "consensual relations" are not strictly prohibited but are discouraged (e.g., University of Minnesota, University of Connecticut, New York University Law School, Massachusetts Institute of Technology).

The University of Virginia called for a total ban on all sexual relationships between faculty and student regardless of the professor's role regarding the student. However, the faculty senate approved a prohibition-only policy rather than the total-ban policy. Thus, this campus prohibits sexual relations between faculty and student when the faculty has some organizational power over the student. The case can be made, however, that a faculty member does not have to be the student's professor in order for that faculty member to be powerful and potentially abuse that power over the student.

All faculty members have an ethical and professional responsibility to provide a learning environment that is respectful of students and fosters the academic performance and intellectual development of students.

The fact that a student is defined as an adult by chronological age can in no way remove the obligation of a teacher or administrator to refrain from engaging in sexual harassment, and the student's adulthood is in no way a proxy for consenting to a relationship. The stories girls and women tell about their "consensual relationships" do not parallel romances or typical stories about sexual affairs; they instead resemble stories depicting patterns of manipulation and victimization, responses identical to those of girls and women who are sexually harassed in a nonconsensual relationship (Zalk et al. 1991).

INCIDENCE OF SEXUAL HARASSMENT

Elementary and Secondary School Students

Research has suggested that most students do not label their experiences as sexual behavior despite the fact the behavior they have experienced meets the legal definition of either quid pro quo or hostile environment harassment (Fitzgerald, 1996; Paludi & Barickman, 1991). A major interpretation of this research finding concerns individuals' lack of understanding of the definition of sexual harassment. Most students still report that sexual harassment does not occur unless there has been some physical assault. Yet most sexual harassment experienced by students does not include assault or perhaps even touching. This finding has suggested to researchers that in order to collect incidence data on sexual harassment, one cannot simply ask "Have you ever been sexually harassed?" Providing respondents with behavioral examples of sexual harassment facilitates more reliable responses (Paludi & Barickman, 1991).

The American Association of University Women (1993) used this methodological approach when collecting incidence data of adolescents' experiences with sexual harassment. In this study, 1,632 students in grades 8 through 11 from 79 schools across the United States were asked: "During your whole school life, how often, if at all, has anyone (this includes students, teachers, other school employees, or anyone else) done the following things to you *when you did not want them to?*"

Made sexual comments, jokes, gestures, or looks.

Showed, gave, or left you sexual pictures, photographs, illustrations, messages, or notes.

Wrote sexual messages/graffiti about you on bathroom walls, in locker rooms, etc.

Spread sexual rumors about you.

Said you were gay or lesbian.

Spied on you as you dressed or showered at school.

Flashed or "mooned" you.

Touched, grabbed, or pinched you in a sexual way.

Pulled at your clothing in a sexual way.

Intentionally brushed against you in a sexual way.

Pulled your clothing off or down.

Blocked your way or cornered you in a sexual way.

Forced you to kiss him/her.

Forced you to do something sexual, other than kissing.

Results suggested that four out of five students (81%) reported that they experienced some form of sexual harassment in school. With respect to sex comparisons, 85% of girls and 76% of boys surveyed reported they had experienced unwelcomed sexual behavior that interferes with their ability to concentrate at school and with their personal lives. The AAUW study also analyzed for race comparisons. African-American boys (81%) were more likely to have experienced sexual harassment than white boys (75%) and Latinos (69%). For girls, 87% of whites reported having experienced behaviors that constitute sexual harassment, compared with 84% of African-American girls and 82% of Latinas.

The AAUW study also suggested that adolescents' experiences with sexual harassment are most likely to occur between sixth to ninth grade. The behaviors reported by students, in rank order from most experienced to least experienced, are as follows:

Sexual comments, jokes, gestures, or looks

Touched, grabbed, or pinched in a sexual way

Intentionally brushed against in a sexual way

Flashed or "mooned"

Had spread sexual rumors about them

Had clothing pulled at in a sexual way

Shown, given, or left sexual pictures, photographs, illustrations, messages, or notes

Had their way blocked or cornered in a sexual way

Had sexual messages/graffiti written about them on bathroom walls, in locker rooms, etc.

Forced to kiss someone

Called gay or lesbian

Had clothing pulled off or down

Forced to do something sexual, other than kissing

Spied on as they dressed or showered at school

Students reported that they experience these behaviors while in the classroom or in the hallways as they are going to class. And the majority of harassment in schools is student to student. However, 25% of harassed girls and 10% of boys reported they were harassed by teachers or other school employees.

Bogart, Simmons, Stein, and Tomaszewski (1992, p. 197) reviewed the sexual harassment complaints brought by students against teachers to the Massachusetts Department of Education. Among the complaints they reported were the following:

A science teacher measured the craniums of the boys in the class and the chests of the girls. The lesson in skeletal frame measurements were conducted one by one, at the front of the class, by the teacher. The print shop teacher, who was in the habit of putting his arms around the shoulders of the young women, insisted, when one young woman asked to be excused to go to the nurse to fix her broken pants' zipper, that she first show him her broken zipper. She was forced to lift her shirt to reveal her broken pants' zipper.

Girls in nontraditional high school programs have reported the following experiences (Stein, 1986, cited by Bogart et al., 1992):

One female in diesel shop refused to go to lunch during her last two years of shop because she was the only young woman in the lunchroom at that time. When she went to the cafeteria, she was pinched and slapped on the way in, and had to endure explicit propositions made to her while she ate lunch. A particular shop's predominantly male population designated one shop day as "National Sexual Harassment Day," in honor of their only female student. They gave her non-stop harassment throughout the day, and found it to be so successful (the female student was forced to be dismissed during the day), that they later held a "National Sexual Harassment Week." (p. 208)

These accounts provide a better picture than do simply percentages of the types of behaviors children and adolescents are experiencing at school.

College and University Students

With respect to the incidence of sexual harassment of college and university students, Dziech and Weiner (1984) reported that 30% of undergraduate women suffer sexual harassment from at least one of their instructors during their four years of college. When definitions of sexual harassment include sexist remarks and other forms of "gender harassment," the incidence rate in undergraduate populations nears 70% (Paludi, 1996).

Bailey and Richards (1985) reported that of 246 women graduate students in their sample, 13% indicated they had been sexually harassed, 21% had not enrolled in a course to avoid such behavior, and 16% indicated they had been directly assaulted. Bond (1988) reported that 75% of the 229 women who responded to her survey experienced jokes with sexual themes during their graduate training, 69% were subjected to sexist comments demeaning to women, and 58% of the women reported experiencing sexist remarks about their clothing, body, or sexual activities.

Fitzgerald et al. (1988) investigated approximately 2,000 women at two major state universities. Half of the women respondents reported experiencing some form of sexually harassing behavior. The majority of these women reported experiencing sexist comments by faculty; the next largest category of sexual harassing behavior was seductive behavior, including being invited for drinks and a backrub by faculty members, being brushed up against by their professors, and having their professors show up uninvited to their hotel rooms during out-of-town academic conferences or conventions.

Research by Paludi, DeFour, and Roberts (1994) suggests that the incidence of academic sexual harassment of ethnic minority women is even greater than that reported with white women. Dziech and Weiner (1984) and DeFour (1996) suggested that ethnic minority women are more vulnerable to receiving sexual attention from professors. Ethnic minority women are subject to stereotypes about sex, viewed as mysterious, and may be less sure of themselves in their careers (DeFour, 1996). Thus, although all students are vulnerable to some degree, male teachers and faculty tend to select those who are most vulnerable and needy. For certain student groups, the incidence of sexual harassment appears to be higher than others (Barickman, Paludi, & Rabinowitz, 1992). For example:

Girls and women of color, especially those with "token" status

Graduate students, whose future careers are often determined by their association with a particular faculty member

Students in small colleges or small academic departments, where the number of faculty available to students is quite small

Girls and women students in male-populated fields, e.g., engineering

Students who are economically disadvantaged and work part-time or full-time while attending classes

Lesbian women, who may be harassed as part of homophobia

Physically or emotionally disabled students

Women students who work in dormitories as resident assistants

Girls and women who have been sexually abused

Inexperienced, unassertive, socially isolated girls and women, who may appear more vulnerable and appealing to those who would intimidate or entice them into an exploitive relationship

Schools most likely to have a high incidence of sexual harassment are ones, according to Sandler and Paludi (1993), that:

Have no policy prohibiting sexual harassment

Do not disseminate the policy or report information regarding sexual harassment

Have no training programs for teachers, staff, and students

Do not intervene officially when sexual harassment occurs

Do not support sexual harassment victims

Do not quickly remove sexual graffiti

Do not sanction individuals who engage in sexual harassment

Do not inform the school community about the sanctions for offenders

Have been previously all-male or have a majority of male students

Employees

Sexual harassment in the workplace is widespread (Levy & Paludi, 1997), with women more likely to experience sexual harassment than men. The U.S. Merit Systems Protection Board (1981) addressed sexual harassment in the federal workplace and found that 42% of all women employees reported being sexually harassed. Merit Systems reported that many incidents occurred repeatedly, were of long duration, and had a sizable practical impact, costing the government an estimated minimum of $189 million over the two-year period covered by the research project.

Results also indicated that 33% of the women reported receiving unwanted sexual remarks, 28% reported suggestive looks, and 26% reported being deliberately touched. These behaviors were classified in the study as "less severe" types of sexual harassment. When "more severe" forms of sexual harassment were addressed, 15% of the women reported experiencing pressure for dates, 9% reported being directly pressured for sexual favors, and 9% had received unwanted letters and telephone calls. One percent of the sample had experienced actual or attempted rape or assault. Merit Systems repeated their study of workplace sexual harassment in 1987 and reported identical results to the 1981 findings.

Research by Barbara Gutek (1985) with women in the civilian workplace reports that approximately half of the female workforce experiences sexual harassment. Based on telephone interviews generated through random digit dialing procedures, Gutek's results suggested that 53% of women had reported one incident they believed was sexual harassment during their working lives, including degrading and insulting comments (15%), sexual touching (24%), socializing expected as part of the job requirement (11%), and expected sexual activity (8%).

Group differences in sexual harassment have been reported in the literture. Fitzgerald and her colleagues (1988), for example, found that women who were employed in a university setting (e.g., faculty, staff, and administrators) were more likely to experience sexual harassment than were women students in the same institution. Gold (1987) reported that her sample of blue-collar tradeswomen experienced significantly higher levels of all forms of sexual harassment (e.g., gender harassment, seductive behavior, sexual bribery, sexual coercion, sexual assault) than did either white-collar professional women or pink-collar clerical women.

LaFontaine and Tredeau (1986) reported similar findings in their sample of 160 women, all college graduates employed in male-populated occupations (e.g., engineering and management). Baker (1989) studied a sample of 100 women employed in either traditional or nontraditional occupations, where traditionality was defined by the sex distribution in the work group. Baker also divided the traditional group into pink- and blue-collar workers. The pink-collar group included women who were secretaries and clerical workers. The blue collar-group included women who were industrial workers. Baker reported that high levels of sexual harassment are associated with having low numbers of women in the work group. For example, machinists reported significantly high frequencies of all levels of sexual harassment, whereas the traditional blue-collar workers reported very low levels. Clerical women reported experiences that were more similar to those of the traditional blue-collar workers than the nontraditional blue-collar workers. Baker also reported that women in the pink-collar and traditional blue-collar groups encountered just as many men as the machinists during the workday but were treated differently. Thus, these results suggest that as women approach numerical parity in various segments of the workforce, sexual harassment may decline.

This perspective has also been raised by Gutek (1985), who argued that sexual harassment is more likely to occur in occupations in which "sex role spillover" has occurred. Gutek's model suggests that when occupations are dominated by one sex or the other, the sex role of the dominant sex influences (i.e., "spills over") the work role expectations for that job. For example, gender stereotypes imply that men should be sexually aggressive and women ready and willing to be sex objects. Thus, sexual harassment may occur when these gender stereotypes spill over into the workplace setting. When individuals act on their thoughts about women and men, they may engage in behavior that is discriminatory. For example, research suggests that women are evaluated less favorably than men for identical performance on a job (Doyle & Paludi, 1995). In addition, men tend to turn away from women and to move away from them, in contrast to their behavior toward other men (Lott, 1996). Furthermore, men have higher expectations for other men's ability than for women's ability; thus, they attribute women's successful performance on the job to luck, cheating, sexuality, or the fact that someone "likes" them. The causal attribution of "lack of ability," however, is used by men to describe women's job performance that is anything less than perfect (Gutek & Koss, 1993; Levy & Paludi, 1997).

The workplace is not insulated from gender stereotyping. For example, women employees may be evaluated by their co-workers and supervisors in terms of their sexuality and their performance as sex objects instead of their merit as a manager or colleague. Gender stereotypes are related to the amount of perceived power one has in the workplace. Stereotypes are more commonly used in describing the behavior of those who are seen as having less power in the organization and thus occupy lower-echelon positions.

Fain and Anderton (1987) noted that some types of sexual harassment are more significantly experienced by women of color than by white women. For example, unwanted pressure for sexual favors was reported by 7.9% of women of color versus 6.6% of white women, and unwanted pressure for dates was reported by 12.3% of women of color and 9.2% of white women. The interface of gender stereotypes and race stereotypes increases sexual harassing behaviors toward women of color (DeFour, 1996).

WHO HARASSES?

Research suggests that men are more likely to engage in sexual harassment than are women. Men who sexually harass are not distinguishable from their colleagues who do not harass with respect to age, marital status, occupation, or job status (Fitzgerald & Weitzman, 1990). Men who harass do so repeatedly to many women, especially when they have not received any training and counseling about the impact of their behavior on others. And men who harass hold attitudes toward women that are traditional, not egalitarian (Zalk, 1996).

Pryor's (1987) research suggested that sexual harassment bears a conceptual similarity to rape. He developed a series of hypothetical scenarios of situations that provided opportunities for sexual harassment if the man so chose. Instructions asked men to imagine themselves in these roles of the men and to consider what they would do in each situation. They were then instructed to imagine that whatever their chosen course of action, no negative consequences would result from their choices.

Results suggested that men who initiate severe sexually harassing behavior are likely to emphasize male social and sexual dominance and to demonstrate insensitivity to others. Furthermore, men are less likely than women to define sexual harassment as including jokes, teasing remarks of a sexual nature, and unwanted suggestive looks or gestures. Men are also more likely than women to agree with the following statements, taken from Paludi's (1993) survey of "atttitudes toward victim blame and victim responsibility":

Women often claim sexual harassment to protect their reputations.

Many women claim sexual harassment if they have consented to sexual relations but have changed their minds afterwards.

Sexually experienced women are not really damaged by sexual harassment.

It would do some women good to be sexually harassed.

Women put themselves in situations in which they are likely to be sexually harassed because they have an unconscious wish to be harassed.

In most cases when a woman is sexually harassed, she deserved it.

Sexual harassment, similar to rape, incest, and battering, may be understood as an extreme acting out of qualities that are regarded as supermasculine in this culture: aggression, power, dominance, and force. Thus, men who harass exhibit stereotypic behaviors characteristic of the masculine gender role in American culture (Doyle & Paludi, 1995).

Lott (1993) and her colleagues have found empirical support for a widely accepted assumption among researchers in sexual harassment: that sexual harassment is part of a larger and more general dimension of hostility toward women and extreme stereotypes of women, including the mythical images of sexual harassment—that sexual harassment is a form of seduction, that women secretly need or want to be forced into sex.

Paludi (1993) noted in her research on why boys and men sexually harass girls and women that the focus should not be on males' attitudes toward females but instead on males' attitudes toward other males, competition, and power. Many of the men with whom Paludi has discussed sexual harassment often act out of extreme competitiveness and concern with ego or out of fear of losing their positions of power. They do not want to appear weak or less masculine in the eyes of other males, so they engage in "scoping of girls," pinching girls, making implied or overt threats, or spying on women. Girls and women are the game to impress other boys and men. When boys are being encouraged to be obsessionally competitive and concerned with dominance, it is likely that eventually they will use violent means to achieve dominance (Paludi, 1993). Paludi also noted that boys are likely to be abusive verbally and intimidating in their body language. Deindividuation is quite common among adolescent boys who, during class changes and lunch break, scope girls as they walk by in the hall. These boys discontinue self-evaluation and adopt group norms and attitudes. Under these circumstances, group members behave more aggressively than they would as individuals.

The element of aggression that is so deeply embedded in the masculine gender role is present in sexual harassment. For many boys and men, aggression is one of the major ways of proving their masculinity, especially among men who feel some sense of powerlessness in their lives (Doyle & Paludi, 1995). The male-as-dominant or male-as-aggressor is a theme so central to many males' self-concept that it literally carries over to their interpersonal communications, especially with female peers. Sexualizing a professional relationship may be the one area where the average man can still "prove" his masculinity when few other areas can be found for him to prove himself in control, or the dominant one in a relationship. Thus, sexual harassment is not so much a deviant act as an overconforming act to the masculine role in this culture (Paludi, 1996).

Can girls and women engage in sexual harassment? The data to date suggest that during adolescence, girls may be likely to harass boys sexually, although the boys may misinterpret or mislabel their experiences. Women teachers and college and university professors are highly unlikely to date or sexually harass their students. As Fitzgerald and Weitzman (1990) concluded, although it is theoretically possible for women to harass men, it is in practice extremely rare. The incidence of women's sexually harassing other women is also small. Many of men's experiences with sexual harassment are with other men. Consquently, men may be reluctant to disclose this information due to homophobic concerns (Levy & Paludi, 1997). Research in this area of same-sex sexual harassment is ongoing and will offer insight on this topic as well as suggestions for policies, procedures, and training programs.

IMPACT OF SEXUAL HARASSMENT ON EMPLOYEES AND STUDENTS

Several reports have documented the high cost of sexual harassment to victimized employees and students. For example, Fitzgerald and Omerod (1993) noted that the impact of sexual harassment can be examined from three main perspectives:

Work-Related Outcomes

In the first Merit Systems study (1981), 10% of the women who reported they were sexually harassed reported changing jobs as a result. In the second study, Merit Systems (1987) noted that over 36,000 federal employees left their jobs due to sexual harassment in the two years covered by their study. This incidence rate included individuals who quit or were fired, transferred, or reassigned because of unwanted sexual attention. Additional research has documented decreased morale and absenteeism, decreased job or school satisfaction, performance decrements, and damage to interpersonal relationships at work or school (Gutek & Koss, 1993).

Psychological Outcomes

The consequences of harasment for employees' and students' emotional well-being include depression, helplessness, extreme sadness, strong fear reactions, loss of control, worry, disruption of their lives, and decreased motivation (Dansky & Kilpatrick, 1997; Gutek & Koss, 1993; Samoluk & Petty, 1994).

Physiological Outcomes

The following physical symptoms have been reported in the literature concerning workplace and academic sexual harassment: headaches, sleep disturbances, disordered eating, gastrointestinal disorders, nausea, weight loss or gain, and crying spells (Dansky & Kilpatrick, 1997; Gutek & Koss, 1993). Victims of sexual harassment can exhibit a "postabuse" syndrome characterized by shock, emotional numbing, constriction of affect, flashbacks, and other signs of anxiety and depression (Fitzgerald, 1993; Salisbury, Ginoria, Remick, & Stringer, 1986). These responses are influenced by disappointment in the way others react and by the stress of harassment-induced life changes such as moves, loss of income, and disrupted work history (Dansky & Kilpatrick, 1997).

A study by the New York Division of Human Rights (1993) documented several direct costs women have experienced as a result of alleged sexual harassment, including legal expenses, medical costs, and psychotherapy costs. This study also reported the number of individuals who lost health benefits, life insurance, pensions, access to day care, or other benefits as a result of the alleged harassment.

Fitzgerald, Gold, and Brock (1990) classifed individuals' responses into two categories: internally focused strategies and externally focused strategies. Internal strategies represent attempts to manage the personal emotions and cognitions associated with the behaviors they have experienced—for example:

Detachment	Individual minimizes the situation or treats it as a joke.
Denial	Individual denies the behaviors and attempts to forget about it.
Relabeling	Individual reappraises the situation as less threatening and offers excuses for the harasser's behaviors.
Illusory Control	Individual attempts to take responsibility for the harassment.
Endurance	Individual puts up with the behavior because she does not believe help is available or fears retaliation.

Externally focused strategies focus on the harassing situation itself, including reporting the behavior to the individual charged with investigating complaints of sexual harassment—for example:

Avoidance	Individual attempts to avoid the situation by staying away from the harasser.
Assertion/Confrontation	Individual refuses sexual or social offers or verbally confronts the harasser.
Seeking Institutional/ Organizational Relief	Individual reports the incident and files a complaint.

| *Social Support* | Individual seeks the support of others to validate perceptions of the behaviors. |
| *Appeasement* | Individual attempts to evade the harasser without confrontation or to placate the harasser. |

Ormerod and Gold (1988), using this classification system, noted that internal strategies represented by far the more common response overall. Most victims do not tell the harasser to stop. Their initial attempts to manage the initiator are rarely direct. Typically harassers are more powerful—physically and organizationally—than the victims, and sometimes the harasser's intentions are unclear. The first or first few harassing events are often ignored by victims, especially when there is no effective and enforced policy statement and investigatory procedures that make it safe to report sexual harassment. Victims may interpret or reinterpret the situation so that the incident is not defined as sexual harassment.

Victims of sexual harassment may fear retaliation should they confront the harasser. The economic reality for most employees and students is that they cannot just leave a workplace or school where they are being sexually harassed.

The AAUW (1993) study reported that fewer than 1 in 10 students who had been sexually harassed told a teacher, although girls are twice as likely as boys to report their experiences. In addition, fewer than 1 in 4 students who had been sexually harassed told a family member about their experiences. The majority of adolescents who did report their experiences told a friend. Still, a sizeable number of students remained silent about sexual harassment.

Malovich and Stake (1990) found that women students who were high in performance self-esteem and held nontraditional gender role attitudes were more likely to report incidents of sexual harassment than women who were high in self-esteem and held traditional gender role attitudes, or women who were low in self-esteem. Brooks and Perot (1991) found that reporting behavior was predicted by the severity of the offense and the student's feminist attitudes. And Gruber and Smith (1995) found that harassment severity, source of harassment, and being in an occupation in which women were a threatening minority were the strongest predictors of reporting.

PSYCHOLOGICAL RESEARCH ON SEXUAL HARASSMENT: A REVIEW AND A CRITIQUE

A great deal of research on sexual harassment has been guided by a series of questions raised by a few researchers. Such questions channel the data researchers look at and the conclusions they draw. Although there are no right or wrong questions to study, there has been an overabundance of research that is victim focused, seeking to answer such questions as the following: Is sexual harassment common? What's wrong with individuals who are harassed? Why do harassed students keep silent about their victimization? Research has thus focused on the supposed inadequacies of the sexually harassed employee and student. Although this perspective has been challenged (see Levy & Paludi, 1997), it and other victim-focused and victim-blaming perspectives continue to influence research, the treatment of sexual harassment in schools and workplaces, and the resolution of sexual harassment complaints in the school or workplace and through the courts.

Researchers must be aware of the implications of the questions they are asking and the underlying assumptions being made about the sexual harassment they are investigating. Their research is used by policymakers and attorneys, those who are supportive of women's complaints and those seeking to discredit them by referring to their psychological inadequacies.

One research formulation is that sexually harassed women suffer from helplessness. Evidence outside the laboratory suggests, however, that sexually harassed students and employees seek help from friends, family, trusted faculty, and therapists, and when there is an effective and enforced policy statement and investigatory procedures, they seek help from the campus or workplace. Fitzgerald and Omerod (1993) identified a variety of coping styles, internal and external. This research-based response contributes to revictimizing women who do come forward. Telling others is important and should be used in any investigation as data about the impact of sexual harassment on the individual.

Other research suggests it is the responses of others, especially from college administrators, to individuals' requests for resolution of the sexual harassment that are inadequate. Rather than continuing to research the problems of sexually harassed students, it might be more profitable to address effective interventions, training programs, and investigatory procedures.

In addition, much of the research on academic and workplace sexual harassment has given little attention to construct validity issues. Researchers have not typically asked questions that sexually harassed students and employees themselves might ask. Researchers have not typically investigated sexually harassed individuals' own conceptions of their experiences. The research studies rely heavily on descriptive situations as research stimuli. Students, for example, are asked if they believe the description of an incident is sexual harassment and how they would respond to the situation presented. To date, there is no research to suggest that how students respond to descriptive situations on paper in any way reflects how they would respond in an actual situation (Stapf, 1997). In fact, we do have evidence that women are more likely to label incidents as sexual harassment when they are describing others rather than themselves.

In these research studies, ambiguous situations are typically presented to college students with no criteria for determining the occurrence of sexual harassment. Consquently, individuals use their own definitions of sexual harassment in making their judgments. Would we obtain similar findings if we provided individuals with criteria for determining sexual harassment and less ambiguous situations?

Morever, the paper descriptions, most of them very brief, do not capture the depth of emotions and interactions that transpire in a real sexual harassment incident. The percentages reported by researchers based on students' responses to these paper descriptions tell us nothing about the severity or the pervasiveness of the sexual harassment—important issues, especially for seeking resolution of sexual harassment through the courts (Paludi, 1997a).

Nor is attention being paid to the reactivity of the measures used. In the process of measuring students' opinions about sexual harassment, students may change their attitudes due to the increased sensitization to issues surrounding sexual harassment. Furthermore, we do not have studies that have paid attention to whether students chose to file a complaint or not file one as a consequence of what they are learning by participating in a research study.

Are the methodologies researchers are using inhibiting students from filing a complaint because they do not see any parallels between the situation described in their research study and what they have experienced in real life? This question is most important for the research that does not define sexual harassment for students but asks them to rely on their own definitions (Stapf, 1998). Barak (1997) points out that this methodological problem is even more apparent when trying to compare incidence rates of sexual harassment across cultures: researchers have not used the same definition or the same measuring instrument in collecting incidence data.

College students may be able to use abstract thought in making connec tions between their own experiences and the experiences of some fictitious victim of sexual harassment (who is typically an employee, not another student, and thus students may be asked to do a task for which they are unprepared). However, when in a sexual harassment situation, students need concrete information. The topic is too emotionally laden to be treated from the academic perspective typically portrayed in the paper-and-pencil measures of sexual harassment (Paludi, 1997a).

We are concerned about using laboratory research findings outside the context of research for research's sake. Very little attention has been paid to the reactivity of the measures used (Paludi, 1997b).

In order to eliminate the dichotomy between research and practice, we recommend the following:

1. Make data collection include a small training program on sexual harassment, including distributing the campus policy statement on sexual harassment.
2. Invite the individual charged with investigating sexual harassment complaints to the research session.
3. Include information to research participants about counseling available for victims of sexual harassment.
4. Notify the counseling center and the investigator of sexual harassment complaints that data will be collected on this issue and may result in students' wanting to discuss their own experiences or topics raised by the research program.
5. Share results of studies with campus administrators and sexual harassment investigators.

The manner in which some researchers have studied sexual harassment has contributed to school and workplace administrators' and others' trying to alter victims' thoughts, feelings, and behaviors with respect to the victimization, to try to have them conform to a victim-blaming perspective. Most research studies ask the following basic questions:

1. Is sexual harassment a common phenomenon?
2. What's wrong with individuals who are sexually harassed?
3. What is the impact on students who have been sexually harassed?

The methodology used to answer these questions is based on contrived situations in paper-and-pencil form. Other questions to address—focused on changing the school or workplace, not the victims and based on victims' own concerns are these:

1. Why do schools and workplaces allow sexual harassment?
2. Why do individuals sexually harass students and employees?
3. Why are policy statements and investigatory procedures inhibitive to individuals who wish to file a complaint of sexual harassment?

It is to these issues that we now turn in the remainder of this chapter.

DEALING WITH SEXUAL HARASSMENT

To deal with sexual harassment in educational institutions and the workplace, the following components have been recommended in the literature (see Levy & Paludi, 1997): an effective policy statement, an effective grievance procedure, and education and training programs for all members of the workplace and campus.

In order to deal with the issue of definitions of sexual harassment, it is necessary to have an explicit policy. Such a policy allows the campus and workplace to uphold and enforce its policies against sexual harassment within its own community (including such severe penalties as loss of pay or position) without requiring victimized individuals to undertake the laborious, protracted, and costly process of seeking redress from the courts. An effective policy statement has these components (Levy & Paludi, 1997; Shattuck & Williams, 1992):

- Statement of purpose
- Definition
- Behaviors that constitute sexual harassment
- Statement of importance
- Statement of campus's/workplace's responsibility
- Statement of individual's responsibility for reporting
- Statement of sanctions
- Statement concerning sanctions for retaliation
- Statement concerning false complaints
- Identification of individuals responsible for hearing complaints

It has also been suggested that the policy statement should be reissued each year by the president or CEO, as well as be placed prominently throughout the campus or workplace. Adding the policy statement to employee, faculty, and student handbooks is recommended.

Procedures for investigating complaints of sexual harassment must take into account the psychological issues involved in the victimization process, including individuals' feelings of powerlessness and isolation, changes in social network patterns, and their wish to regain control over their personal and professional lives. These procedures need to include the following:

- Those who are responsible for conducting investigations
- Confidentiality
- Due process

- Role of witnesses
- Time frame for completion of investigation
- Role of counsel
- Instructions for communicating with complainant
- Procedures for documentation
- Disciplinary actions and sanctions
- Closure

It has been suggested that the most important feature of an effective policy statement on sexual harassment for any workplace and educational institution is the training programs designed to implement this policy (Levy & Paludi, 1997; Paludi & Barickman, 1991). Effective training programs send a clear message to everyone that the sexual harassment policy must be taken seriously and that sexual harassment will not be tolerated. Successful training programs have the following components incorporated into their design and implementation:

- The president supports and participates in it.
- Attendance at the training session is mandatory and at the written invitation of the president.
- Training sessions are provided for groups of individuals working together in a department.
- Resources are provided for participants in training sessions.
- Training sessions must be held annually.
- Training sessions must be at least three hours in length and provided for the entire workplace or school within a short time period.
- Training sessions must build in time for questions from individuals who wish to speak privately to the trainer.
- The participants' concerns about sexual harassment are assessed prior to the training session.
- Follow-up surveys must be conducted.
- Training programs should include females and males as participants.

Sexual harassment training involves much more than a recitation of individuals' rights and responsibilities and what the law and workplace or school policy require. Training also requires dealing with individuals' assumptions and misconceptions about sexual harassment and their anxieties about the training itself. Thus, training sessions must devote ample time to dealing with the participants' feelings, misconceptions, and questions. All sessions must be completed within a relatively short time frame so as not to place undue concern on individuals. (Additional suggestions for training programs may be found in Levy & Paludi, 1997, and Paludi & Barickman 1998.)

Thus, to deal effectively with sexual harassment, researchers, educators, and advocates have recommended taking an ecological perspective (Bond, 1988): the development and monitoring of an effective policy statement prohibiting violence, an effective and enforced investigative procedure, and sexual violence awareness education and training programs for all members of the workplace or campus community in which they can explore individuals' beliefs, attitudes, and behaviors that may predispose, enable, and reinforce violence. The goal of these approaches is the promotion of multiple prevention strategies that impact the workplace or campus environment as well as the surrounding community.

Paludi (1997b) has provided an example of an ecological approach to dealing with sexual violence on campus. Campuses have multiple constituencies with divergent needs. For example, research suggests that administrators are concerned about the school's liability; undergraduate students typically are not. Faculty are concerned with issues surrounding academic freedom; students are typically not interested in academic freedom in the same way as are faculty. Students are concerned with preserving their reputations; faculty too are concerned with these but for themselves, not for the students for the most part.

An ecological approach to providing training programs for each of these constituencies reflects each group's divergent needs. Topics specific to each constituency are addressed in addition to the standard topics of legal definitions, explanatory models, and behavioral examples. We recommend that training be offered in the following sequence:

1. Revising and reissuing the policy statement to all members of the campus community, taking into account the scientific research on the psychology of the victimization process and the recognition of divergent perceptions and attitudes about sexual harassment because of sex, faculty or student status, race, and power differentials.

2. Revising and reissuing of investigatory procedures to all members of the campus community, taking into account issues of confidentiality, due process, and prompt investigation.

3. Providing extensive training of investigators of complaints of sexual harassment. Since training programs may prompt flashbacks, it is important to have all procedures in place prior to training.

4. Training counselors in student services.

5. Training counselors in the employee assistance program.

6. Training president and cabinet.

7. Training divisional deans.

8. Training administrators.

9. Training student peer support groups.

10. Training faculty peer support groups.

11. Training employee peer support groups.

12. Training faculty.

13. Training students.

14. Training employees.

In order to provide options for individuals who wish to use services in the community, we recommend a campus-community program that includes the following elements:

- A support group in the community co-facilitated by clergy, therapists, attorneys, researchers, and advocates.

- A mentoring program between students and alumni.

- Invitations to students to attend meetings of local organizations (e.g., American Association of University Women, Business and Professional Women, League of Women Voters).

- Guest speakers from the community (e.g., attorney specializing in Title VII or Title IX, therapist, human resources specialist, affirmative action officer).

Paludi (1996) has developed procedures for facilitating faculty development seminars so that faculty can incorporate issues related to sexual harassment in their courses. The main goal of such teaching is to educate students about various aspects of sexual harassment so that they can learn to label their own experiences accurately and seek campus-wide assistance for their experiences. Thus, faculty can work with their campus's sexual harassment trainer in providing information about theoretical and empirical work on the psychology of sexual harassment as well as their campus's policy and investigatory procedures.

Within this ecological approach, Paludi has recommended the development of brochures, posters, and bookmarks that are displayed on the campus, including in residence halls. The bookmarks, complete with information relating to definitions, impact, and assistance, are distributed during registration each term.

All of these strategies have the goal of making sexual harassment more visible and breaking the silence that surrounds the issue on college campuses.

We recommend conducting research on whether the prevention programs have reduced the incidence of sexual victimization or reduced the likelihood that individuals on campus will sexually victimize another person. To date, we do not have many prevention programs on campus sexual violence that rigorously assess their effects. Recommendations for evaluating prevention programs, and taking into account methodological considerations, include the following:

- Representative sampling of trainers and participants.
- Use of relevant and psychometrically sound measures.
- Assessment of potential negative effects of training programs.
- Measurement of generalization across settings and time.

Funding for research on sexual violence must be increased. Furthermore, faculty who conduct research on sexual violence must be supported by their campuses and not discriminated against in tenure and promotion decisions because of their research focus. Furthermore, faculty members who handle investigations of sexual violence should be supported through course reductions.

Finally, we ask workplace and campus administrators to consider their motivation for implementing prevention programs on sexual violence. Many programs exist for the sole purpose of limiting legal liability. The programs can make a significant impact on the social problem of sexual violence.

REFERENCES

American Association of University Women. (1993). *Hostile hallways.* Washington, DC: Author.

Bailey, N., & Richards, M. (1985, August). *Tarnishing the ivory tower: Sexual harassment in graduate training programs.* Paper presented at the Annual Meeting of the American Psychological Association, Los Angeles.

Baker, N. (1989). *Sexual harassment and job satisfaction in traditional and nontraditional industrial occupations.* Unpublished doctoral dissertation, California School of Professional Psychology, Los Angeles.

Barak, A. (1997). Cross-cultural perspectives on sexual harassment. In W. O'Donohue (Ed.), *Sexual harassment: Theory, research, and treatment.* Boston: Allyn & Bacon.

Barickman, R. B., Paludi, M. A., & Rabinowitz, V. C. (1992). Sexual harassment of students: Victims of the college experience. In E. Viano (Ed.), *Victimization: An international perspective*. New York: Springer.

Bogart, K., Simmons, S., Stein, N., & Tomaszewski, E. (1992). Breaking the silence: Sexual and gender-based harassment in elementary, secondary, and postsecondary education. In S. Klein (Ed.), *Sex equity and sexuality in education*. Albany: State University of New York Press.

Bond, M. (1988). Division 27 sexual harassment survey: Definition, impact, and environmental context. *The Community Psychologist, 21*, 7–10.

Brooks, L., & Perot, A. (1991). Reporting sexual harassment: Exploring a predictive model. *Psychology of Women Quarterly, 15*, 31–47.

Dansky, B., & Kilpatrick, D. (1997). Effects of sexual harassment. In W. O'Donohue (Ed.), *Sexual harassment: Theory, research, and practice*. Boston: Allyn & Bacon.

DeFour, D. C. (1996). The interface of racism and sexism on college campuses. In M. A. Paludi (Ed.), *Sexual harassment on college campuses: Abusing the ivory power*. Albany: State University of New York Press.

Doyle, J., & Paludi, M. A. (1995). *Sex and gender: The human experience*. (3rd ed.) Dubuque: Wm. C. Brown/Benchmark.

Dziech, B., & Weiner, L. (1984). *The lecherous professor*. Boston: Beacon Press.

Fain, T. C., & Anderton, D. (1987). Sexual harassment: Organizational context and diffuse status. *Sex Roles, 17*, 291–311.

Fitzgerald, L. (1990). Sexual harassment: The definition and measurement of a construct. In M. A. Paludi (Ed.), *Ivory power: Sexual harassment on campus*. Albany: State University of New York Press.

Fitzgerald, L. (1993). Sexual harassment: Violence against women in the workplace. *American Psychologist, 48*, 1070–1076.

Fitzgerald, L. (1996). Sexual harassment: The definition and measurement of a construct. In M. A. Paludi (Ed.), *Sexual harassment on college campuses: Abusing the ivory power*. Albany: State University of New York Press.

Fitzgerald, L. F., Gold, Y., & Brock, K. (1990). Responses to victimization: Validation of an objective policy. *Journal of College Student Personnel, 27*, 34–39.

Fitzgerald, L. F., & Omerod, A. (1993). Sexual harassment in academia and the workplace. In F. L. Denmark & M. A. Paludi (Eds.), *Psychology of women: A handbook of issues and theories*. Westport, CT: Greenwood.

Fitzgerald, L. F., Shullman, S., Bailey, N., Richards, M., Swecker, J., Gold, Y., Omerod, A., & Weitzman, L. (1988). The incidence and dimensions of sexual harassment in academia and the workplace. *Journal of Vocational Behavior, 32*, 152–175.

Fitzgerald, L. F., & Weitzman, L. (1990). Men who harass: Speculation and data. In M. A. Paludi (Ed.), *Ivory power: Sexual harassment on campus*. Albany: SUNY Press.

Fitzgerald, L. F., Weitzman, L., Gold, Y., & Ormerod, M. (1988). Academic harassment: Sex and denial in scholarly garb. *Psychology of Women Quarterly, 12,* 329–340.

Gold, Y. (1987, August). *The sexualization of the workplace: Sexual harassment of pink-, white-, and blue-collar workers.* Paper presented at the annual conference of the American Psychological Association, New York.

Gruber, J., & Smith, M. (1995). Women's responses to sexual harassment: A multivariate analysis. *Basic and Applied Social Psychology, 17,* 543–562.

Gutek, B. (1985). *Sex and the workplace.* San Francisco: Jossey-Bass.

Gutek, B., & Koss, M. P. (1993). Changed women and changed organizations: Consequences of and coping with sexual harassment. *Journal of Vocational Behavior, 42,* 28–48.

Haring-Hidore, M., & Paludi, M. (1991). Power, politics, and sexuality in mentor-protégé relationships: Implications for women's achievement. In S. Klein (Ed.), *Sex and sexuality in education.* Albany: State University of New York Press.

Kenig, S., & Ryan, J. (1986). Sex differences in levels of tolerance and attribution of blame for sexual harassment on a university campus. *Sex Roles, 15,* 535–549.

LaFontaine, E., & Tredeau, L. (1986). The frequency, sources, and correlates of sexual harassment among women in traditional male occupations. *Sex Roles, 15,* 423–432.

Levy, A., & Paludi, M. A. (1997). *Workplace sexual harassment.* Englewood Cliffs, NJ: Prentice-Hall.

Lott, B. (1993). Sexual harassment: Consequences and realities. *NEA Higher Education Journal, 8,* 89–103.

Lott, B. (1996). The perils and promise of studying sexist discrimination in face-to-face situations. In M. A. Paludi (Ed.), *Sexual harassment on college campuses: Abusing the ivory power.* Albany: State University of New York Press.

Malovich, N. J., & Stake, J. E. (1990). Sexual harassment of women on campus: Individual differences in attitude and belief. *Psychology of Women Quarterly, 14,* 63–81.

Mead, M. (1978). A proposal: We need new taboos on sex at work. In B. Dziech & L. Weiner (1984). *The lecherous professor.* Boston: Beacon Press.

New York Division of Human Rights. (1993). Survey of the costs of sexual harassment. In J. Avner, *Sexual harassment: Building a consensus for change.* Final report submitted to Governor Mario Cuomo. Albany, NY.

Ormerod, A., & Gold, Y. (1988, March). *Coping with sexual harassment: Internal and external strategies for coping with stress.* Paper presented to the annual conference of the Association for Women in Psychology, Newport, RI.

Paludi, M. A. (1993, October). *Sexual harassment in corporate America.* Paper presented at the Columbia Conference on Sexual Harassment, New York.

Paludi, M. A. (Ed.). (1996). *Sexual harassment on college campuses: Abusing the ivory power.* Albany: State University of New York Press.

Paludi, M. A. (1997a, October). *Ivory power.* Paper presented at Middlebury College, Middlebury, VT.

Paludi, M. A. (1997b, September). *The campus as a violent institution for women: From the research lab to campus and community intervention.* Paper presented at the Higher Education Conference, San Antonio, TX.

Paludi, M. A., & Barickman, R. B. (1991). *Academic and workplace sexual harassment: A manual of resources.* Albany: State University of New York Press.

Paludi, M. A., & Barickman, R. B. (1998). *Sexual harassment, work, and education: A resource manual for prevention.* Albany: State University of New York Press.

Paludi, M. A., DeFour, D. C., & Roberts, R. (1994). *Academic sexual harassment of ethnic minority women.* Research in progress.

Petrocelli, W., & Repa, B. (1995). *Sexual harassment on the job: What it is and how to stop it.* Berkeley, CA: Nolo Press.

Pryor, J. (1987). Sexual harassment proclivities in men. *Sex Roles, 17,* 269–290.

Salisbury, J., Ginoria, A., Remick, H., & Stringer, D. (1986). Counseling victims of sexual harassment. *Psychotherapy, 23,* 316–324.

Samoluk, S., & Petty, G. (1994). The impact of sexual harassment simulations on women's thoughts and feelings. *Sex Roles, 30,* 679–699.

Sandler, B., & Paludi, M. A. (1993). *Educator's guide to controlling sexual harassment.* Washington, DC: Thompson.

Shattuck, C., & Williams, C. (1992). *Employers' guide to controlling sexual harassment.* Washington, DC: Thompson.

Stapf, D. (1997). *Attributions about peer sexual harassment among college students.* Senior honors thesis, Union College.

Stites, M. C. (1996). Consensual relationships. In M. A. Paludi (Ed.), *Sexual harassment on college campuses: Abusing the ivory power.* Albany: State University of New York Press.

U.S. Merit Systems Protection Board. (1981). *Sexual harassment of federal workers: Is it a problem?* Washington, DC: U.S. Government Printing Office.

U.S. Merit Systems Protection Board. (1987). *Sexual harassment of federal workers: An update.* Washington, DC: U.S. Government Printing Office.

Zalk, S. R. (1996). Psychological profiles of men who harass. In M. A. Paludi (Ed.), *Sexual harassment on college campuses: Abusing the ivory power.* Albany: State University of New York Press.

Zalk, S. R., Paludi, M. A., & Dederich, J. (1991). Women students' assessment of
    consensual relationships with their professors: Ivory power reconsid-
    ered. In M. A. Paludi & R. B. Barickman, *Academic and workplace sex-
    ual harassment: A resource manual.* Albany: State University of New
    York Press.

PART V

SEXUAL VICTIMIZATION: LEGAL AND LEGISLATIVE RESPONSES

6

The Law and Workplace Sexual Harassment

Anne C. Levy

Although it offers perhaps one of the most imperfect solutions to the problem of workplace sexual harassment, the law has continued to be one of the prime motivators for change in this area. Because it exacts an increasingly severe penalty on those who perpetrate it and do not take adequate actions to prevent it, the law is often the preferred choice for victims as a source of compensation and a feeling that they have, at least in some small but meaningful way, taken a stand against the power that once seemed overwhelming. The law is often seen as the great leveler of power, giving those who are usually not on equal footing with their aggressors the chance to level the playing field. Unfortunately, this field can often exact its own toll on the victims, especially those unfamiliar with the workings of the law. To learn to deal more expertly with the legal system, victims and those who are working with them will benefit greatly by a better understanding of the laws that protect victims of sexual harassment.

THE LEGAL SYSTEM GOVERNING SEXUAL HARASSMENT LAWSUITS

Perhaps the first aspect of the law in the United States that must be understood is that there are two separate court systems, one federal and the other individually in each of the fifty states. Although the scheme of exactly which cases are heard in each of these systems can be complex, it is enough to know that generally federal courts deal with cases involving the U.S. Constitution or national laws passed by the federal Congress or lawsuits involving parties who live in different states. State courts deal with cases involving the states' constitutions, laws passed by the state legislature, or lawsuits brought under common law. Occasionally, lawsuits allege a violation of a variety of laws, both state and federal. In these circumstances, federal and state courts each have the power to decide all of the claims if the judge decides that this will better serve the interests of justice. In both systems, there are hierarchies of courts, with a variety of avenues for appealing decisions made in the lower courts.

The lowest-level courts, called the district courts in the federal system and by a variety of names (including municipal, circuit, and district courts) in the states, are the places where trials are held and juries or judges make decisions based on the evidence presented to them and the applicable law. Once this decision is made, the parties may choose to appeal the decision to an appeals court and finally to a supreme-type court.

In the federal system, the appeals courts are called the federal circuit courts of appeal. The country is divided into sections or *circuits* and cases heard in district courts will be appealed to the appropriate circuit court for that section. Often in the area of sexual harassment, the decisions that influence the law the most come from these circuit courts. The final decider of cases in the federal system, if it chooses to take a case, is the U.S. Supreme Court. There are not many cases that the U.S. Supreme Court is required to hear, and it usually denies *certiorari*, or permission to argue the case at the highest court, to most parties. In the area of sexual harassment, there have only been a few cases heard by the Supreme Court, leaving most of the pivotal decision making to the circuit courts. District courts situated in each circuit must adhere to the decisions of its circuit court of appeals, but circuit courts need not follow the same rule as each other. This can result in a situation called a "conflict in the circuits," with different results in lawsuits, depending on which circuit court is hearing them. Often the Supreme Court will have to resolve the issue, resulting in uniformity in all federal courts. In the area of sexual harassment, there have arisen a number of such conflicts, only one of which has been decided by the Supreme Court.

Understanding of the law and its processing of sexual harassment complaints also requires a basic knowledge of the overall U.S. justice system. Our common law system derives from the English system of justice. In 49 of the 50 United States, Louisiana being the only exception, there are three types of laws that come into play when the legal system undertakes to deal with problems: common law, statutory law, and constitutional law. Each of these areas will provide a variety of *causes of action* (or legally recognized reasons to sue) for *plaintiffs* (those who are bringing the lawsuit). In any one lawsuit, any combination of these may be involved.

Common law is judge-made law or rules that have evolved through the many hundreds of years that cases have been brought before decision makers. Although these rules evolve, many remain fairly constant, giving a good indicator of how judges will deal with certain situations. Common law is usually decided in state courts, which means that there may be some conflicts between the decisions of one state's courts and another's. Lower courts in any one state must follow the rules set down by the higher courts in that same state, but no state must follow the common law rules of any other state, so the common law is less consistent than one might like. Nevertheless, the judges retain the ability to make decisions based on changing times, truths, and facts and to recognize when justice requires a certain outcome in a particular case.

An example of a common law lawsuit is one that alleges a *tort* or a legally recognized reason for one private party to sue another for damages suffered because of some wrongdoing. There are a number of tort causes of actions, including many found in sexual harassment lawsuits: intentional or negligent infliction of emotional distress, assault, battery, and negligent or intentional interference with contractual relations. These causes of action provide for some benefits for victims beyond those provided by statutory law, often including no limits on the amount of money damages that can be awarded for pain and suffering. Of course, the common law rules set in each state will influence how the courts will decide each case, sometimes resulting in plaintiffs' winning in one state but not in another, even when the facts are basically the same.

The same inconsistent results can occur in the second area of law—*statutory law*. This involves the bringing of lawsuits that allege a violation of a law or statute written by the national Congress or a state legislature. In the area of sexual harassment, the applicable federal law is usually Title VII of the Civil Rights Act of 1964, which made discrimination on certain bases illegal in the employment setting. Many states also have their own antidiscrimination laws, but in the area of sexual harassment, quite often decisions with regard to the federal law strongly influence the state courts in interpreting their own statutes. Although statutory law is written by legislatures, courts are also involved, as it is usually their job to interpret the laws and determine whether the statute has been violated in certain situations.

The third area of law is *constitutional law*, or interpretation of the requirements of a federal or state constitution. Courts are often called on to determine whether certain actions violate constitutional limits on government. In workplace sexual harassment situations, a constitutional violation can be alleged only when the employer is some arm of the government, because constitutions place restrictions on only governmental actions, not those of private parties.

ILLEGAL WORKPLACE SEXUAL HARASSMENT

Although the various manifestations of sexual harassment are many, the law recognizes two types of sexual harassment situations for purposes of employment discrimination lawsuits. The earliest cases usually involved the quid pro quo type of sexual harassment, while today many more allege that an employer maintains a sexually hostile environment.

It was the federal courts' interpreting the requirements of Title VII of the Civil Rights Act of 1964 that first outlined the limits and requirements for cases of each type, with many state courts following their lead in interpreting their own state statutes. Title VII states that it is illegal for an employer to fail or refuse to hire or to discharge any individual, or otherwise to discriminate against any individual with respect to compensation, terms, conditions, or privileges of employment, because of such individual's race, color, religion, sex, or national origin. The U.S. Supreme Court has approved the lower courts' view that both quid pro quo and hostile environment sexual harassment constitute discrimination with regard to the terms, conditions, or privileges of employment on the basis of sex and, thus, violate Title VII.

The Equal Employment Opportunity Commission (EEOC), the federal agency charged with carrying out the requirements of Title VII, has defined illegal workplace sexual harassment:

Unwelcome sexual advances, requests for sexual favors, and other verbal or physical conduct of a sexual nature constitute sexual harassment when (1) submission to such conduct is made either explicitly or implicitly a term or condition of an individual's employment, (2) submission to or rejection of such conduct by an individual is used as the basis for employment decisions affecting such individual, or (3) such conduct has the purpose or effect of unreasonably interfering with an individual's work performance or creating an intimidating, hostile, or offensive working environment.

Sections 1 and 2 refer to quid pro quo situations: section 3 defines hostile environment harassment. Although the EEOC definition includes only the words "conduct of a sexual nature" when describing harassing behavior, "sexual" harassment need not be of this kind. In recent years, the agency has made clear that it interprets Title VII as prohibiting behavior that has no overt sexual overtones but "denigrates or shows hostility or aversion toward a person because of their gender."

Both quid pro quo and hostile environment harassment may be alleged in the same lawsuit, but often different standards have to be met for each. While there is some overlap between the two types of sexual harassment cases, they are viewed quite differently in the law, each with its own requirements and problems for victims and employers.

Quid Pro Quo Sexual Harassment

The term *quid pro quo* is a legal contract term that means "something for something," referring to the requirement that for a contract to be binding, there must be something given by each side. In sexual harassment situations, this involves the unwelcomed offering of workplace benefits in return for sexual favors of some kind. Because of its nature, it is almost always alleged only when there is a disparate power between the victim and the perpetrator. This is perhaps the most easily recognized of the two types of sexual harassment, as few will claim not to understand that such situations violate the law.

In quid pro quo cases, the biggest problem victims have is getting the judge or jury to believe that such an offer did take place and that they suffered some damages because of their refusal of the offer. These damages could be a lost promotion, false negative evaluations, or any number of other workplace actions a person with power can inflict on a subordinate. This requires that the victim be believed by the judge or jury, because the other side often denies such an offer, and also that the judge or jury be convinced that the actions were related to the refusal of the offer. In other words, the plaintiff must establish that an offer was made, that it was rejected, and that the damage the victim suffered was because of the rejection and not because of some other factor. While this is not always easy and testifying can be very difficult when faced with an overly vigilant defense attorney, it has been found that judges and juries are surprisingly good at seeing through false claims from either side in the vast majority of cases.

There are a number of reasons that a lawsuit alleging the quid pro quo type of harassment is better for a victim than one claiming hostile environment. First, many courts are more comfortable recognizing the illegal offer situation as a violation of the law than they are with defining behavior as creating a hostile environment. In addition, the employer has a higher standard of liability in these types of cases than in those alleging hostile environment. When a victim proves her or his case under the quid pro quo theory, the law imposes what is called *strict liability*. This means that the employer is liable, regardless of any actions it may have taken to try to prevent the occurrence. In such situations, the employer is liable for the damages, even if it has a strong policy against such behavior and strictly forbids managers to make such offers. This is not the case in cases involving hostile environment.

In the quid pro quo arena, a new issue has recently arisen: the question of whether a victim must have suffered some loss of benefit or a workplace detriment of some kind in order to bring a lawsuit. In other words, is the law violated only when the victim suffers a loss or also merely by the unwelcomed "offer" itself? Most courts have accepted the view that the actions are what violates the law in a quid pro quo case, although a small minority have said that statutes are violated as soon as the offer is made. This could be important, because an employee who goes along with the "contract" and thus suffers no tangible workplace detriment or one who refuses the offer but does not incur the detriment might not have a quid pro quo lawsuit. Even so, there could be pain and suffering damages, which can be awarded in most sexual harassment lawsuits. Victims who do not have tangible workplace detriments are not without a recourse, however; they could also claim that the offer creates a sexually hostile environment, the second type of workplace sexual harassment lawsuit allowed under current law.

Hostile or Discriminatory Environment Sexual Harassment

The less understood and more complex type of sexual harassment case involves behavior that is alleged to have created a work environment discriminatory to one's gender. This could mean that it is more difficult for women to work or succeed in the workplace because of sexual behavior or any other conduct that denigrates or demeans women. This type of harassment is difficult for the law to handle because these cases involve the complexities of psychological and sociological issues, including the differences in perspectives between the genders. While they are the more complex of the two types of illegal harassment, discriminatory environment situations are the ones that are usually involved when the term is used in today's workplace. For employers, they represent both a problem and an opportunity. Although the behavior may be more subtle and difficult to root out than in the quid pro quo situations, the law does give more protection from liability for companies that develop policies and programs designed to prohibit and punish behavior that makes the environment discriminatory and encourages victims to come forward when harassing behavior occurs. The term most often used to describe this type of harassment is "hostile or intimidating environment," but this often does not bring understanding as to what behavior is prohibited. For most workers, hostile and intimidating behavior is overt and has a malicious intent. This need not be the case, as a discussion of the requirements for a finding that the environment is discriminatory will show. For purposes of understanding how the law deals with these situations, there are two general criteria that must be understood: whether the conduct affects a term, privilege or condition of employment and whether the conduct is unwelcome.

Does the Behavior or Conduct Affect a Term, Condition, or Privilege of Employment?

Logically, every action, event, or policy that denigrates or demeans a person on the basis of gender is viewed as sexual harassment. In order to violate the law, the behavior or conduct must be serious enough to affect a term or condition of employment. Although the courts have had some difficulty defining when this occurs, it is often stated that this means that "trivial" (in the words of the law, not me) sexual harassment cannot be the basis of a sexual harassment lawsuit. When behavior is serious enough to violate the law is a question that has plagued the courts for many years; even the U.S. Supreme Court appears not to be able to put its collective finger on the answer. Often the result depends on the perspective used to judge the behavior.

In its first case dealing with work environment sexual harassment, *Meritor Savings Bank v. Vinson* (1986), the U.S. Supreme Court approved the use of Title VII in such situations and noted that for sexual harassment to be the basis of a lawsuit, it must be "sufficiently severe or pervasive to alter the conditions of the victim's employment and create an abusive working environment." The justices did not identify when that plateau would be reached, but they did note that the allegations in Vinson "which include not only pervasive harassment but also criminal conduct of the most serious nature—are plainly sufficient to state a claim for 'hostile environment' sexual harassment." The victim in that case had definitely endured more than "trivial" behavior, having been forced into intercourse with her supervisor, Sidney Taylor, 40 or 50 times, having been fondled in front of other employees, and having been followed into the ladies' restroom, where her supervisor exposed himself.

Although the behavior in *Vinson* was easy to identify as sufficiently serious to reach the level of legal liability, subsequent cases in the lower courts had inconsistent results. The only guidance that appears to have been given was the Supreme Court's quoting of the EEOC guidelines, which state that every case must be viewed based on "the record as a whole" and "the totality of circumstances, such as the nature of the sexual advances, and the context in which the alleged incidents occurred." Courts have indicated that decisions as to the pervasiveness of the harassment must include evidence as to the severity of the behavior, how often it occurred (once a month, once a year, once a day), and the time frame in which it occurred (over a month, over a year, for several years). In some further explanation of how it views the severity question, the EEOC has indicated that it will usually assume that any unwelcome physical contact would be severe enough on its own to constitute a violation of the law, although this has not been tested in the courts.

Because the Supreme Court has given little guidance as to "how much was too much," it often depends on the sometimes biased perceptions of the judge or jury as to the point at which the law is violated. Results often depend on the resolution of a variety of thorny issues, including the effect of gender differences, the effects necessary in order to reach legal liability, and the interplay of the perpetrator's intent and the effect on the victim. Because it is now the least controversial issue, we will look at the intent-versus-effect issue first.

The EEOC's definition of sexual harassment includes behavior that has the intent *or* effect of depriving the victim of equal employment opportunity. This means that even if the perpetrator did not intend to harass anyone but the behavior had this result, it would be illegal. While a government agency's interpretation of the laws it is given the power to carry out is given deference when the courts have to interpret situations under those laws, it is also true that judges have the ultimate decision making as to the intent of those who made the law. Thus, if a court decided that the EEOC had misinterpreted Congress's intent in making effect the key, it could overturn the agency's rule. In this area, however, courts have accepted that the effect of behavior is what is key, not whether someone intended for it to be harassment. The U.S. Supreme Court in *Vinson*, while not specifically stating that it agreed with that specific wording, did quote the EEOC's definition in deciding that "hostile environment" was intended to be illegal under Title VII. Although it was not quoting the definition in order to answer that specific issue, the law usually assumes that a court is expressing approval of the entire language when it uses it in a decision. This is probably why almost all courts have assumed this to be a resolved issue, and few arguments about benign intent are now heard in such cases as a defense to liability, although lack of intent may reduce the damage amount. A second and much thornier issue has involved the effect that one might observe when the harassment has reached the level of affecting a term or condition of employment. Because it is probably impossible to pinpoint the level of behavior that would create a discriminatory work environment, the courts have been more focused on what tangible results occur when it does reach that level. There appears to be a universally held belief in the courts that certain effects will be apparent when the harassment goes beyond "trivial" and reaches the level of legal liability.

For many years after *Vinson*, the courts wrestled with this problem. The EEOC had stated in its definition that one effect that may be expected is that a victim's work performance may suffer. The definition also adds the wording, "or creates an intimidating, hostile, or offensive working environment," leaving open the door to a finding that the law is violated even if there is no interference with work performance. This only added to the confusion.

Obviously inconsistent results were being seen. In one court, a number of egregious incidents were judged inadequate, and in another, one or two "lesser" behaviors were found to be enough. One of the biggest problems appeared to be how severe the effects needed to be in order for the environment to violate the law. Many courts indicated that the conduct must be serious enough to affect the psychological well-being of the reasonable person, and a few appear to have required that it must seriously affect his or her psychological well-being. Understandably, due to the lack of psychological training of most lawyers, judges, and jury members, determining either of these would be difficult, but certainly the serious effect standard would require much more egregious and persistent harassing behavior than merely *an* effect. The U.S. Supreme Court decided in 1993 that it would try to give better guidance in this area, although it is debatable whether this was accomplished in its decision in *Harris v. Forklift Systems*.

In the *Harris* case, the lower court had found that Ms. Harris had not made out a case for legal liability because she had not proved that "his" behavior was "so severe" as to be expected to affect her psychological well-being seriously. The Supreme Court found that this was too high a standard, noting that "Title VII comes into play before the harassing conduct leads to a nervous breakdown." It also noted that although the actions of the supervisor in the *Vinson* case were especially egregious, that case did not "mark the boundary of what is actionable."

Unfortunately, the Court in *Harris* was not especially clear after that point about the boundaries of actionable harassment. Noting that there can be no mathematically precise test, the justices held that the law must strike a middle ground between conduct that is "merely offensive and requiring the conduct to cause a tangible psychological injury." Where is that middle ground, and how can a judge or jury determine when the threshold has been met?

The only guidance given on the question of how much is too much harassment was a statement by the Court that a variety of effects might be expected when terms or conditions of employment were affected by workplace conduct. For example, stated the justices, behavior that reaches the level of legal liability might be expected to "detract from employees' job performance, discourage employees from remaining on the job, or keep them from advancing in their careers." This may seem to be a helpful answer, but it still leaves open the question of when these occur—at what level of abusive behavior? Interestingly, the Court noted that even without such effects, Title VII could be violated and that there did not need to be "concrete psychological harm."

In conclusion, the Supreme Court stated that "whether an environment is 'hostile' or 'abusive' can be determined only by looking at all the circumstances. These may include the frequency of the discriminatory conduct; its severity; whether it is physically threatening or humiliating, or a mere offensive utterance; and whether it unreasonably interferes with an employee's work performance." Finally, it noted that the judging of when Title VII is violated must be done on both an objective and subjective level. The behavior must be serious enough that a reasonable person would find the environment to be hostile or abusive and the victim herself must "perceive the environment to be abusive." In other words, if reasonable people would think this was enough and it had an abusive effect on this victim, the standards had been met in a case.

The *Harris* opinion left open a variety of questions. Perhaps the most important was the one the lower courts had been debating for some time. When determining whether the environment was hostile or abusive, whose eyes should reasonable people be looking through? Perspective is important in determining the effect of a variety of behaviors in the workplace, as the American Psychological Association has argued, the difference between the genders makes this a pivotal question in every case. Is the effect on the "reasonable woman" to be determined when the victim is a woman?

The law has always used the term "reasonable person" or "reasonable man" in setting standards for acceptable behavior. Many commentators have argued that both of these tests are gender biased because they view conduct through the perspective and biases of males. In the area of discriminatory environment sexual harassment, many argue that this bias can result in injustice toward female victims. Is there a difference in how behavior affects men and women? Can the same conduct have a discriminatory effect on one gender but be viewed as trivial if directed at the other? A number of psychologists and sociologists suggest a vast difference in this area between men and women, and they are often called on by lawyers to present expert testimony to show judges and juries the importance of that difference in perspective.

While there is probably little difference in the effect of overtly demeaning or insulting conduct between the genders, it is in the area of sexual behavior and displays in the workplace that perspective becomes a vital issue. According to much courtroom testimony, women are affected quite differently from men when sexuality becomes part of the work environment. In the cutting-edge case of *Robinson v Jacksonville Shipyards* (1991), for example, the court found the following testimony from psychologist and professor Dr. Susan Fiske to be highly credible:

Men and women respond to sex issues in the workplace to a degree that exceeds normal differences in other perceptual reactions between them. For example, research reveals a near flip-flop of attitudes when both men and women were asked what their response would be to being sexually approached in the workplace. Approximately two-thirds of the men responded that they would be flattered; only fifteen percent would feel insulted. For the women the proportions are reversed.

The sexualization of the workplace imposes burdens on women that are not borne by men. Women must constantly monitor their behavior to the existence of the sexual stereotyping either by becoming sexy and responsive to the men who flirt with them or by becoming rigid, standoffish, and distant so as to make it clear that they are not interested in the status of sex object.

Two major effects of stereotyping were described by Dr. Fiske. One effect is selective interpretation. The individual who engages in stereotyping of another person because of that person's membership in a minority group selectively interprets behavior of the other person along the lines of the stereotypes applied to the group. Thus, an employer may respond to a complaint by a female employee by stereotyping her as "an overly emotional woman," and thereafter ignore her complaints as exaggerated or insignificant. . . . A second effect of stereotyping is denigration of the individual merit of the person who is stereotyped. The presence of stereotyping in the workplace affects the job turnover and job satisfaction of the members of the group subjected to stereotyping.

Kathryn Abrams, a legal commentator who is often quoted in judicial opinions in this area, explains the situation this way:

While publicly disseminated pornography may influence all viewers, it remains the expression of the editors of *Penthouse* or *Hustler* or the directors of *Deep Throat*. On the wall of an office, it becomes the expression of a coworker or supervisor as well.

In this context the effect of pornography on workplace equality is obvious. Pornography on an employer's wall or desk communicates a message about the way he views women—a view strikingly at odds with the way women wish to be viewed in the workplace. Depending upon the material in question it may communicate that women should be the objects of sexual aggression, that they are submissive slaves to male desires, or that their most salient and desirable attributes are sexual. Any of these images may communicate to male coworkers that it is acceptable to view women in a predominantly sexual way. All of the views to some extent detract from the image most women in the workplace would like to project: that of professional, credible coworker.

A number of courts have noted that they must view the behavior using the perspective of a reasonable person of the same gender as the alleged victim in order to uphold the intent of Title VII. Included in these are at least four federal circuit courts. One judge noted that any other approach did not make sense because it would permit employers to "sustain ingrained notions of reasonable behavior fashioned by the offenders."

Because the Supreme Court has not decided the issue, however, courts remain free to use whichever standard they wish. A variety of approaches are articulated in opinions, including the "reasonable woman," "reasonable person," and "reasonable victim" standards, yet even some of those who use the term "person" note a difference in certain behaviors' effects between the genders. Thus, it appears that the courts are moving more toward accepting, as the APA has always argued, that the perspective used will make a great deal of difference in the outcome of work environment sexual harassment cases. For this reason psychologists and sociologists are usually in high demand as expert witnesses in sexual harassment lawsuits, and most judges and juries rely on their testimony to help them understand the complexities involved in determining whether this behavior reaches the level of legal liability.

Interestingly, a variety of seemingly unrelated conduct can be joined in one lawsuit, often resulting in a finding that, when taken together, the behaviors create a discriminatory work environment. This is often seen in situations where the conduct itself may be deemed "trivial," yet the company's inadequate and sometimes abusive response when it is reported or observed adds to the seriousness. The employer then can be liable because the behavior and the inadequate response, when viewed as a pattern, are said to reach the level of legal liability—in other words, affect a term or condition of employment.

Is the Conduct or Behavior Unwelcome?

A second and important issue in the determination of the legal liability question in sexual harassment cases is whether the victim welcomed the behavior. This is true in both quid pro quo situations and in work environment cases, although it appears more in the latter. Determining the welcomeness of behavior can also be a complex matter, with the interplay of possible gen-der differences in responses to harassment, but it appears that most judges and juries are willing to assume that in most cases, behavior is not wel-comed by the victim, absent evidence to the contrary.

This element of work environment sexual harassment cases was dis-cussed by the U.S. Supreme Court in the *Vinson* case. The lower court had determined that the intimate or sexual relationship was a voluntary one on the part of the victim. The Supreme Court justices noted that there was a necessary difference between voluntary and welcomed and added that "the fact that sex-related conduct was 'voluntary' in the sense that the complain-ant was not forced to participate against her will, is not a defense to a sexual harassment suit brought under Title VII." The key, according to the high court, was whether the victim by her conduct indicated that the alleged sex-ual advances were unwelcome, "not whether her actual participation in sex-ual intercourse was voluntary."

In reality, it may be difficult to conceptualize the difference between un-welcome and involuntary, especially with regard to the problem with the whole concept of free will. For the high court, the unwelcome element ap-pears to center on whether, given a real choice, unfettered by power differ-entials and fear of reprisals, the victim would have chosen for this behavior to have occurred. Perhaps this can be explained by comparing it to a rape situation, where the victim, fearing for her life or further bodily harm, does not scream or try to fight off her assailant. While the Supreme Court feels that, in one sense of the word, it might be said that the victim voluntarily had intercourse, it certainly could not be said that she welcomed the rape.

As in the case of the effect of behavior, the welcomeness does not appear to be an important issue in situations where behavior is overtly demeaning. It can hardly be argued that anyone welcomes statements or behavior that belittle or deride her or his abilities in the workplace. With regard to sexual behavior, however, there seems to be more difficulty.

When can it be said that a victim welcomes sexuality and sexually based comments or conduct in the workplace? Women who have been subjected to such conduct often note that they feel uncomfortable yet do not know how to respond. Is it necessary for a person to manifest that behavior is un-welcome in order for a judge or jury to conclude that it was? If so, how must this be exhibited? Overtly? Is silence adequate?

The Supreme Court in *Vinson* noted that this inquiry presents "difficult problems and proof and turns largely on credibility determinations." It also noted that the correct inquiry would be whether the victim "by her conduct indicated that the alleged sexual advances were unwelcome." While this would appear to require that there be some overt manifestation by the victim that does not seem to be the fact in most cases.

There are a number of ways that people respond to behavior that makes them uncomfortable. Some psychologists and sociologists argue that gender differences play an important role in response. They believe that men are far more likely to express their disapproval than women and that a standard requiring overt manifestation that behavior is unwelcome would unreasonably obstruct lawsuits by the usual victims of work environment sexual harassment—women. For this reason and others, most courts appear to give wide latitude in this area. In fact, many seem to assume that a victim does not welcome the behavior, absent evidence to the contrary.

In cases where the welcomeness of the behavior is an issue, evidence from experts is often presented. Once again, psychologists and sociologists can be helpful to judges and juries in understanding why certain responses, such as silence or even begrudging participation, might be ways of dealing with difficult situations. It is argued that women especially are prone to "grin and bear it" in the hope that the behavior will subside, unfortunately making it appear to some that the conduct is welcomed. Often it takes an expert to explain the difference in psychological responses to such situations.

While the victim's own behavior can be an ambiguous indicator of welcomeness, the Supreme Court in *Vinson* did open the door to a potential use of such evidence in work environment cases. The victim in that case had argued that evidence of her "dress and personal fantasies" should not have been allowed in the lower court hearing. The high court stated that evidence of a complainant's sexually provocative speech or dress was not irrelevant as a matter of law, which means that a district court is free to allow it if the judge determines that it is relevant to that particular case. Of course, it also means that a judge may refuse to allow it if there is a determination that the potential for unfair prejudice outweighs its relevance. Once again, expert testimony can be helpful in showing a judge that such evidence is of little relevance in determining that the behavior was welcomed.

Recent cases and the EEOC have added some new insights into the welcome versus unwelcome factor and evidence relevant to such a determination. For example, a number of cases have made it clear that a person's behavior outside the workplace cannot be used against him or her in a work environment sexual harassment case. The case that most illustrates this principle involved a victim who had posed for pin-up pictures. The circuit court overturned a district court that had allowed the evidence to be brought in by the defendant to prove that the victim welcomed sexual behavior in the workplace. The higher court stated that how a person behaved outside the workplace was irrelevant to how she wished to be viewed and treated in a professional environment.

In addition to differentiating between work and nonwork behavior, the EEOC has expressed the view that a person may welcome behavior from one person yet still make a claim that the same conduct was from another not welcomed. Perhaps a victim is dating a co-employee and engages in sexually based conversations with that person. That does not mean, according to most sources, that the same conversation would be welcomed from anyone else. It is possible to choose those with whom such behavior will be allowed.

Although a person may choose with whom to engage in certain conduct, in situations where behavior had been welcomed—for example, where a consensual intimate or close relationship had existed but is no longer welcomed (perhaps the relationship is over)—the alleged victim must have overtly manifested to the other that a change has occurred. In other words, the person who no longer wishes to be the object of such conversations or behavior must tell the former "friend" that such conduct is no longer welcomed. If it occurs after this is made clear, it may be viewed as unwelcomed, despite the earlier participation.

The determination of welcomeness, just like that of whether the behavior is "serious" enough to violate the law, is not always an easy one. Nevertheless, both must be determined in order for a victim to be successful in a sexual harassment lawsuit. Even if these are proved, however, it is not certain that the plaintiff will win a work environment case brought under Title VII or most state statutes. In addition, the judge or jury must find that someone is liable under the statutory law for the violation. Usually this requires a finding of employer liability for the conduct.

A CLOSER LOOK AT LIABLE PARTIES

Usually under the common law, anyone who has been at fault for inflicting damage on another person may be sued for those damages. This is the same in sexual harassment situations. Any co-worker or supervisor who has caused damage may be named as a defendant in a lawsuit that alleges such common law claims as intentional infliction of emotional distress. This is not the case, however, when there is an alleged violation of a statute. In those situations, the statute itself will note who can be sued.

In Title VII and in most state statutes, the parties named as potentially liable are employers, employment agencies, or labor organizations. Normally the employer is the one who is named and from whom plaintiffs wish to secure damages. In that situation, it must be proved that the employer is liable for the behavior, a determination that is made separately from any other in a sexual harassment lawsuit.

Employer liability for quid pro quo sexual harassment is easily proved. Because the courts and the EEOC agree that strict liability is the standard, if there is a determination that an unwelcomed illegal offer was made and, in most courts, that some detriment was incurred, then the employer will be liable for the damages. It is somewhat different in the case of work environment sexual harassment.

Employers are not viewed as strictly liable for work environment harassment. Their liability in those situations is expressed somewhat differently. First, most courts agree that when co-workers only are involved in the harassment, the standard is whether the employer knew or should have known of the behavior and failed to take prompt remedial action. An employer is normally deemed to know when one of its supervisors knew, such as when she or he views the conduct or when a complaint is addressed to him or her. An employer should have known when the conduct is so prevalent that a reasonable employer who is paying ordinary attention to the work environment would have known. In addition, the courts usually look to see whether there is a strong sexual harassment policy and procedure in place and, if not, will often find that the employer would have known, even if it actually did not, if it had such a program in place. Thus, it is determined that the employer should have known in those circumstances also.

When a supervisor is involved in the conduct, the standard is more conducive to the victim. Then, according to the Supreme Court in *Vinson*, agency principles apply. Understanding this requires a short discussion of the law of agency, which is not always as clear-cut as many people, especially nonlawyers, might like.

When a person (called the *principal*) gives authority to someone else (called the *agent*) to act on her or his behalf, the law of agency governs the rights, responsibilities, and liabilities of all of the parties. Usually the principal is liable for the actions of the agent with regard to third parties when the agent is going about the business she or he has been given the authority to do or is involved in activities deemed necessary in order to carry out the principal's business. The law also sometimes allows third parties to sue the principal for damages when the activity is neither authorized nor necessary. This can occur when the principal has made it appear to the third party that the agent has this authority or when the principal places the agent in a position, because of the authority granted to the agent, to cause damage to the third party.

Consider work environment sexual harassment situations involving a supervisor. When the supervisor is involved in harassing behavior, it is often argued that the employer, here the principal, by giving the supervisor unrestricted authority over the workplace and the work environment, has either led the workers to believe that the supervisor is authorized to do as he or she wishes or has at least placed them in a position (by giving them the responsible position) that the worker can be damaged by his or her own actions. Thus, most courts will find that an employer is liable for its supervisor's work environment harassment, unless it puts into place a system for removing such indications of authority.

The system that courts and the EEOC require for the removal of this potential for liability is a strong sexual harassment policy and procedure, designed not just to allow reporting but also to encourage victims to come forward. There are many requirements that must be met in putting together such a program (see Levy & Paludi, 1996, for further discussion), but basically it must adequately describe the prohibited conduct, lay out the discipline for violations, set up a confidential procedure for investigating, and allow for a variety of reporting possibilities for suspected violations. When such a program is in place, if the victim did not use the internal procedures or the response was deemed adequate when a report is made, the court will usually dismiss the lawsuit, finding that although a violation may have occurred, the employer is not liable; it did all it could do to remedy the problem.

Under Title VII, the possibility of individual liability for those who are involved in the harassing behavior is small. The Supreme Court has not addressed the issue of whether the law is intended to allow lawsuits against individual persons, so there is no definitive answer, but most courts appear to believe that only the actual employer, an employment agency, or a union can be sued. Occasionally a court allows individuals to be named if they are in high positions, had responsibility for carrying out the company's sexual harassment policy, and did not do so. This type of liability is far from settled, but usually the victim has the best possibility of receiving adequate restitution for her or his damages from the employer, anyway.

DAMAGES FOR SEXUAL HARASSMENT

The damages that can be claimed in a sexual harassment lawsuit depend on the bases under which the victim is suing. For example, in a lawsuit alleging a violation of common law, such as intentional infliction of emotional distress, the money damages are usually unlimited unless a particular state legislature has placed a limit (called a *cap*) on the amount that any plaintiff can receive in such lawsuits. Under statutes, however, the damages are determined by the specific wording of the law or the court's interpretation of the legislature's intent.

Title VII has been seen as very specific on the damages that can be claimed. A successful victim can first receive what the law calls *equitable damages*—those that are required to make up for lost opportunities caused by the harassment. These may include an order to institute sexual harassment programs, back pay (up to a usual limit of two years), pay while the victim recovers from psychological injury, reinstatement to a lost position, or the awarding of a denied promotion or lost seniority. In addition, attorney fees can be awarded. Since 1991, when it was amended, Title VII also allows a victim to receive pain and suffering damages and, in the case of intentional discrimination, punitive damages. The pain and suffering damages are capped on a sliding scale, depending on the size of the company. This sliding scale allows up to: $50,000 for businesses with 15 to 100 employees, up to $100,000 for 101 to 200 employees, up to $200,000 for 201 to 500 employees, and up to $300,000 for more than 500 employees.

CONCLUSION

While giving a victim the only real opportunity to regain what she or he has lost, the law also requires that some rather high standards be met before it can step in. Although the best change in the workplace will come with training, communication, and understanding, the law, as always, is uniquely able to get the attention of those who may be reticent to move into a new era. Victims with the courage to come forward often find it offers them a chance to even the stakes, giving them the power that was denied them elsewhere to succeed and contribute in the work world.

REFERENCES

Cases

Burns v. McGregor Electronic Industries, 989 F.2d 959 (8th Cir. 1993).
Ellison v. Brady, 924 F.2d 892 (9th Cir. 1991).
Harris v. Forklift Systems, 114 S.Ct. 367 (1993).
Karibian v Columbia University, 14 F.3d 983 (2d Cir. 1994).
Meritor Savings Bank v. Vinson, 477 U.S. 57 (1986).
Robinson v. Jacksonville Shipyards, 760 F. Supp. 1486 (M.D. Fla. 1991).

Article

Abrams, K. (1989). Gender discrimination and the transformation of workplace norms. *Vanderbilt Law Review 42* 1183.

Book

Levy, A. C., & Paludi, M. A. (1996). *Workplace sexual harassment*. Englewood Cliffs, NJ: Prentice Hall.

7

Sexual Victimization: Responses of the U.S. Congress

Michael R. Stevenson

The response of the U.S. Congress to the victimization of women has been necessarily piecemeal. Three prime examples dealt with victims of rape and family violence. The Privacy Protection for Rape Victims Act of 1978 reformed federal rape laws to focus on the defendant's conduct rather than the survivor's past sexual history. The Family Violence Prevention and Services Act of 1984 encouraged and funded shelters for battered women. And the Victims of Crime Act of 1984 created a fund to compensate survivors out of the fines paid by criminals. It granted priority compensation to rape and domestic violence survivors (Biden, 1993).

This approach to legislation concerning survivors of sexual crimes is due, in part, to constitutional constraints on the power of the federal government. Put simply, powers not specifically granted to Congress are left with the states and the people (Wells, 1996). One can argue that states are better equipped to legislate in this area and that it is outside the purview of the federal government to do so, unless there is a compelling federal interest. In the examples described here, Congress has argued that sexual victimization is a federal issue because these crimes violate survivors' civil rights or influence interstate commerce. Occasionally Congress attempts to influence state law by restricting the use of federal funds.

VIOLENCE AGAINST WOMEN ACT OF 1994

After six years of debate, the Violence Against Women Act of 1994 (VAWA) became the first comprehensive federal effort to combat violence against women. Compared with the Civil Rights Act of 1964 and the Americans With Disabilities Act, VAWA has been touted as "one of this country's greatest civil-rights achievements" (Frazee, 1995).

The statute provides that "all persons within the United States shall have the right to be free from crimes of violence motivated by gender" (42 U.S.C.A. 13981(b)) and requires that such crimes be "due, at least in part, to an animus based on the victim's gender" (42 U.S.C.A. 13981 (d)(1)). In other words, to be a crime under this law, the perpetrator must have targeted the victim based on gender. Although intended primarily to protect women in cases of domestic violence, the law is gender neutral and would allow court action regardless of the gender of the perpetrator or the victim.

The bill became law in spite of criticism from a variety of sources. Federal judges worried that its passage would overburden federal courts that were already backlogged. This expected flood of litigation never materialized. Others claimed that domestic violence is an area of family law best left within the jurisdiction of state authorities. One civil rights group claimed that gender bias is too difficult to prove (Frazee, 1995).

Sally Goldfarb (1993), counsel for the Legal Defense and Education Fund of the National Organization for Women (NOW), argued that "the fact that a bill to enhance the rights of women is met with a concern for overloading the federal courts adds a disturbing note of sexism to the debate. . . . The fact that violence against women is widespread would seem to argue in favor of, not against, passing legislation to remedy it" (Goldfarb, 1993, p. H10365). An incensed Representative Patricia Schroeder quipped, "Are they saying it's better for women to put up with this rather than flood the court system?" (quoted in Frazee, 1995).

Senator Orin Hatch, a staunch supporter of the law, used the perpetrators' motives to differentiate the roles of federal and state governments. "If a man rapes a woman while telling her he loves her, that's a far cry from saying he hates her. A lust factor does not spring from animus" (Siegel, 1996, p. 2205). In other words, "Those acts of rape and domestic violence that are motivated by hate properly concern women's status as equal citizens of the United States, while those acts of rape and domestic violence that are motivated by love (or lust) are matters of purely local concern having no bearing on women's status as federal citizens or persons entitled to equal protection of the laws" (Siegel, 1996, p. 2205). Goldfarb (1993) claimed that "federal remedies such as VAWA are needed to reinforce state remedies and to provide a 'back-up' when the state justice system is unable to protect victims' rights adequately" (p. 10364).

Defining violence against women as a form of sex discrimination, the VAWA made gender-based violence a violation of civil rights and entitled victims to compensatory and punitive damages and attorney fees. Under VAWA, crossing state lines to abuse a fleeing spouse or partner became a federal offense. The possession of firearms by persons facing a restraining order on domestic abuse was prohibited. VAWA also gave victims of violent crimes the right to speak at the sentencing hearings of their assailants.

The criminal provisions and the provision ordering states to enforce each other's protective orders in domestic violence cases went into effect on September 13, 1994. Since then, VAWA has been widely ignored by prosecutors. Few cases have been brought, and victims of domestic violence continue to have difficulty getting restraining orders enforced outside of the state where they were issued (Lardner, 1996).

In addition to the criminal provisions, VAWA created a host of grants and training programs to educate police, prosecutors, and judges about violence against women. It authorized funding for new crisis centers, improved lighting for unsafe streets and parks, and a domestic violence hot line (1–800–799–SAFE). It also requires a variety of institutions to collect data and create and submit reports documenting the extent of crimes covered by the law. After signing VAWA into law, President Clinton established the Violence Against Women Office at the Department of Justice. The president also frequently referred to passage of this bill and recited statistics on the number of calls to the hot line during the 1996 presidential campaign.

Although not fully funded, the bill authorized $1.6 billion in spending over six years (Kennedy, 1995; Reske, 1995; Siegel, 1996). Provisions requiring judicial education and training of court personnel on domestic violence and one calling for gender-bias studies in the federal courts were among the sections left unfunded. According to Lardner (1996), "Judges are the least accountable of all public officials, and many prefer to keep it that way" (p. C3).

Examples of judicial gender bias are numerous. In one Florida court, the judge rejected a woman's request for a restraining order against her ex-husband whom she claimed had raped her. When she burst into tears and ran from the courtroom, the judge had her arrested and jailed for a day. A Missouri judge sometimes asked women in his court if they liked being beaten. Another Florida judge, when told that a man had poured lighter fluid on his wife and set her on fire, began singing, "You light up my life." Without the studies authorized by VAWA, the extent of gender bias in the courts is difficult to determine.

The new law has already been challenged in federal court. In one case, a Connecticut woman sought damages from her husband as a result of 17 years of gender-based violence. In the other, a student at Virginia Tech brought suit against two football players she had accused of rape. In the

Connecticut case, the judge refused to dismiss the suit, ruling VAWA was constitutional. In the Virginia case, U. S. district judge Jackson L. Kiser ruled that it was unconstitutional for Congress to allow women the right to sue their attackers for damages. This decision applies only to the Western District of Virginia, but it is likely to be cited by lawyers throughout the country until higher courts rule on the law. It is interesting to note that Judge Kiser is also known for the decision, eventually reversed by the Supreme Court, allowing the all-male Virginia Military Institute to receive state funds as long as a separate program for women was created (Becker-Lausen, 1996; Shear, 1996).

DRUG-INDUCED RAPE PREVENTION ACT OF 1996

Rohypnol, known as the "date-rape drug," is a member of a class of drugs that is used to treat sleep disorders and anxiety disorders and to control seizures. Although not approved for import, sale, or use in the United States, it is a legitimate therapeutic agent that has been approved in several other countries. It is available in Mexico for as little as 50 cents a pill (Congress approves, 1996).

Rohypnol is being abused by addicts to enhance low-quality heroin and in combination with cocaine. It is also used by some for recreational purposes. However, it is best known in the United States for its use to facilitate rape. Drinks spiked with the drug, called "roofies," are illicitly given to unsuspecting victims before they are sexually assaulted.

Rohypnol is a sedative 10 times more powerful than Valium (Importing of, 1996). In addition to intoxicating the victim, the drug has disinhibiting effects and causes memory loss, precluding recall of the crime and the attacker's identity (The new international, 1996).

In October 1996, Congress passed a bill to increase penalties for the illicit use and trafficking of Rohypnol (Congress approves, 1996). Under this act, persons convicted of distributing a controlled substance to an individual with the intent to rape and without their knowledge shall be imprisoned not more that 20 years and fined up to $2 million. The bill also provides stronger penalties for "manufacturing, distributing, dispensing, or possessing with the intent to manufacture, dispense, or distribute" large quantities of Rohypnol (Hatch, 1996).

Interestingly, Senator Joseph Biden (1996) argued that a penalty of up to life in prison for the use of any intoxicant to commit a sexual crime in any federal jurisdiction (Title 18 2241 (b) (2)) was already on the books. In addition to the Drug-induced Rape Prevention Act, there has been some interest in the Senate, as well as the Department of Health and Human Services, to reclassify Rohypnol as a drug with no accepted medical use, similar to heroin and LSD (Importing of, 1996).

INTERSTATE STALKING PUNISHMENT AND PREVENTION ACT OF 1996

During the early 1990s state legislatures began passing laws prohibiting stalking, "harassing or threatening behavior which an individual engages in repeatedly, such as following a person, appearing at a person's home or place of business, making harassing phone calls, leaving written messages or objects or vandalizing a person's property" (Thomas, 1992, p. 2).

Most stalkers are heterosexual men whose victims are usually their former lovers or spouses. Without antistalking laws, such behavior would not be considered a criminal violation, and the victim's only recourse is a civil protection order. Such court actions order an individual to refrain from contacting or coming within the vicinity of another person. The target of a protection order can be fined or incarcerated for violating the order. Civil protection orders are difficult to obtain and to enforce and may not provide sufficient protection for victims. Under the civil protection system, the victim is responsible for initiating legal action. This can be time-consuming, expensive, and emotionally burdensome. Antistalking laws invoke the criminal law system and place the burden of enforcement on the state rather than the victim (Thomas, 1992).

Although most states have some form of antistalking statute, stalkers could not be charged if they went to another state without federal intervention. As a result, Senator Kay Bailey Hutchison introduced a bill making stalking a federal crime if a person traveled across a state line while stalking or if the behavior occurred on an Indian reservation, a military base, or other federal property. Under the statute, it is a felony to cross a state line with the intent to injure or harass, and in the course of, or as a result of, such travel, place the victim in reasonable fear of death or serious bodily injury to the victim or a member of the victim's immediate family, or in violation of a protective order. The victim need not be the offender's spouse or intimate partner, as was the case in previous legislation.

As surprising as it may seem, this legislation stirred considerable acrimony. The bill stalled in the Senate for months. Eventually Senator Frank Lautenberg proposed an amendment to the bill that would prohibit anyone convicted of domestic violence from possessing a firearm. The senator said in a speech on the Senate floor:

It is truly remarkable. The Senate is being held hostage and so is the American public for one reason and one reason only: So that we do not take away guns from wife beaters and child abusers. We want to make sure they can get their gun if they want it. That is why some 2,000–plus women a year get killed by men who have already beat them up, have been hauled into court, and in many cases convicted of misdemeanors, and then they want their gun back. Around here, we want to make sure those nice boys can get their guns. . . . It is pretty simple. My amendment stands for the simple proposition that if you beat your wife, if you beat your kid, you should not have a gun. It says "beat your wife, lose your gun; abuse your child, lose your gun." It is pretty simple. It is little more than common sense. (Lautenberg, 1996, S9458)

Senator Hutchison was supportive of the Lautenberg amendment. However, it was August before the bill was brought to the floor of the Senate for debate. The end of the 104th Congress was only weeks away, and there was little time to amend the bill in the Senate and return it to the House for further debate. Rather than let the amendment prevent the bill from becoming law, Senator Hutchison asked that the two issues be separated such that the antistalking bill could be delivered to the president before the end of the legislative session. Although the Senate eventually passed the bill with the Lautenberg amendment intact, opposition in the House prevented the bill from moving forward. In the end, the original version of the bill was passed into law as an amendment to a piece of unrelated legislation.

CHILD SEX OFFENDER REGISTRATION AND NOTIFICATION LAWS

Named for an 11-year-old Minnesota boy who was abducted from his home and never found, an amendment to the 1994 federal crime law, the Jacob Wetterling Crimes Against Children and Sexually Violent Offender Registration Act, required states to register and track convicted sex offenders for 10 years after their release from prison and to notify law enforcement officials when criminal sex offenders moved into their communities. This law allowed, but did not require, states to make public notification of the whereabouts of paroled sex offenders (Harris, 1996; Gray, 1996).

Megan Kanka was a seven-year-old New Jersey girl who was allegedly raped and murdered by a neighbor twice convicted of sexual offenses. Her story sparked state legislators to enact a state law, named Megan's Law in her memory. This action was followed by federal legislation of the same name, which required states and localities to inform communities when dangerous sexual offenders are about to be released from prison.

Since passage of the Jacob Wetterling Act, all states except Massachusetts and the District of Columbia have adopted a registration and tracking system for paroled sex offenders. However, few states have adopted laws that require public notification. The federal version of Megan's Law requires states to publicize information about child molesters and sexually violent offenders. However, it allows local lawmakers to set guidelines on the amount of publicity offenders will receive and how the information will be disseminated. Failure to enact state laws would result in a reduction of federal crime-fighting funds (Gray, 1996; Ingram, 1996).

Taking this issue further, President Clinton endorsed a Senate proposal to create a national registry of sex offenders. Such a database would make it easier for law enforcement agencies to track offenders across state lines. The Senate bill would require the FBI to establish a database to track the whereabouts and movement of every person convicted of a criminal offense against a minor, every person convicted of a sexually violent offense, and every person who is considered a sexually violent predator (Amendment to HR 1533).

Sex offender registration and notification laws are based on two unsupported premises. Federal legislators have assumed that convicted sex offenders are a greater threat to children than other classes of people and that child sex offenders are more likely than others to become repeat offenders. As is the case with nonconsensual sexual behavior between adults, most children are sexually abused by someone they know and trust. In the case of children, this is most often a member of their family or a close family friend. The majority of these cases are never reported, and the perpetrators are not prosecuted. As a result, their names would never appear on a sex offender register. Perhaps more important, focusing on convicted offenders "may divert the discussion on intrafamilial sexual abuse and prevent the perpetrators of this abuse from being discovered" (Earl-Hubbard, 1996, p. 852).

Contrary to the data presented to Congress during the debate on these laws, success rates for intensive treatment programs can be over 90 percent. Furthermore, requiring that convicted child sex offenders register and requiring public release of this information could result in decreased reporting of the crime, decreased participation in treatment, and, in the end, increased incidence of the behaviors the laws are intended to deter or punish. These laws may also be ineffective because "the penalties for not registering are negligible, and the intrusion and risks associated with compliance so severe, that many offenders do not register, and law enforcement lacks the resources or time to locate or investigate those who do not comply or who submit false information" (Earl-Hubbard, 1996, p. 861).

State and federal child sex offender registration and notification laws may be challenged in court under the Eighth, Fifth, and Fourteenth amendments to the Constitution. The Eighth amendment prohibits the infliction of cruel and unusual punishment, excessive fines, and excessive bail. The Fifth and Fourteenth Amendments prohibit the government from depriving an individual of life, liberty, or property without due process of law.

Although consensus has not yet been reached (Fein, 1995; Martone, 1995), requiring individuals to register with the government can be construed as punishment, and the vigilantism and public humiliation that can result from community notification may be deemed cruel and unusual. In addition, community notification may deprive the offender of "liberty." Offenders are rarely provided the opportunity for a hearing. As a result, community notification requirements may lead to the deprivation of liberty without due process. Disclosure of private information, such as the offender's home address and telephone number, and interference with family relations and job opportunities have been construed by the courts as deprivation of a liberty interest. In striking down the law, the New Jersey Supreme Court held that the community notification provision in New Jersey's Megan's Law imposed extra punishment on people already sentenced for their crimes (Van Natta, 1996) and implicated an offender's liberty interest because the law allowed the publication of private information (Earl-Hubbard, 1996).

Although developed in reaction to real pain and sorrow, sex offender registration and notification laws may be both unconstitutional and ineffective. They may lull communities into a false sense of security, create a climate of vigilante justice, and deflect attention and scarce resources from children who face an intrafamilial or unregistered abuser. They may also prevent convicted abusers from seeking treatment (Earl-Hubbard, 1996; Martone, 1995).

FEMALE GENITAL MUTILATION

Female genital mutilation (FGM) is a crude and painful ritual, often performed without anesthetic by untrained people, which involves removing portions of a young woman's genitals. The practice has been imported to the United States by immigrants from Africa and the Middle East. It is considered by some as a way to perpetuate customs that regulate and keep control over the body and sexuality of the individual. Family honor, cleanliness, protection against spells, insurance of virginity and faithfulness to the husband, or simply terrorizing women out of sex are used as justifications for the practice (Sarkis, 1995).

Senator Harry Reid has long been an opponent to this practice, claiming that "if there were ever an example of sexism, this is it" (Congressional Record, S4287). In 1994, he facilitated the passage of a "sense-of-the-Senate" resolution condemning the ritual. Since then, he has introduced legislation to outlaw the procedure on numerous occasions In 1996, he proposed an amendment outlawing female genital mutilation in the United States and making it a basis for asylum—Specifically, "whoever knowingly circumcises, excises, or infibulates the whole or any part of the labia majora or labia minora or clitoris of another person who has not attained the age of 18 years shall be fined under this title or imprisoned not more than 5 years, or both" (Congressional Record, S4490).

Senator Reid eventually modified the amendment so that it simply outlaws female genital mutilation, stripping it of the provision that would make female genital mutilation a justification for asylum by women fleeing cultures where the procedure is practiced. In support of Senator Reid's efforts, Senator Alan Simpson, a leading figure on immigration issues, described female genital mutilation as "a serious issue. It is an issue of assault. It is an issue of culture" (Congressional Record, S4490).

As Senator Simpson explained, the problem with using female genital mutilation as a justification for pleas of person seeking asylum is that when the asylee is joined by her family, sometimes this includes the perpetrator. Senator Simpson expressed interest in holding hearings on the issue of asylum and added that criminalizing the act in the United States would solve a large part of the problem.

The Immigration and Naturalization Service (INS) believes that claims for asylum on the basis of female genital mutilation should be considered on a case-by-case basis. Although the INS established guidelines in 1995 allowing the use of female genital mutilation as a justification for asylum, it has taken some time for the INS to act favorably on such a case. In fact, while debate in the Senate continued on this issue, Fauziya Kasinga, a 19-year-old woman from Togo, became the first woman to be granted political asylum in the United States to avoid being subjected to female genital mutilation. The Board of Immigration Appeals, the highest immigration court in the country, ruled 11 to 1 in her favor.

In an extension of her remarks on the House floor, Representative Patricia Schroeder, author of a House bill to outlaw FGM, described the case:

While in several INS detention facilities, Fauziya was shackled in chains, tear-gassed and beaten, and forced to spend her 18th and 19th birthdays in prisons intermingled with drug users and murderers. Thus, the decision the 11 Board members took in stating that FGM, an explicit violation of human rights, is a basis for political asylum is long overdue. (Congressional Record, E1103)

Thanks to the efforts of Congresswoman Schroeder and Senator Reid, FGM became illegal in the United States as of March 29, 1997. The provisions were included in the Department of Defense appropriations bill signed into law by President Clinton on September 30, 1996. In addition to outlawing the procedure, the bill included language that will discourage financial investment in foreign governments that have no education initiative concerning FGM. It also requires INS to notify immigrants and nonimmigrants entering the United States from countries where FGM is practiced of the health and legal consequences of FGM.

CONCLUSION

Efforts to improve the lives of survivors of sexual victimization are not always successful. For example, some women's advocacy groups have claimed that violence against women constitutes the largest category of hate crime (Jacobs & Henry, 1996). However, the Hate Crimes Statistics Act, which requires the attorney general to collect data "about crimes that manifest evidence of prejudice based on race, religion, disability, sexual orientation, or ethnicity" and has resulted in a federal data base on bias-motivated crime, does not include gender (Congressional Record, S5458). Adding gender as a counted category has been debated for some time (Fernandez, 1991), but there is little hope that such data will be gathered under this act by the federal government in the near future. In spite of the advances made under VAWA, if members of Congress cannot agree on whether or how to count hate crimes against women, it is unlikely that other hate crimes statutes in the U.S. Code will soon be amended to include gender.

Notwithstanding notable failures, the U.S. Congress has not been blind to the needs of survivors of sexual victimization. Through the dedication of enlightened members of congress and Congressional staff, laws protecting survivors and the judicial system as a whole have gradually improved. However, as budgets continue to tighten proponents of further reform face an uphill battle.

My experience as an adviser to a U.S. senator underscored the need for an expanded role for scholars in the policymaking process. I was repeatedly faced with congressional staff who did not understand the value of research findings or what the social and behavioral science might have to offer. Staff rely heavily on information provided by the media, advocacy organizations, personal networks, and analysts who work within the government. They have neither the time nor the expertise to do their own in-depth analysis. As Smith and Torrey (1996) suggest,

The burden of communication rests with the behavioral and social scientists to demonstrate that they have valuable, concrete evidence that can be used to address social issues. The use of evidence by the public and its elected officials will help ensure a more rational dialogue on societal issues. (p. 612)

The academic and scholarly communities need not remain disconnected from policymakers. If we want research findings to provide the basis for sound policy decisions, publishing in refereed journals is not enough. Researchers and scholars must be willing to provide research findings to legislative staff and advocacy networks in forms they can use. We must share what we learn from our research with those in positions of power and we must learn to work with the media. We must also convey to students the importance of understanding how research findings are useful in the policy-making arena and encourage those with the interest and aptitude to pursue careers in public policy.

ACKNOWLEDGMENT

I am deeply indebted to the American Psychological Association Congressional Fellowship Program for the opportunity to serve as a senior congressional fellow in the office of U.S. Senator Paul Simon from August 1995 to August 1996.

REFERENCES

Becker-Lausen, E. (1996, October). Violence victims fight civil hurdles: Suites challenge a federal law that addresses gender-based violence. *APA Monitor*, p. 22.

Biden, J. (1996). Violence against women: The congressional response. *American Psychologist, 48*(10), 1059–1061.

Congress approves bill that bans date-rape drug. (1996, October 4). *USA Today*, p. 3A.

Earl-Hubbard, M. L. (1996). The child sex offender registration laws: The punishment, liberty deprivation, and unintended results associated with the scarlet letter laws of the 1990s. *Northwestern University Law Review, 90*(2), 788–862.

Fein, B. (1995). Community self-defense laws are constitutionally sound. *ABA Journal, 81*, 38.

Fernandez, J. M. (1991). Bringing hate crimes into focus. *Harvard Civil Rights—Civil Liberties Law Review, 26*(1), 261–293.

Frazee, D. (1995, August 24). Court TV we'd like to see: A plain English guide to the Violence Against Women Act. *On the Issues: The Progressive Woman's Quarterly* (online journal).

Goldfarb, S. (1993, November 20). Statement of NOW Legal Defense and Education Fund on the Violence Against Women Act, H.R. 1133 before the Subcommittee on Civil and Constitutional Rights; Committee on the Judiciary, House of Representatives. *Congressional Record—House*, 103rd Cong. 1st Sess. H10363.

Gray, J. (1996, May 10). Senate approves measure requiring states to warn communities about sex offenders. *New York Times*, p. A28.

Harris, J. F. (1996, June 23). President endorses sex offender registry; Reno to report on a national tracking system. *Washington Post*, p. A19.

Hatch, O. (1996, August 2). The Drug-Induced Rape Prevention Act of 1996. *Congressional Record—Senate*, 104th Cong. 2nd Sess. S9593.

Importing of sedative rohypnol nixed. (1996, April 25). *Facts on File, 56*, p. 285.

Ingram, C. (1996, June 12). Bill to publicize locations of sex offenders gains; Children: State Senate panel approves version of federal "Megan's law." Failure to enact legislation could lead to loss in crime-fighting funds. *Los Angeles Times*, p. A3.

Jacobs, J. B., & Henry, J. S. (1996). The social construction of a hate crime epidemic. *Journal of Criminal Law and Criminology, 86*, 366–391.

Kennedy, E. (1995, March 21). President Clinton implements the Violence Against Women Act. *Congressional Record—Senate*, 104th Cong 1st Sess. S4210.

Lardner, G. (1996, June 2). The stalking game: Our anti-abuse laws are tougher, but our prosecutors aren't. *Washington Post*, p. C3.

Lautenberg, (1996, August 2). Lautenberg amendment to the stalking bill. *Congressional Record*, 104th Cong. 2nd Sess. S9458–S9460.

Martone, E. (1995). Mere illusion of safety creates climate of vigilante justice. *ABA Journal, 81*, 39.

Reske, H. J. (1995, January 20). An untested remedy for abused women. *ABA Journal*, p. 20.

Sarkis, M. (1995). *What is FGM?* http://hamp.hampshire.edu/mnbf94/whatisFGM.htm/.

Shear, M. (1996, July 30). Judge rejects U.S. law for abuse victims: Allowing women to sue ruled unconstitutional. *Washington Post*, p. A1.

Siegel, R. B. (1996). "The rule of love": Wife beating as prerogative and privacy. *Yale Law Journal, 105*, 2117–2207.

Smith, P. M., & Torrey, B. B. (1996, February 2). The future of the behavioral and social sciences. *Science, 271*, 612.

The new international threat of date-rape drug trafficking. 104th Cong., 2nd
    Sess. (1996) Testimony of Senator Joseph R. Biden, Jr., Committee on
    Foreign Relations, Subcommittee on the Western Hemisphere.
Thomas, K. R. (1992, September 26). *Anti-stalking statutes: Background and
    constitutional analysis.* (Congressional Research Service Report No.
    92–735 A).
Van Natta, D. (1996, March 22). Law tracking sex offenders faces setback. *New
    York Times*, B1.
Wells, W. G. Jr. (1996). *Working with Congress: A practical guide for scientists
    and engineers* (2nd ed.). Washington DC: American Association for the
    Advancement of Science.

PART VI

SEXUAL VICTIMIZATION: RESOURCES FOR TEACHING, RESEARCH, AND ADVOCACY

8

Parental Kidnapping and Child Abuse: What Is the Appropriate Intervention?

Donna Linder

The majority of missing children in America have been abducted not by a stranger but by a relative or parent. This phenomenon is explored in depth in the *National Incidence Studies of Missing, Abducted, Runaway, and Thrownaway Children in America* (NISMART) (Klain, 1990), a study conducted by the U.S. Department of Justice, Office of Juvenile Justice and Delinquency Prevention (OJJDP). According to the NISMART research, an estimated 354,100 children were abducted by a parent or family member in 1988. This is a staggering figure with profound implications regarding the challenge courts face to meet the needs of children and parents.

EFFECTS OF KIDNAPPING ON CHILDREN

An article in the *Missing Children Minnesota Journal* (1995) is particularly eloquent on the effect of kidnapping on a 2 ½-year-old girl. The article is a victim impact statement presented by a mother at a criminal court hearing. Her daughter was abducted out of the country by the father and kept for 22 months. The mother described her little girl prior to the abduction as a happy, generous, outgoing child who loved dolls, loved having her picture taken, and was generally well adjusted. (We note that although this story is about an abducting father, parental abduction is not sex specific. The current Child Find of America statistics indicate that of the parents who call the hot lines searching for their children, 65% are fathers and 35% are mothers.)

When the little girl was returned 22 months later, she was thin and pale and covered with bug bites. Her baby teeth were decayed and black, she was biting her nails, and she no longer knew any English. She hung her head and growled when anyone spoke to her. She ate with her hands; she did not know how to turn on water faucets; she did not know how to use a toilet; and she took frequent cold bird baths in the tub. The mother described her as wild and animal-like-snarling, growling, and breaking everything she could get her hands on.

In the seven months since she has been home, her behavior has swung between passive and baby-like and highly aggressive. She regressed to the age she had been when she was abducted, wearing a diaper and crying and wanting to be rocked. At the same time she became terribly protective of her house, her food, and her dolls, often yelling at her dolls and telling them to shut up. She wet her bed and had nightmares.

This is a heartbreaking story, and fortunately not all abducted children are subjected to such severe neglect and abuse. Nonetheless, research shows that victims of abduction may experience serious psychological consequences upon their return, such as mistrust of intimate relationships, constant anxiety, guilt for not stopping the abduction or for loving the abductor, fear of abandonment, a feeling of responsibility for the abduction, cognitive or language problems, developmental delay, and stress-related ailments (Tedisco & Paludi, 1996). In addition to the emotional turmoil, many children suffer from inadequate schooling, poor nutrition, unstable lifestyles, and isolation and loneliness.

LINKS AMONG FAMILY VIOLENCE, CHILD ABUSE, AND PARENTAL KIDNAPPING

Awareness of the damage inflicted on children by parental kidnapping, itself a form of child abuse, reveals the direct links among family violence, child abuse, and parental kidnapping. Domestic violence occurs at all levels of society and is the leading cause of injury to women in the United States. Child abuse is present in 70% of families in which there is spouse abuse, and the severity of the child abuse generally parallels the severity of the spouse abuse (Klain, 1995). It is important to recognize that both battered parents and batterers abduct their children and that they do so for very different reasons.

Abused parents frequently attempt to protect themselves by fleeing with their children. Although flight to avoid abuse is clearly not a solution to the violent relationship, many battered parents see it as their only option. Unfortunately, the risk of abuse to children increases as the battered parent attempts to leave and the abusive parent seeks to continue domination over the family.

Batterers often abduct children as the ultimate weapon against their partners, especially following separation where abduction or the threat of abduction is the only "battering technique" left.

APPROPRIATE INTERVENTION STRATEGIES

Parents who are searching for their children and parents who are on the run with their children are in crisis. Intervening in parental abduction situations is particularly challenging because of the immediacy of the problem and the multitude of factors involved. The process of assessing the appropriate intervention must take into account who the individuals are; the dynamics of their relationship in relation to substance abuse, domestic violence, and their ability to cooperate with each other; the parents' marital status; the custody status in the court; and the motivation for abduction.

Not all parental abductions are motivated by domestic violence. Callers to the hot lines at Child Find also cite the following reasons: dissatisfaction with the court-ordered custody decision, denial of visitation, nonpayment of child support, revenge or retribution for the breakup of the relationship, and anger or dislike for the other parent's new partner or lifestyle.

Given the myriad influences at play in families where abduction is a problem, there is a range of appropriate intervention strategies: psychological and substance abuse counseling, mediation, legal representation, police and FBI investigation, and support from other parents who have experience with parental abduction.

The remainder of this chapter discusses Child Find of America's 10-year experience with mediating parental abductions and its current focus on creating a national parental support network for cases for which mediation is not an appropriate intervention.

MEDIATION OF PARENTAL ABDUCTION SITUATIONS

Recognizing the potential value of mediation in parental abduction situations that do not involve domestic violence, Child Find of America developed a free, over-the-phone mediation program in 1986 to help prevent and resolve parental abductions. A toll-free 800 number (1-800-292-9688; callers outside the United States must call the business line at 1-914-255-1848) offers free professional mediation services to parents who have abducted their child, who are contemplating abducting their child, or whose court-ordered custody or visitation is being denied. Since many family abductions involve transporting the child to another state, phone mediation can be especially effective when face-to-face mediation is impractical or impossible.

All parents who call Child Find's hot line describe complex family dynamics, and many of them are struggling with custody issues made more complicated by a lack of uniform cooperation between states in court procedures. Child Find's mediation program is not intended to serve parents who are disputing custody, unless that dispute threatens or has resulted in the abduction of a child. The focus of the program is on the legal environment of the child.

Central to Child Find's mediation program are pro bono mediators, most of whom are practitioner members of the Academy of Family Mediators (AFM). These professionals offer parents the opportunity to resolve conflicts that have caused or could cause the abduction of a child. Child Find's mediation program has been supported by the National Institute for Dispute Resolution, several foundations, and a three-year $225,000 competitive grant from the U.S. Department of Justice, Office of Juvenile Justice and Delinquency Prevention.

How the Mediation Program Works

Parents calling the 800 hot line initially speak with Child Find's mediation coordinator who screens each call, explains the mediation program, and encourages the caller to try the mediation process. When a caller agrees to mediation, the coordinator assigns a volunteer professional mediator to the case. The mediator contacts the parent who initially called Child Find; ascertains his or her circumstances and goals for mediation; contacts the other parent and offers mediation; screens cases for allegations of abuse, secures the commitment to mediate from both parents; interacts with police, attorneys, or court officials where appropriate; and distributes to the parents and Child Find any agreements reached through mediation. Child Find also has a mediation consultant who is available to advise the pro bono mediators and mediation coordinator as they work with parents. The mediation coordinator is selected from the roster of Child Find's volunteer mediators and serves a two-year term.

Protocols for Offering Mediation

The parents who call Child Find's mediation program are all in pain, and many feel that this program is their last hope. Consequently, Child Find strives to offer mediation to as broad a group of parents as possible. Our current protocols for providing mediation services are as follows:

1. Mediation services to searching (left-behind) parents who are being denied their court-ordered custody or visitation. Some of these parents know where their child is, and our mediator contacts the restraining parent directly. Other parents may have an idea of where their child may be or may have reason to believe that a relative has contact with the restraining parent and the child. In these cases, the mediator reaches out to the abducting parent through the family in order to offer mediation.

2. Mediation to all in-flight (restraining) parents. The welfare of a child who is in hiding with a parent is often seriously jeopardized. These children may not be attending school regularly or at all, they may not be allowed outside to play, and they may move and change names frequently. They are always transient, and their living conditions may be desperate. Therefore, it is not necessary for custody to have been established in order for Child Find to offer mediation to the parent who is on the run with a child. Our focus is on assisting parents to create a healthy environment for their children, and our coordinator offers mediation to all in-flight parents.

3. Mediation to parents who are contemplating abduction. The mediation coordinator screens these calls carefully to determine whether mediation is the appropriate intervention. Some callers are seeking legal advice. Others relate stories of domestic violence or substance abuse. In these situations, the coordinator makes referrals to the appropriate programs or agencies that can help these parents.

4. Mediation on international parental abductions on a case-by-case basis. Child Find's mediation program has been effective in resolving international parental abductions. Over-the-phone mediation has been particularly appropriate when parents are separated by long geographical distances and time zones. As a charity, Child Find may be able to help in circumstances where other types of agencies or organizations might encounter political or cultural barriers.

Factors Influencing Parental Abduction Mediation

The Child Find of America mediation program operates on three premises: (1) the collaborative process of mediation is a viable alternative to the adversarial process of litigation for resolving disputes involving the welfare of children; (2) parents who may not be able to cooperate with each other on their own to resolve parenting issues may be able to do so with the aid of a mediator; and (3) parents know better than anyone else what is best for their family, through mediation, they may be able to create the best parenting agreement for their family.

Factors that influence the outcome of these parental abduction mediations are basic: the parents' willingness to cooperate with the process and with each other, the presence of domestic or substance abuse, and the timing of the intervention. Ideally, we like to see these parents gain access to parenting classes and to mediation before their circumstances become so desperate that abduction appears to be the only option. In the meantime, Child Find is reaching out to professionals who intervene on behalf of children so that they will know our mediation program exists and who it serves.

WHEN MEDIATION IS NOT A VIABLE ALTERNATIVE: THE PARENTAL SUPPORT NETWORK

Family mediators are generally in agreement that mediation is not an appropriate intervention in most domestic violence situations. We know that the dynamics of domestic violence do not place parents in equal positions of power, and mediation is not advisable if a parent has been a victim of violence by the other parent. The playing field simply is not level, and the abused parent has a greater need for an advocate than for a neutral mediator. Therefore, other forms of family intervention besides mediation are urgently needed to protect children from kidnapping and the resulting abuse.

Child Find is proposing a team approach in its efforts to help parents resolve their conflicts. In this ideal vision, this team would be a national parental support network consisting of our volunteer mediators; pro bono attorneys, therapists, and social workers in each state; and other parents who have been involved in parental abduction situations. The goal of the national parental support network is to give parents for whom mediation is not an option appropriate referrals to individuals and agencies that can effectively intervene in their specific circumstances.

There is an urgent need for pro bono legal advice and representation for families with children. Legal Aid cannot handle the volume of family law custody cases and, in some counties, does not even take domestic law cases. Most of the callers to the Child Find hot lines cannot afford to pay an attorney or have exhausted their financial resources in an extended custody battle. And many parents involved in a parental abduction situation are contending with complicated legal issues that cross over state lines, which may necessitate legal representation in two states.

Less well known is the existing need for support services for families who are reuniting with a missing child. The story outlined at the beginning of this chapter poignantly describes the moment-to-moment chaos arising from the abducted child's emotional turmoil on returning home. Child Find anticipates that the national parental support network will augment its work in locating missing children. The network will provide parents with contacts to professionals who can guide them as they help their child adjust to the security and stability of their home. The network will also act as a self-help service for parents by putting them in touch with other parents who have experienced the pain of losing a child and the struggle to help that child reunite with the family.

SOME HAPPY ENDINGS

A father from Florida called for help in finding his two sons. He was convinced that the mother's family was involved in hiding her and the boys, and asked if Child Find would help him talk to the family. Our mediator spoke with the father and developed some strategies for contacting the mother's family. Although the mother would not return the mediator's calls, the maternal grandmother agreed to encourage communication between the parents. When the mediator next spoke with the grandmother, she reported that the father and mother had talked with each other "without screaming" and that the children were back with their father. She said that the parents plan to work out a parenting plan through the courts.

A mother in Pennsylvania called Child Find for help finding her 2-year-old son, who had been abducted by his father. The parents, who were never married, had been separated for a year and had an informal parenting agreement where the child lived with his mother during the week and visited with his father at the father's parents' house over the weekend. The mother said that she and the father were scheduled to go to custody mediation when he ran with the child. The mother asked for our help in contacting the paternal grandparents in an effort to offer the abducting father the opportunity to mediate. At first the grandfather was suspicious of our mediator's motives and credentials. After speaking with the Child Find office, he agreed to talk with our mediator. He told the mediator that he and his wife had been trying to get custody of the child themselves. When the mediator next spoke with the mother, the child had been returned to her. The mother said that the mediator's intervention with the grandfather gave "authenticity" to her plea for her child and her promises to seek visitation for the father.

A father in Ohio called Child Find in 1996 saying that his ex-wife had never honored his court-ordered "liberal" visitation awarded to him in 1990. He said that the last time he saw his three children was in April 1993, and the last time he spoke with them was on Thanksgiving 1994. The father said he is tired of waiting for things to change, that he felt very frustrated and was considering kidnapping the children. He called for mediation in hopes that it would prevent him from abducting his children. Our mediator spoke with both parents. The mother, who was angry at first, became cooperative and revealed that the reason she was denying the father his visitation was that she had never received her support payments. Subsequent conversations with the mediator revealed that the father had been making his payments, and the state confirmed that he had been making them, but the mother had never received them. Once the confusion over the child support was clarified, the parents easily agreed to specific times for phone calls and visits between the children and their father. The parents expressed their appreciation for the mediator's help in working out a specific parenting schedule. They also made plans to work together to track down the support payments.

We received a call from a mother in France. The father, in California, was refusing to return their 13-year-old son after the child's summer visit with him. The parents had never married, and there were no court orders for custody or visitation. The parents had a standing agreement that the child would spend summers in California, and this was the first time this verbal agreement had broken down. The father said that he was concerned about learning disabilities he thought his son might have and about the mother's lifestyle in France. The mediator helped the parents discuss these concerns and assisted them in finding a therapist who could test the child for learning disabilities and other adjustive disorders. The therapist found the boy to be healthy and free of any dysfunction. Following this evaluation, the mediator brought the parents together on a conference call with himself and the therapist. The therapist counseled the parents over the phone and provided them with factual information about their son. This conference call enabled the parents to reach some agreements about how they would relate with each other in the future about their child. The child returned to France shortly after.

CONCLUSION

Parental abduction is a frequent occurrence in the United States today—much more frequent than stranger abduction (Tedisco & Paludi, 1996). Parents who abduct their children do so for completely personal and unique reasons—among them, an attempt to protect themselves and their children from family abuse, an expression of extreme frustration with an ex-spouse or ex-partner, or dissatisfaction with the legal remedies available to parenting issues. Each act of parental abduction is also a desperate attempt to maintain contact with their child. Unfortunately, parental abduction has been shown to have serious consequences on children's physical and mental health.

Appropriate intervention in parental abduction situations, which is dependent on a multitude of factors, includes counseling, legal advocacy, mediation, police and FBI investigation, and parental support. Child Find of America's parental abduction mediation program is 10 years old. Free, professional, over-the-phone mediation is offered to parents who have taken their children, are considering taking their children, or whose court ordered-custody or visitation is being denied.

When mediation is not a viable intervention, Child Find is proposing a national parental support network that consists of mediators, social workers, therapists, lawyers, and parents. The goals of this network are to refer parents to agencies and individuals who can effectively intervene in their family situation, guide parents during reunification after Child Find has located their missing child, and improve the parents' ability to help themselves through contact with other families who have experienced kidnapping and reunification.

REFERENCES

Klain, E. J. (1990). *National incidence studies, missing, abducted, runaway, and thrownaway children in America.* Washington, DC: U.S. Department of Justice.

Klain, E. J. (1995, March). *Parental kidnapping, domestic violence, and child abuse: Changing legal responses to related violence.* Alexandria, VA: American Prosecutors Research Institute's National Center for Prosecution of Child Abuse Parental Kidnapping Project.

One mother's pain . . . one daughter's pain: The sad realization of parental abduction. (1995–1996, Winter). *Missing Children Minnesota Journal*, 3–4.

Tedisco, J. N., & Paludi, M. A. (1996). *Missing children: A psychological approach to understanding the causes and consequences of stranger and non-stranger abduction of children.* Albany: State University of New York Press.

9

One Woman's Story: The Development of S.E.S.A.M.E.

Mary Ann Werner

Educator sexual abuse, like all other victimization, has at its core a traumatizing violation of trust and an inherent imbalance of power. Betrayal by a school staff authority figure is an offense committed by an individual. Compounding this blow is the betrayal rendered by the entire publicly supported educational establishment. This treachery is based on the institution's failure to fulfill the victim's and the public's expectation of protection, accountability, compassion, and rectification.

The disadvantage of power inequity for the student begins when the teacher uses his or her authority to manipulate and seduce. Educator sexual abuse victims and their families are repeatedly disadvantaged by institutional power from disclosure on to any possible activism in attempts to right the wrong done to them.

As the parent of two adult sons sexually victimized by their former high school teacher, I can personalize the effects of educator sexual abuse. This chronicle will, primarily, reflect betrayal at the institutional level.

At the time of the accidental disclosure of our older son's prior sexual abuse by his teacher, I processed the information much akin to receiving a medical diagnosis for some baffling, recurrent symptoms over a long time period. Here was the explanation for Frank's repeated withdrawals from our family. Here was a reason for his inability to progress with life's normal milestones: a decent paying job; close, sustaining friendships; or an intimate relationship. His silences, his difficulties with academics, and his aloneness now became understandable. Frank's seeming lack of will and caring, about himself and life in general, now had a basis. His defeatist posture, with head hung low and eyes that avoided contact with us all, at last took on meaning to me.

As I would with any family medical problem, I sought out professional advice and did my own research. Educator sexual abuse however, can present a patient (victim) who refuses treatment, an invading pathological agent (perpetrating teacher) that disappears on the microscope slide, and a breeding environment for the pathogen (educational institution) that defies evaluation by defensively blocking all access to itself.

I felt as if I were shadow boxing with no sense of direction of where and how to strike, no firm ground to stand on, no ropes to define boundaries, and no cheering crowds urging support and perseverance. I collapsed into a lonely, exhausting abyss.

During sleepless nights, I replayed Frank's infancy, childhood, adolescence. During his high school years I was doing . . . what? Involved in a business partnership with my husband that consumed us seven days a week. Frank participated in what sports? We attended how many parent-teacher conferences? What was said during those meetings? When did Frank refuse to take the school bus for the long, boring rides to our rural high school? When did this teacher start picking Frank up at our driveway? Why didn't I question Frank's Sunday afternoons spent at Mr. Zim's house watching TV football? How could I have been so lax? Stupid? Trusting?

Day after day I pulled out old appointment calendars and family photo albums. What grade was Frank in when he was seventeen? What were the other kids doing that year? Was that the year my husband's sister died? Josephine was married that spring. Frank was in the wedding. Clean cut; good posture; trim, muscular, karate-disciplined body—a far cry from the prone, defeated body huddled under bed covers upstairs that day 10 years later.

The family snapshots that shook me most were two taken at Frank's high school graduation party at our home. One showed Frank with his arm around his steady girlfriend. The other showed Mr. Zim and his wife bearing gifts for the happy graduate.

I still tremble when the force of this emotional craziness hits me. How did a 17- and 18-year-old kid survive such a bombardment of sexual conflict? Months later, when I was told of the earlier suicide of another 18-year-old close student friend of Mr. Zim, I fully understood the depth of such a sexual conflict.

I took long solitary walks. I teared up when a neighbor casually told of her 27-year-old son's fast-rising career in Texas, his marriage, and his new house. At our home, as cocky as a 17-year-old, Frank went on interviews for entry-level jobs. His returns in my borrowed car were quiet and difficult to watch. Ten vital developmental years had been stolen from him, as surely as if he'd been in a coma.

I didn't want to socialize. I only wanted to read about child abuse, write in my journal, and be by myself. I was grieving with no death notice to alert friends (or myself). I suppose I grieved the loss of a dream for my child and the loss of my self-esteem as a "good" mom. I was on the bottom. I was what I saw in Frank's unwashed, uncombed hair, neither of us comprehending and both of us miserable.

A regular churchgoer, I now found myself clenching my fists during homilies. They sounded so smug. I looked around at the members of the congregation, thinking, "You patsies! You believe that goo? I'm hurting. Why aren't you helping me?" But of course no one knew about Frank. Still, church made me angry. I tried other denominations. Finally, one Sunday I walked out in the middle of a service.

This anger at the church puzzled me. Over a year went by before I could connect my crisis of faith to the betrayal I felt from another institution, the educational establishment. I had been raised in a religion that greatly discouraged the questioning of authority—the church's certainly, as well as parental, school, and governmental. I'd meekly followed that tenet, only gradually dispelling its authenticity as I adopted more of a feminist mindset. Belatedly I woke up. The church was *my* nonoffending parent, or so I rationalized. I did what I was told. Why didn't it protect me and my family? I miss the comfort of its bosom. I miss the shared goals and projects of its people, people who graced my life with dependable relationships. I've not returned to the faith community. I doubt I will. Good folks ask for me. I just feel alien in their midst. I doubt if any would understand. I don't explain, content that I have pieced together the reason that I dread all church functions. Even with an understanding of my motive, breaking with my church has left a major void in my life.

For one year, the State Education Department Office of Teaching investigated Frank's allegations against his former teacher. Our family heard of other victims, including our younger son, Jay. Days before his high school graduation, Jay had managed to rebuke Mr. Zim's sexual advances. Abuse experts contend, though, that even just a one-time event can cause sexual confusion and loss of self-esteem. Jay's life since his days as class president, honor society member, and salutatorian would verify this contention. He drank his way through college. Even after many years of sobriety, Jay's life is a continuing economic, career, and relationship struggle.

A third victim disclosed his victimization by Mr. Zim to the State Education Department. Jim, however, faded away. Drugs and alcohol had taken too great a hold on him. Jim just didn't care anymore. Then there was that suicide. Another classmate of Jay admitted to having been a very special friend of Zim's. More names surfaced. Men, though, won't tell because they don't see themselves as victims. Even if a man ever does conceive of his sexual involvement with a former teacher as one of victimization, even then he won't report. This is unfortunate, for abuse experts tell us that boys are sometimes at greater risk for sexual abuse outside the home than girls. I wanted to scream. Sometimes I did.

The school nurse told me that "there had been so many rumors." A woman in town told me that she'd "never allow" her boys to go to Zim's house. How did she know something was fishy about Zim? One of our daughters told me that her close friend had been sexually abused by their eighth-grade teacher. I felt vindicated. Someone else's mom had had this happen to her child. "Can I call Mrs. Farmis?" No way. She blamed Connie, and "laid down the law." I sank. I thought I had found someone who understood. I kept feeling so terribly isolated.

Isolation and ambiguity plagued me like clay on my feet. Each step I took was uncertain and lonely. My sons had a right, and a need, to be in control of the consequences of their disclosure, both as to how they'd deal with it internally and exactly who should be told about their past and when. Intellectually I understood how important this was for them. I promised to keep their confidence. In an attempt to counteract the loneliness that I was experiencing, though, I sought out a few select close friends. Guilt compounded guilt. Even the naturalness of talking openly with our daughters about their brothers became a dilemma. Finally, all the immediate family knew. What a relief! Love and support flowed freely and was welcomed and treasured by all of us.

Within days, the ambiguity and isolation gripped me yet again. As outraged as our daughters were, the girls' loyalty to their brothers brought reprimands to me for any telling beyond the strictly defined boundaries of family, one trusted school district employee, and, for procedural information only, the State Department of Education investigator. Was I now to be the betrayer of our sons' trust? The fire within me had to be banked. It sizzled but was not extinguished.

The assurance of confidentiality by the local rape crisis center presented me with an outlet. I poured out my frustrations to their staff and devoured the books on their resource shelves. As I acquired information about child sexual abuse, I had to do mental gymnastics of translating child to adolescent, girl to boy, home to school, father to teacher. I wrote to the authors of books and journal articles, looked up addresses of child abuse prevention organizations, and combed used book stores for books on rape, true crimes containing plots of incest, child sex rings, and other weird and unfamiliar plots. My many requests for interloan books and articles on sex-related topics created a degree of curiosity at our small town library.

I graduated from my private journal writing to writing anonymous letters. I even rented a box at a neighboring post office. Such was the stigma of being a male victim of sex abuse!

I pondered this phenomenon. I'd read that a major effect of same-sex child offenses is sexual confusion, definitely not an indication or precursor of sexual orientation. Research shows that most men who sexually abuse boys are heterosexual. I learned to distinguish pedophiles, ephebophiles, heterosexuals, and homosexuals. Homophobia lost its abstraction for me. It became a tangible, heavy weight in my life. It blocked my sons' recovery and stagnated all progress necessary for essential changes within our school system. I connected society's unacknowledged subordination and suspicion of women to its persuasive homophobia. My emerging feminist soul bristled. My mother's heart raged. The enormity of the forces conspiring against our sons' healing hit me hard.

The search for criminal or civil justice was fruitless. Even if the offenses had been within the time constraints of the statute of limitations, the ages of the victims were considered to be legally consensual. Attorney after attorney shrugged their shoulders and sent us bills. Our chaos and pain was invalidated. It was so very easy to dismiss our churning guts and accept society's view of "no harm done."

Acting upon the complaints of three victims, the professional practice division of our state department of education initiated an investigation of sexual misconduct allegations against Mr. Zim. During this year-long procedure, at the direction of our local school district board of education, Mr. Zim remained at his classroom teaching post. This callous disregard for the safety of current students, and apparent ignorance of the damage inflicted on young sex abuse victims, was indicative of a series of similar responses generated from the entire multilayered, complex educational institution.

My disappointment at the insensitive disregard of the legal system was paltry compared to the betrayal I felt by the educational system. I had always respected the schools to which I had entrusted our children. Parent-Teacher Association symbolized in my mind a partnership between home and school. Together we cared for our kids. I dutifully signed homework, report cards, and excuse notes. I attended all parent-teacher conferences and went on numerous class trips. Home and school, I sincerely believed, exercised a joint endeavor to nurture the minds and futures of not only our children, but all children. I had good cause to anticipate child-centered, alarmed reactions from the schools. How naive I was!

With each defensive legalistic reply or silent nonresponse that the educational system gave us, I felt devastated. My regard for schools as authorities on the welfare of children was shattered. I felt duped and stupid. As the student victims were manipulated, seduced, and betrayed by an authority figure in their young lives, their teacher, so I felt tricked and betrayed by the entire educational institution.

It seems that I had to reconstruct my entire life history. Was every axiom I had accepted on trust as fragile as the faith I had placed in the school system? My church was set aside in this recasting of myself. I've become a cynic of government, law, and all do-gooders. From innocent trust of all, I found myself questioning the motive of each charitable request and every "expert" opinion.

The maternal guilt I wallowed in for failing to protect my offspring offered little internal space for a development of self-trust. Ever so gradually, though, self-reliance and respect have nudged out the guilt. I was eventually able to place the blame on the teacher offender and on his collaborating, politicized education bureaucracy.

With increased regard for my own gut feelings, however, came paralyzing ambivalence about whose lead to follow. My sons had retreated from their initial public disclosure. They sought only to be left alone. Their recovery was theirs alone to flesh out. My outrage at injustices done, deceits not countered, and changes in institutional attitudes not begun was not their cause—not now, and perhaps not ever. Was I to negate the tensing of my innards and the roar in my head in deference to our sons' pace of healing?

Writing became my means of coping. Personal journal contemplations and questionings allowed me to pick and tear at the scars and woundedness I felt. I wrote letters to school officials, union leaders, and board of education associations. After giving a vague overview of our story, I pleaded with one and all to talk about the issue of educator sexual abuse. The ratio of answers I received to these pleas was fewer than 1 in 20. The journaling and letters nevertheless served to clarify my thoughts and release my frustration, sadness, and increasing anger.

In addition to the consideration of our sons' right to privacy, I myself needed the distance that written communication provided. My confidence was fragile, my emotions still brittle. I lacked validation and support. The family and a few close friends genuinely cared. My intensity, however, began to outstrip their need to tend to their own lives, full of pressing concerns. Intellectually I understood their withdrawal. My sense of isolation, though, increased with each passing day. Yet I couldn't let go.

Soon I embarked on every conceivable avenue of accessing the educational bureaucracy. The state department of education had worked out an agreement with Zim's union attorney that Zim, "in lieu of any admission of guilt or administrative hearing, would surrender his teaching certificate and resign his staff position." They got rid of a bad apple from their midst. The victims remained hanging, with no notice of their plight, no restitution for essential therapy costs, no outreach to the possible scores of undisclosing victims. Tossed aside, former students, their mandate notwithstanding. No compassion or accountability expressed.

There was no recognition of why the survivors were distraught, no comprehension of why the letter of recommendation written by the principal for the teacher offender was a slap in the face to the victims and their families, as well as a danger to all youngsters in Zim's future path. The continuous arrogance and apparent stupidity of those who claim to be champions of children had me stamping my feet in tantrum pitch of disillusionment and outrage. My word processor spit out flashes of fire. My unskilled typing fingers slowed down my sputtering and simmered down my anger, righteous though this anger was and is.

My husband and I had been public school teachers. We were aware of self-serving individuals and bureaucratic foul-ups. The hypocrisy of the sell of "our highest priority is our students," the complexity, power, and mammoth size of the institution, and the knee-jerk, adversarial, "circle-the wagons" defensiveness, however, totally floored us. As individuals we were intimidated. As taxpayers we were irate. As voters we were disheartened. As parents of adult children injured by a school staff member, and later discarded, demeaned, and further violated by the credentialing and employing institution, we were stunned, saddened, and ourselves violated.

Any conversation with either of our sons left me depressed. Any encounter with anyone in the educational establishment left me furious. I was back to shadow-boxing. I still had no cheering crowd urging support and perseverance. I knew the enemy better, though—its strength and its skill.

I needed to focus and direct my complaints to those who might care and who would have the power to influence change in the status quo. I needed people with similar complaints to legitimize this call for change. Above all, I needed to be validated, supported, and cheered on.

Again I pressed the keys of my word processor. I set my desk-top copier purring. Postage and printing costs pinched our limited income, but this discomfort compared poorly to my resolve to confront a blatant injustice inflicted on students and former students. The institution whose existence and mandate is the welfare of children has to face up to its obligation. The sexual abuse of its charges, its students, by its staff members has to be acknowledged, prevented, and rectified.

The general media and even sexual abuse survivor newsletters are silent on the issue. I carefully worded notices to survivor, child protection, and sexual assault organizations so as not to be accused of tainting the "apple pie" image of teachers and schools. I stressed anonymity and the need for "numbers" to effect change in policies and legislation. Ever so slowly replies filtered back to me. "I thought I was the only one, ever." "He was my eighth-grade teacher. I loved him." "She gave me the attention I craved. Where, how, to whom, can I report her?" "Will they believe me?" "Thank you. Thank you for listening, for understanding." Each tortured account confirmed my suspicions that educator sexual abuse is not a singular event occurring once in a blue moon.

I thought that my hesitancy to be named in a news account, because of my sensitivity to our sons' privacy, was an unusual dilemma. The stigma of sexual abuse victims, though, prevents most victims and survivors from full disclosure. Families and jobs could be put at risk. For parents of young victims, disclosure places their children as targets for harassment by their peers and by their teachers. Societal misinformation and denial of educator sexual abuse is formidable. One feels impotent to change this resistance to openness and truth.

Direct spoken communication of our family's pain and the need for systemic change to counteract educator sexual abuse began for me with the public input segment of our local school board meetings. I read my pleas for accountability in a tense, wavering voice. My knees shook. My jaw tensed as the three stock answers were routinely given: (1) silence; (2) an astounding exposure of ignorance about child sexual abuse; and (3) "We've done all we can. It's time that you put this all behind you."

Appearances before the Governor's Commission for Education Review and a legislative hearing on educational issues gave me opportunities to gain speaking experience, but garnered no responses at all.

An opportunity to speak out at an incest survivors' forum challenged me to look inside myself. In writing this speech I had to face exactly how educator sexual abuse had affected me. I saw that I too had been victimized. I too needed to be healed. I too had to work on recovery from severe internal conflicts, guilt, depression, isolation, violation of self, grief, rejection, betrayal, and anger. Without taking away the impact of the trauma done to young students, I could speak in my own right as a trauma survivor. I accepted the enthusiastic applause as that of my peers. I was not just a hysterical, irate mom. Here, at last, was the cheering crowd to urge me on in my battle for justice. I floated back down from the podium.

As a product of an upbringing that stressed the evil of pride rather than the goodness of positive self-esteem, applause is a two-edged sword for me.

Am I exploiting victims for my personal gratification? Public acclaim is both desired and dreaded. It validates the cause of that which I deem worthwhile. It draws attention to those I love dearly, violating the privacy they cherish and deserve. To juggle both tugs of conscience, I attempt selective activism and choose my words very carefully. Ambivalence and internal conflict continue to be issues in my healing process.

Speaking out breaks down an isolation that can be crippling. The stroking of the ego, and the empowering feedback that it generates are essential for the prevention of burnout and despair.

Openness and honesty stimulate a decrease in the splintering of self that results from the keeping of secrets. Sharing our stories can normalize them somewhat. Fear and secrets are heavy burdens indeed. Support from other survivors is invaluable in correctly placing the blame on the offender. Trust, after all, is a requirement of life. It is a requirement for me in my acceptance of the choices that others make. Trust is essential too in the letting go of superfluous, self-imposed responsibility that burdens and constricts. Speaking out, risky, painful, humiliating, and conflicting as it is, can be a beginning of a reconstructed wholeness of life.

My correspondence with educator sexual abuse survivors was growing. I was in contact with men and women throughout the United States. It was time to name this project, to clarify its goals, and to publicize its existence. S.E.S.A.M.E. (Survivors of Educator Sexual Abuse and Misconduct Emerge) was born.

S.E.S.A.M.E.'s founding purposes include:

- Outreach and support.
- Information and public awareness.
- Increased reporting of offenders.
- More realistic statistical gathering for effective lobbying.
- Encouragement of professional research of educator sexual abuse.
- Use of organization to enable anonymity in the telling of stories that can inform about offender strategies of seduction and grooming.
- Become our own advocates in the drafting of preventative laws and policies.
- Place emphasis on *child-centered* attention to the problem of educator sexual abuse by decision making authorities.

The prevailing difficulty of outreach for S.E.S.A.M.E. speaks to the insidiousness of the devastation, dynamics, and denial of educator sexual abuse itself. Its survivors suffer isolation and lack of validation as victims of abuse. The status, charisma, and manipulative seduction of the offending teacher are confusing to the young and continue to be so into adulthood. Educational institutions successfully hand-feed denial of the existence of the problem to the general society. A public that entrusts its children to the care of schools wants to believe that these are safe environments.

The stigma that beleaguers all sexual offense victims becomes even more impairing for survivors of educator sexual abuse. Teachers are generally respected public figures. Manipulative offenders charm their superiors, parents and students alike. Student victims become enamored by the attention of this older man or woman. Historically there has been no equally powerful voice or standard contradicting the authority of the teacher's illicit enticements.

With all this, victims and survivors can well ask themselves, "Why me?" Then, "Why tell?" It would appear that only blame, ridicule, reprisal, and heartache will result from disclosing. Reporting to an authority of any stripe seems senseless. "After all, he was my boyfriend then. If I turn him in now, I'll be hurting him and his family."

The historical silence about the wrongness and the abusiveness of teacher-student sexual relationships continues. Unless survivors have sought therapeutic counseling, they are not hearing the message that they have been wronged. S.E.S.A.M.E. has extremely limited access to these undisclosing, non-self-identifying victims.

This difficulty in reaching survivors is compounded for males, If, as experts state (and I thoroughly believe), boys are at greater risk of sexual abuse outside the home, then there are at least as many male survivors as females. Our homophobic society defeats and frustrates the disclosure and reporting by male victims of all sexual offenses; this contributes to the educational institution's denial of the problem and disallows recovery treatment and healing from the trauma for men. This is an extremely serious situation.

S.E.S.A.M.E. promises confidentiality. By speaking as an organization, survivors' voices can still make a difference—for themselves and for the safety of all current and future students.

Because education is in the public domain, advocacy for educator sexual abuse victims and survivors becomes a legislative lobbying issue. The powerlessness of victimhood is no match for the political realities of our lawmaking bodies. The heightened, emotionally charged life of a recovering sexual abuse survivor has trouble connecting with the precise, legalistic (and political) thought processes of legislative minds and the language of proposed bills.

The protection of children and justice for victims and survivors would appear to be a popular issue for legislators to back. Elected officials, however, are beholden to the voting and financial power of many self-interest groups. Notably strong among these groups are various elements of our complex educational institution. Old rivalries within this educational complexes spring to defend their opposing positions. The issue of prevention of educator sexual abuse can end up being ignored, used as a political football for gain, and be co-opted by any member of fringe radical groups. Legislative lobbying is both an extremely delicate mine field and a frustratingly slow process.

Aligning S.E.S.A.M.E.'s cause with established child abuse or sexual assault prevention coalitions is an alternative to going alone. At times the long tenure of these coalitions contributes to a seemingly defeatist attitude. This "maybe in ten years" tone can turn off idealistic survivor advocate neophytes.

Pointing out grave deficiencies in any organization, being a whistleblower, is a most unpopular position. Child advocacy and sexual assault prevention programs court the assistance and monetary support of segments of the vast educational institution. S.E.S.A.M.E.'s whistle-blowing on educational systems might cause these coalitions to consider the possible risk involved in any alteration of existing working relationships.

The origins of these social action groups also create a challenge to them as they attempt to adjust S.E.S.A.M.E.'s mission of directing the public's attention to educator sexual abuse. Child abuse prevention committees have traditionally battled against unsafe home situations. Abuses of fiduciary relationships, by persons in authority such as teachers, is only beginning to be viewed as a possible social problem. With their plates already overflowing, underfunded and understaffed, child protective advocacy groups are unable to embrace S.E.S.A.M.E.'s goals adequately.

The feminist foundation of the sexual assault coalitions, while admirable and fundamental to their hard-fought measure of success, unfortunately and unwittingly creates yet another barrier for male victims to overcome. If my supposition that victims and survivors of educator sexual abuse divide about equally between males and females, then half of S.E.S.A.M.E.'s potential constituency is neglected. This neglect of recognition, services, and support for male victims is not the sexual assault coalition's alone, but that of all of society.

Politics and negotiating go hand in hand. The newly found voice of educator sexual abuse victims can quickly be discouraged and threatened. Recovery issues of powerlessness, loss of control, isolation, anger, and trust can resurface many times as educator abuse survivors enter the world of knockabout politics. For the vast majority of survivors, political activism is a daunting endeavor. To be precise, patience and craftiness run contrary to the emotionalism, impulsiveness, desired honesty, and fragility of the most recovered of survivors. The mutual support and seriousness of mission that S.E.S.A.M.E. promotes is of great value to all educator sexual abuse survivors, activists and nonactivists alike.

In general, I believe abuse survivors try to make sense out of their trauma, hopefully to have some good come out of their pain, to see change. For this reason the revocation of an offending teacher's certification provides no closure for the survivor. There has been no change in the system. Kids are still at risk. Administrators might still look the other way. A few teachers will still offend until they finally get caught.

Offenders must be punished, criminally and administratively. Pro-active preventative measures must be implemented as well.

Following is testimony I gave before a legislative hearing board for our state:

Concrete proposals to facilitate routine preparedness for the possibility of educator sexual misconduct:

1. Break the silence!

By considering educator sexual abuse as an anticipated hazard in the operation of school systems, opportunities can be provided for decision makers to listen to what survivors have learned by their own experiences, for example, the seduction phase. Guidelines can then be established, codes of ethics drawn up, at-risk teachers counseled, and other such preventative techniques studied. Research is essential; nonpolitical think tanks arranged; the public, students, and staff informed about potentially dangerous situations and behaviors. All of the above must be worked out in an open, calm, nonaccusatory atmosphere.

2. Modify college and graduate teacher preparation programs.
    a. Admissions procedures need to be attentive to emotionally immature applicants.
    b. Course work needs to include the study of professional standards and ethical behavior, boundary issues, and adolescent psychological and sexual development.
    c. Counseling resources need to be provided to give students opportunities to work out unresolved problems, and to aid them in sorting through their motivation for entering the teaching profession.

3. Screening of candidates for teaching and school staff positions.
    a. Mandated fingerprinting and criminal record searches would demonstrate the state's commitment to zero tolerance of educator sexual misconduct. It is not a fail-safe measure, however.
    b. Trained, sensitive interviewers need to scan for at-risk personalities.
    c. Prior employment must be extremely well researched.

4. New teachers and experienced staff. Beginning staff need support, to be reminded about appropriate boundaries, and have ample opportunities for counseling. Older teachers need intervention for stress, burnout, and "crossing-the-line" behaviors with students.

5. Increase funding for the Department of Education Office of Teacher Moral Conduct to improve the speed and quality of its services and investigation.

6. Local policies.

    a. State-mandated unified student sexual harassment policies for all districts would alert the entire public that the state is united with the local school in upholding their combined responsibility to provide a safe environment for their pupils.

    b. To demonstrate the depth of its concerns about educator sexual abuse, such mandated policies and procedures should:

        (1) Call for a rapid response to any allegation of educator sexual abuse, harassment, or exploitation.

        (2) Removal of the alleged perpetrator from contact with all students during the inquiries.

        (3) The use of an outside trained investigator, be it police, child protective agent, or private—all of whom must be unbiased and fair to the alleged offender, and victim, and school system.

        (4) Even if the alleged offense does not rise to the level of a crime, it must be considered very serious and worthy of immediate, expert attention and follow-through.

        (5) The victim and his family must be given a list of resources, rights, and options, including the student's choice to change classes or school or have a home tutor.

        (6) A trained victim's advocate should be appointed and the victim immediately referred to the local rape crisis center and community mental health agency.

        (7) Have a penalty—

            (a) For all staff who don't report suspected misconduct by a colleague.

            (b) For any retaliation against staff who do report.

            (c) For students or staff who harass the victim or his family.

            (d) For an administrator who does not report the allegation to the Department of Education and local district attorney and police immediately.

            (e) For the reporter of any known false accusation.

        (8) Provide for the thorough dissemination of the policy, at regularly stated intervals, to the entire school and at-large community.

        (9) Provide for the education of each school board member as to the contents, importance, and obligations incurred by the policy.

(10) Undertake a concerted, widespread effort to search out undisclosing victims of the same, or other, perpetrator of educator sexual abuse.

(11) Give delayed disclosing survivors of educator sexual abuse an urgent, respectful, serious response, and, if still teaching, remove this alleged perpetrator from children immediately. If the teacher is no longer in the same school, cooperate in the search for his whereabouts.

7. Laws must be enacted to:

a. Provide for funding for the implementation of the mandated local student sexual harassment policies.

b. Provide funding for long-term therapy for the victims and survivors of educator sexual misconduct with provisions for limited counseling for their parents.

c. Provide for adequate legal recourse via the Department of Human Rights for victims of educator sexual abuse in equal strength as to that available to workplace and college campus sexual harassment victims.

d. Give criminal status for sexual offenses by persons in authority, such as teachers, *against students of any age*.

As taxpayers and consumers of the education system, educator sexual abuse survivors cannot defect from the institution. We have a self-interest as well—our recovery. Our healing, the reclamation of our own self-worth, demands honesty. As our personal conscience prods us to not lie, so, individually and collectively, we must prod the educational institution to be forthright, fair, and just as they care for their charges, our children.

To be worthy of the public trust placed in it, the educational institution must meet our expectations of protection, accountability, compassion and rectification for wrongs it may have done.

The isolation so keenly felt by all educator sexual abuse victims, survivors, and their families contributes immensely to society's denial of this problem. Breaking this isolation, and the silence it perpetuates is key to the reinstitution of the proper weight, the worthiness, of the welfare of students and former students, into the structure, and the spirit, of our country's educational institutions.

Teaching about Sexual Harassment in the Undergraduate Psychology Curriculum

Michele A. Paludi,
Lindsay Doling, and Lauren Gellis

Research suggests that approximately 50% of undergraduate women experience quid pro quo sexual harassment (e.g., not receiving the grade earned for failing to comply with faculty's sexual requests). This incidence rises to approximately 75% when hostile environment sexual harassment cases are included (e.g., faculty making unwanted sexual comments about a student's body or sexual activity; faculty member fondling a student) (see Fitzgerald & Omerod, 1993; Paludi, 1996a). For example, in one large-scale study of 2,000 students at two universities by Fitzgerald et al. (1988), half of the women college students reported experiencing sexual harassment. The majority had experienced sexist comments by faculty; the next largest category of sexual harassment was seductive behavior, including being invited for drinks and offers for backrubs by faculty members, being brushed up against by faculty, and having their professors show up uninvited to their hotel rooms during out-of-town academic conventions.

Barickman, Paludi, and Rabinowitz (1992) noted that although all college students are vulnerable to some degree, faculty tend to sexually harass those students who are most vulnerable and needy. Research has further noted that sexual harassment can affect college students in three major areas: career development, physical health, and emotional health (Dansky & Kilpatrick, 1997; see Chapter 5, this volume). For example, research has documented decreased morale and absenteeism, decreased school satisfaction, performance decrements, and damage to interpersonal relationships on campus. The emotional consequences of sexual harassment include depression, helplessness, strong fear reactions, and decreased motivation.

Physical symptoms associated with sexual harassment include headaches, sleep disturbances, gastrointestinal disorders, eating disorders, and crying spells. Researchers and clinical reports suggest a postabuse syndrome characterized by shock, emotional numbing, constriction of affect, flashbacks, and other signs of anxiety and depression (Quina, 1996; Rabinowitz, 1991).

Although the incidence of sexual harassment among college students is high, with significant impact on several areas of their emotional and physical well-being, students are not likely to label their experiences as sexual harassment, despite the fact that the behaviors they are experiencing fit the legal definition of sexual harassment (Fitzgerald, 1996). Consequently, they may not label their stress-related responses as being caused or exacerbated by the sexual harassment. Furthermore, students may not be aware that their experiences should be reported to campus authorities since they do not know whether their experiences meet the legal definition of sexual harassment.

To assist students with labeling their experiences as sexual harasment and assist them reporting the victimization, researchers and trainers (e.g., Biaggio & Brownell, 1996; Paludi & Barickman, 1991, 1998) have recommended that colleges have an effective and enforced policy statement prohibiting sexual harassment; have an effective and enforced investigatory procedure that ensures confidentiality and prevents retaliation for reporting; and provide training and education for all members of the campus community.

With respect to this last component, several kinds of intervention have been identifed For example, Biaggio and Brownell (1996) and Barickman, Paludi et al. (1992) suggested that individuals within the campus (e.g., residence hall advisers, department chairs) be targeted for attendance at workshops at which they can be informed about the policy statement and procedures for dealing with sexual harassment at their campus. In addition, items relating to sexual harassment can be placed on teaching evaluations. Paludi and Barickman (1998) suggested the following interventions:

Include information about sexual harassment in new student orientation classes;

Hold a "sexual harassment awareness week";

Require that student leaders attend workshops on sexual harassment;

Encourage sororities and fraternities to present programs on sexual harassment;

Include information on sexual harassment in packets for transfer students;

Encourage faculty to incorporate discussions of sexual harassment in their courses.

It is this last suggestion of Paludi and Barickman that we address in this chapter. Specifically, we outline ways psychology faculty can teach about sexual harassment in their courses. The main goal of such teaching is to educate students about various aspects of sexual harassment so that they can learn to label their own experiences accurately and seek therapeutic support for their experiences. Thus, faculty can work with their campus's sexual harassment trainer in providing information about theoretical and empirical work on the psychology of sexual harassment as well as campus policy and investigatory procedures.

In Table 1 we identify examples of topics related to sexual harassment that can be incorporated into several courses in the psychology curriculum. Because of the sensitivity of the issues that are discussed in a unit on sexual harassment, we make the following pedagogical recommendations:

1. Faculty should alert the campus sexual harassment investigator about the material on sexual harassment about which they are teaching. Students may experience flashbacks to their own experiences during a class lecture on sexual harassment. In addition, they may choose to discuss their experiences confidentially with the investigator.

2. Faculty should prepare an informational sheet for their students for this unit. This sheet should contain the names, office numbers, and telephone numbers of the following individuals at their campus: the sexual harassment investigator or adviser, the sexual harassment counselor, therapists and support groups in the community that deal with sexual harassment, and campus security.

3. Faculty must distribute a copy of the campus sexual harassment policy. We recommend inviting the investigator of complaints to their class so that students can meet her or him and begin to develop a sense of trust of this person.

4. Faculty should announce the content of this unit on their syllabus and in class for several meetings prior to the beginning of the unit on sexual harassment. For students for whom this material will be emotionally difficult, faculty should not make attendance at this class mandatory.

5. We recommend notifying the counselors in student services about the unit on sexual harassment and asking them to be available for consultations immediately following the class discussions. Faculty should inform students that the counselors will be available following class.

6. While some students may laugh when tense or when discussing sensitive topics, do not permit laughter during this unit. If it occurs because of discomfort we recommend saying something similar to the following: "Sometimes we may giggle or laugh when we are uncomfortable with a topic. We should not interpret laughter as only meaning that we find the topic silly" (also see Paludi, 1996b).

Table 1
Suggestions for Incorporating a Unit on Sexual Harassment
into Courses in the Undergraduate Psychology Curriculum

Course	Suggested Topics
Statistics/Experimental	Methodology used to obtain incidence rates; reliability and validity issues; comparisons of incidence rates across cultures and/or college majors and occupations
Developmental	Sexual harassment incidence rates across the life cycle; parental socialization of aggression and passivity; sex education, effect of sexual harassment on children's and adolescents' development; race comparisons in incidence rates of sexual harassment in colleges and workplaces
Social	Aggression and power; attitudes toward victim blame and victim responsibility; sexual harassment as portrayed in the popular media; gender roles displayed in dating relationships; deindividuation as a way to understand why individuals harass; interface of racism and sexism in sexual harassment; interface of homophobia and sexism in sexual harassment
Clinical	Posttraumatic stress disorder; profiles of sexual harassers; therapeutic interventions with victims and perpetrators of sexual harassment
Psychology of Women/ Psychology of Gender	Pornography and sexual harassment; interpersonal power and gender; feminist therapeutic approaches; feminist analyses of the origins of sexual harassment
Industrial/Organizational	Development of effective policies and procedures to discourage sexual harassment; characteristics of effective investigations of sexual harassment; communications programs for workplaces
Psychology of Addiction	Abusive relationships; peer sexual harassment; relationship between drug abuse and sexual assault; repeated victimizations

7. The class should be reminded of the statistics concerning the incidence of sexual harassment, incest, battering, and rape. This information should be related to the potential number of women and men in the class who may have experienced sexual victimization.

8. We recommend discussing sexual harassment later in the term rather than toward the beginning. By the end of the term, students (especially in smaller classes) have had an opportunity to get to know each other and develop a sense of mutual trust.

9. We recommend that students read current research about issues related to sexual harassment. Table 2 lists books and book chapters that may be used for this purpose.

10. Audiovisual material on sexual harassment is listed in Table 3. We recommend using these videos in conjuction with faculty-guided discussions. A list of sample discussion questions for this purpose is presented in Table 4.

Table 2
General Resources on Sexual Harassment

Barickman, R. B., Paludi, M. A., & Rabinowitz, V. C. (1992). Sexual harassment of students: Victims of the college experience. In E. Viano (Ed.), *Victimization: An international perspective.* New York: Springer.

DeFour, D. C. (1996). The interface of racism and sexism on college campuses. In M. A. Paludi (Ed.), *Sexual harassment on college campuses: Abusing the ivory power.* Albany: State University of New York Press.

Dziech, B., & Weiner, L. (1984). *The lecherous professor.* Boston: Beacon Press.

Levy, A., & Paludi, M. A. (1997). *Workplace sexual harassment.* Englewood Cliffs, NJ: Prentice Hall.

Lott, B., & Reilly, M. E. (Eds.). (1996). *Combatting sexual harassment in higher education.* Washington, DC: NEA Professional Library.

O'Donohue, W. (Ed.). (1997). *Sexual harassment: Theory, research, and treatment.* Boston: Allyn & Bacon.

Paludi, M. A. (Ed.). (1990). *Ivory power: Sexual harassment on college campuses.* Albany: State University of New York Press.

Paludi, M. A. (Ed.). (1996). *Sexual harassment on college campuses: Abusing the ivory power.* Albany: State University of New York Press.

Paludi, M. A. (1997). Sexual harassment in schools. In W. O'Donohue (Ed.), *Sexual harassment: Theory, research, and treatment.* Boston: Allyn & Bacon.

Table 3
Audiovisual Material for Classroom Use

Intent vs. Impact
BNA Communications Inc.
9439 Key West Avenue
Rockville, MD 20850

No Laughing Matter: High School Students and Sexual Harassment
Massachusetts Department of Education
1385 Hancock Street
Quincy, MA 02169

Sex, Power, and the Workplace
KCET Video
4401 Sunset Boulevard
Los Angeles, CA 90027

Sexual Harassment: Building Awareness on Campus
The Media Education Foundation
26 Center Street
Northampton, MA 01060

Sexual Harassment—Crossing the Line
Cambridge Career Products
P.O. Box 2153, Department CC13
Charleston, WV 25328

Sexual Harassment: Issues and Answers
College and University Personnel Association
1233 20th Street, NW
Washington, DC 20036

Sexual Harassment in the Schools
Northwest Women's Law Center
119 South Main Street, Suite 330
Seattle, WA 98104

Sexual Harassment on Campus: Current Concerns and Considerations
Center for Instructional Services
Old Dominion University
Norfolk, VA 23529

You Are the Game: Sexual Harassment
Indiana University
Audio Visual Center
Bloomington, IN 47405

Your Right to Fight: Stopping Sexual Harassment on Campus
Affirmative Action
State University of New York at Albany
Albany, NY 12222

Table 4
Sample Discussion Questions for Audiovisual Material

Do you believe the behavior described in the video illustrates sexual harassment?

If you believe this is sexual harassment, what kind of sexual harassment do you believe this case illustrates: quid pro quo or hostile environment sexual harassment?

How do you think the individuals involved feel? Scared? Upset? Angry? Embarrassed? Powerless?

Do you believe there is miscommunication between the individuals in the cases?

What do you think the individuals should do?

If you observed this situation occurring, what, if anything, would you do?

What services would be available at this campus to assist with the situations described in this video?

If you were the student in this situation, what services would you want, if any, to assist you?

Do you believe the sex or sexual orientation of the individuals involved in the cases makes any difference in your evaluation of the situation?

Do the individuals involved in the cases have a responsibility to behave differently? Explain.

What outcome would you like to see in this case?

For faculty not comfortable with teaching about sexual harassment, we recommend a guest lecturer to provide the information—perhaps the campus investigator of sexual harassment complaints, a faculty colleague, or a colloquium speaker. Information about potential speakers is presented in Table 5.

Table 5
Organizations for Supplying Speakers

American Educational Research Association
1230 17th Street, NW
Washington, DC 20036

Canadian Association against Sexual Harassment
Dr. Carole Pond
Sexual Harassment Office
University of Saskatchewan
104 Qu'Appelle Hall Addition
Saskatoon, Saskatchewan, Canada S7N 0W0

Equal Employment Opportunity Commission
2401 E Street, NW
Washington, DC 20506

National Network of Minority Women in Science
Association for the Advancement of Science
1776 Massachusetts Avenue, NW
Washington, DC 20036

National Organization for Victim Assistance
1757 Park Road, NW
Washington, DC 20010

National University Continuing Education Association
Division of Women's Education
One Dupont Circle
Washington, DC 20036

9 to 5
YWCA
140 Clarendon Street
Boston, MA 02139

Sociologists against Sexual Harassment
Dr. James Gruber
Sociology Department
University of Michigan
Dearborn, MI 48128

Women Employed
22 West Monroe, Suite 1400
Chicago, IL 60603

There are several benefits to teaching about sexual harassment in the psychology curriculum: assisting students in accurately labeling their experiences as sexual harassment or not sexual harassment; providing information about campus policy and procedures; indicating how the campus, psychology department, and faculty in general are committed to maintaining a harassment-free and retaliatory-free learning environment; and providing necessary information that can carry over to students' experiences in the workplace.

Students' comments about the approach we recommend include the following:

I registered for this course on gender so I could learn more about sexual harassment and other types of sexual violence. Learning about sexual harassment from an academic perspective helped me to understand what I was feeling emotionally because of my own experiences. Next year I will be a residence adviser. I can use the handouts you provided—with organizations and phone numbers—with the students.

I never knew there was empirical research on teens' experiences with sexual harassment. I'm glad you discussed this issue in our seminar on adolescent development. I want to go into high school guidance counseling. This information will be helpful to me in my future work with adolescents.

If I had to describe this material we learned to a friend, I would say: emotional: because of the issues we discuss and because it is likely that you will think more about yourself; thought-provoking: not only do you think about the issues in general, but you also consider how you personally fit into these issues; informative: you learn a great deal about many aspects of our society and about ourselves.

I think that distributing the lists were good—most times people would feel uncomfortable asking for certain phone numbers because they wouldn't want people to know they had problems. However, if they are given a list, they don't have to worry about anything.

Although we have outlined some pedagogical techniques for the undergraduate psychology curriculum, our material can be (and has been) integrated into other undergraduate courses in the academy as well as into graduate psychology courses. Students have reported benefiting from an increased understanding of sexual harassment. Some have worked with their respective campuses in forming peer support groups for student victims of sexual harassment and other forms of sexual victimization. For additional resources, we recommend Lott and Reilly (1996), Levy and Paludi (1997),

O'Donohue (1997), Paludi and Barickman (1991, 1998), and Paludi (1996a).

REFERENCES

Barickman, R. B., Paludi, M. A., & Rabinowitz, V. C. (1992). Sexual harassment of students: Victims of the college experience. In E. Viano (Ed.), *Victimization: An international perspective*. New York: Springer.

Biaggio, M., & Brownell, A. (1996). Addressing sexual harassment: Strategies for prevention and change. In M. A. Paludi (Ed.), *Sexual harassment on college campuses: Abusing the ivory power*. Albany: State University of New York Press.

Dansky, B., & Kilpatrick, D. (1997). Effects of sexual harassment. In W. O'Donohue (Ed.), *Sexual harassment: Theory, research, and practice*. Boston: Allyn & Bacon.

Fitzgerald, L. M. (1996). Sexual harassment: Definition and measurement of a construct. In M. A. Paludi (Ed.), *Sexual harassment on college campuses: Abusing the ivory power*. Albany: State University of New York Press.

Fitzgerald, L. F., & Omerod, A. (1993). Sexual harassment in academia and the workplace. In F. L. Denmark & M. A. Paludi (Eds.), *Psychology of women: A handbook of issues and theories*. Westport, CT: Greenwood.

Fitzgerald, L. F., Shullman, S., Bailey, N., Richards, M., Swecker, J., Gold, Y., Omerod, A., & Weitzman, L. (1988). The incidence and dimensions of sexual harassment in academia and the workplace. *Journal of Vocational Behavior, 32*, 152–175.

Levy, A., & Paludi, M. A. (1997). *Workplace sexual harassment*. Englewood Cliffs, NJ: Prentice Hall.

Lott, B., & Reilly, M. E. (Eds.). (1996). *Combatting sexual harassment in higher education*. Washington, DC: NEA Professional Library.

O'Donohue, W. (Ed.). (1997). *Sexual harassment: Theory, research, and treatment*. Boston: Allyn & Bacon.

Paludi, M. A. (Ed.).(1996a). *Sexual harassment on college campuses: Abusing the ivory power*. Albany: State University of New York Press.

Paludi, M. A. (1996b). *Exploring/teaching the psychology of women: A manual of resources* (2nd ed.). Albany: State University of New York Press.

Paludi, M. A. & Barickman, R. B. (1991). *Academic and workplace sexual harassment: A manual of resources*. Albany: State University of New York Press.

Paludi, M. A., & Barickman, R. B. (1998). *Sexual harassment, work, and education: A resource manual for prevention*. Albany: State University of New York Press.

Quina, K. (1996). The victimization of women. In M. A. Paludi (Ed.), *Sexual har-assment on college campuses: Abusing the ivory power.* Albany: State University of New York Press.

Rabinowitz, V. C. (1991). Coping with sexual harassment. In M. A. Paludi (Ed.), *Ivory power: Sexual harassment on campus.* Albany: State University of New York Press.

Zalk, S. R. (1996). Men in the academy: A psychological profile of harassment. In M. A. Paludi (Ed.), *Sexual harassment on college campuses: Abusing the ivory power.* Albany: State University of New York Press.